CW00348769

The News
Revolution
in England

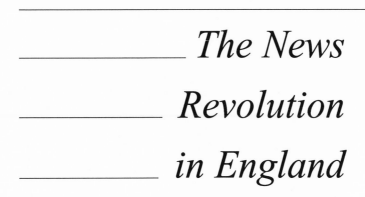

The News
Revolution
in England

CULTURAL DYNAMICS OF DAILY INFORMATION

C. JOHN SOMMERVILLE

New York   Oxford
Oxford University Press
1996

Oxford University Press

Oxford   New York
Athens   Auckland   Bangkok   Bogota   Bombay
Buenos Aires   Calcutta   Cape Town   Dar es Salaam   Delhi
Florence   Hong Kong   Istanbul   Karachi
Kuala Lumpur   Madras   Madrid   Melbourne
Mexico City   Nairobi   Paris   Singapore
Taipei   Tokyo   Toronto

and associated companies in

Berlin   Ibadan

Copyright © 1996 by Oxford University Press, Inc.

Published by Oxford University Press, Inc.
198 Madison Avenue, New York, New York 10016

Oxford is a registered trademark of Oxford University Press

All rights reserved. No part of this publication may be reproduced,
stored in a retrieval system, or transmitted, in any form or by any means,
electronic, mechanical, photocopying, recording, or otherwise,
without the prior permission of Oxford University Press

Library of Congress Cataloging-in-Publication Data
Sommerville, C. John (Charles John), 1938—
The news revolution in England : cultural dynamics of daily
information / C. John Sommerville.
p.   cm.
Includes bibliographical references and index.
ISBN 0-19-510667-9
1. English newspapers—Great Britain—history.   I. Title.
PN5115.S66   1996
072'.09—dc20   95-51528

1 2 3 4 5 6 7 8 9

Printed in the United States of America
on acid-free paper

To
M.E.H.
and to the memory
of
N.W.H.

Preface

It will not take long for the reader to sense a polemical element in this study, but its thrust may be puzzling to those who are bracing themselves for some of the usual criticisms of the media. This book is only interested in the effect of periodicity (regular publication schedules) on how information is processed and on the relation between readers and writers. The point might be missed by those who feel they must reinterpret my point to bring it more in line with media criticisms of their own, and this may explain a certain insistence in my presentation. I do not intend to criticize, as others have done, the way the news was processed. And I will not question the importance of news per se, as opposed to periodical news. Rather, I am questioning whether it is possible for periodical news and an information industry dependent on planned obsolescence to offer an adequate sense of things.

This is not another history of journalism from the standpoint of the intentions of journalists or politicians, but rather a consideration of the journalistic product. We will attempt to infer the effects of that product on the audience, whether found in magazines, scholarly or literary journals, advertisers, "comic" papers, essay journals, or newspapers. Partly, it is about how the public lost the initiative in investigating their world. For we will see how vibrant public opinion could be at a time when there was only one, official newspaper, to play against the sounding board of the coffee-house—a periodical medium in its own right. And we will see how communications media began to develop into communications mechanisms.

So this book does not repeat previous criticisms of the press, valid as they may be. Earlier critics have usually assumed that the news can be fixed, by greater objectivity, better research, real impartiality, or the like. I do not believe periodical news can be fixed, since its flaw is in its essential characteristic. This may lead readers to assume that I want to turn the clock back to an unacceptable past. This is true only in the sense that I accept the view that a communications system is basic to a society, and that some of the dysfunctional characteristics of modern societies will continue so long as they are held together by periodical media rather than by cultures of a more natural growth. If this seems cryptic, I hope the chapters to follow will make things clearer.

Given that the study draws from cultural history, literary criticism, critical social theory, mass communications theory, and even the philosophy of religion, my debts to those who have offered aid are great. I am most grateful to the Institute for Advanced Study (and the National Endowment for the Humanities), which supported me through the writing stage, and to my fellow Members in 1993–94. In particular, I was helped by discussions with Howard Weinbrot, Sachiko Kusukawa, Maria Pia Di Bella, Wesley Kort, George Lindbeck, Sebastian deGrazia, Sarah Hanley, and Barbara Shapiro. The pleasure with which I remember my year in Princeton is also due to the encouragement of David Hackett, Natalie Zemon Davis, Daniel Hardy, Robert Wuthnow, Diogenes Allen, Richard Fenn, Peter Paret, Robert Cathey, and James Bratt. The project was aided in various ways by Michael MacDonald, Sir Keith Thomas, Robert Webb, David Martin, Joad Raymond, William Chamberlin, Steven Pincus, and Adrian Johns. Robert Thomson, Peter Dimock and an anonymous reviewer offered suggestions on the manuscript, which I have tried to incorporate. Once again, I am glad to acknowledge the encouragement and comments of my department, which listened uneasily to a presentation of part of this material, as well as of seminar participants at Cambridge, Oxford, and the University of London. As always, my biggest debt is due to my family, Susan, Eden and Henry, who are my only indulgent audience.

Dates are given in the usual manner, using the old calendar but beginning the year at 1 January rather than 25 March. Dates of newspapers are given by the last date listed, so that a paper dated 18–21 May is cited as from 21 May. Page numbers are not cited for periodicals that were no longer than the standard eight quarto pages of the traditional newsbook.

Readers who want a finding list for the periodicals discussed can now turn to Carolyn Nelson and Matthew Seccombe's *British Newspapers and Periodicals, 1641–1700: A Short-Title Catalogue of Serials Printed in England, Scotland, Ireland, and British America* (New York: Modern Language Association of America, 1987). For the eighteenth century, *The Times* of London's *Tercentenary Handlist of English and Welsh Newspapers, Magazines and Reviews* (1920), and R. S. Crane and F. B. Kaye's *A Census of British Newspapers and Periodicals, 1620–1800* (London: Holland, 1966, orig. 1927) are still useful.

Gainesville, Florida   C.J.S.
December 1995

Contents

The News

Revolution

in England

ONE

The Strangeness of Periodical News

There is a common saying that, whoever discovered water, it wasn't a fish. That is how *we* are with periodical news. Daily news is the element in which we swim, so we think of it as a part of nature. For many of us, having news daily seems necessary to being socially *conscious*, much less "informed." We can hardly imagine a time, a little more than three centuries ago, when there was *not* a daily budget of published news from all over. And we can hardly imagine how differently people's minds worked when that was the case.

Periodical news reports are such a large element in our thinking that we may not have thought about what a strange way they are of acquiring our understandings of politics, science, religion, history, social affairs, values. Indeed, the periodicity of our thinking deserves attention as a main cause of some of our social and cultural dysfunctions. Periodical publication has a dynamic of its own, and its effects on our consciousness go beyond those of the so-called print revolution. We may speak of a comparable "news revolution" in seventeenth-century England and other parts of Northern Europe, which began a long erosion of knowledge, as knowledge was then conceived. This study explores the ways in which periodical—and eventually daily—publication began to produce its characteristic distortions and how it has played out.

When news was only a *part* of what people read, it did not have such a drastic effect. Now that people take in very little that is not in the form of daily reports, the effects are more apparent. Complaints about the media are widespread these days, but they are usually about various kinds of bias or incompetence in the press. That is, the critics take daily news itself for granted, and only complain of how the product is processed. We will be looking for the ways that periodicity in publishing (or broadcasting) constitutes a bias all by itself, and asking whether its decontextualizing and deconstructing effects are part of its essential nature.

3

Essentially, daily publication cuts things out of a larger reality in order to dispose of them and clear the decks for tomorrow's edition. There can be little historical or philosophical scale in such reports, because every day's events must be presented as deserving of equal attention. Each day's edition costs the same, after all. You wouldn't buy it tomorrow, because tomorrow's news will supercede today's. Much of the population shares a sort of addiction to this process, which is what news industry profits depend on.

And this brings us to the main point. Periodicity is about economics. There can be news without its being daily, but if it were not daily, a news *industry* could never develop. The industry's capital assets would lie idle waiting for news of significance to print. Periodicity is a marketing strategy, a way of holding property in information—information of the most ordinary sort. Beyond that, it is a way of turning everything into information of the most ordinary sort. Obviously, it is necessary to do certain things to knowledge in order to commodify it in this way.

In tracing the beginnings of the "news revolution" we will be expanding on the hints of those historians who have sensed that news media helped to create a new kind of reading public, even a new society. What social theorists call "communicative action" does seem to be the basis of society itself, and the public created by news was not simply the audience for printed books. Early editors learned very quickly how to make knowledge *disposable* to insure a steady market. What this does to reporting about government, politics, philosophy, manners, literature will be a theme of our study.

First, however, there are preliminaries to consider, such as a definition of news. We normally think of news as a particular kind of historical reality, which could probably be defined analytically.[1] That is a mystification of the subject. If journalists are experts on anything, it is their audience, and not some other aspect of reality. Viewed "phenomenologically," news is simply what made it into today's paper or news broadcast. There are now 180 countries, 5 billion people, and thousands of things that "happened" yesterday. Only the ones that actually made the paper became news. Tomorrow will have its own news, so the rejected events will *never* be news. Of course, they might be part of later *historical* reconstructions of our time. One might be inclined to think, in such a case, that the journalists just blew it—if you thought news was of the same nature as history. But news is not about history, really, but about profits, when publishers are thinking clearly, and we shall see that English publishers were thinking clearly from the very beginning.

Definitions should come from general usage, and this is what we mean by "news" when we are not being confused with such notions as unimportant news or unreported news. There is no such thing as unreported news, because news is not natural. Events are natural but periodical news is a manufactured product. Of course, that is true of "history" too. History is what historians make out of everything left from the past. News is what newswriters squeezed into today's paper. If there is a point to histories, it is ultimately philosophical; the point of newspapers is to be recycled—the first product with planned obsolescence.[2]

Our second preliminary point is that there is no necessity of thinking of news as *daily*. It used to come along irregularly when people, exercising their own judgment, decided that something they heard was unusually interesting or important, and passed it on. People maintained their normal standards of honor and truth in spreading this news, so everyone knew about how far to trust the information. They were not awed by the institutional stature of giant news corporations. That changed in the seventeenth century, when people got used to the idea that there was an absolutely regular quota of news, which was vouched for by transcendent sources. Daily news then became a steady stream of perceptions, the stream of society's consciousness. One participated in society in a new way.

Third, not all of the content of the many kinds of periodicals appearing in the seventeenth century (or now) is news, in the accepted sense of important social or political events. This study will be interested in all of it, however, because it all partakes of the same urgency with which we invest politics. *Everything* becomes strange when it is cut out of reality in the same way as political or commercial reports are, so that our science, religion, ethics, and arts are becoming as curious as our politics. And it bears remembering that this cultural tempo, like our political tempo, is for the convenience of publishers.

Fourth, our most common mistake in thinking about news is to imagine that the most important events are those that get the most publicity. The reverse may be true. Powerful people do not usually like publicity. Celebrities like publicity, and the media have learned that customers will pay as much or more to read about celebrities as about the powerful. Given the accessibility of celebrities, reporters may concentrate on them while the powerful go about their business. So there is a good chance that the news will *not* cover what historians will later write about our times.

Those who hope that the news will keep them informed about the powerful forces in the world should consider that power might be *defined* as the ability to keep oneself out of the news.[3] And further, an *elite* can be defined as a group that is able to monopolize a certain class of information, and keep it out of circulation. For even today all *important* news is transmitted orally, within elites. If important news is what gives one person an advantage over others, then it follows that valuable news is something you have to pay a lot for, one way or another. What is left over becomes the contents of the media.[4]

It is doubtless true that over the centuries media attention has helped the public to monitor and challenge elites. In time, this attention has eroded the power of some of those elites, but only at the point when the press itself became big business, an elite with secrets of its own. What the balance sheet would show of the new distribution of power, and whether the public has a right to feel included in the power structure because of its news consciousness, should get more attention than it has.

If all of this seems obvious, the question becomes why no one has tried to analyze the effects of periodicity, along with the various other complaints of journalistic performance. The answer is probably that others have approached the history of the press with other things in mind. Those who described what they called the "print revolution" and its effects on our consciousness were interested in the appearance of the book.⁵ They did not treat newspapers as a different category, or treat them at all. Periodical publications used the same letterpress technology as books and it did not strike scholars that they represented any great difference in their effects on consumers. But newspapers did not evolve from books. Newspapers descended from newsletters or from letters in general, and early editors maintained essential features of this more continuous medium.⁶

Critical social theorists have sometimes remarked on news as a part of what is wrong with modern society, but they stop their analysis too soon, before considering its most essential characteristic. Having uncovered the hegemonic designs of publishers, these critics give the impression that the press is only being misused. But it should be crucial to Jürgen Habermas's analysis of social communication, for example, if the news industry immediately and necessarily became one of the constraining structures that "colonized" the public sphere.⁷ Alvin Gouldner need not have puzzled over how the news business could betray the interests of capital by regularly printing criticism of the system. He only needed to reflect that this particular industry holds its *property* in the news.⁸

Critical theorists ordinarily assume that since news organizations take basic institutions for granted, they cannot truly have an unsettling influence.⁹ But we cannot afford to forget that the product of the news industry is change—of some kind. Horkheimer and Adorno pointed out long ago that ceaseless, superficial (cultural) change can mask the fact that nothing "real" (or social-structural) is changing: "Tempo and dynamics serve this trend. Nothing remains as of old; everything has to run incessantly, to keep moving. For only the universal triumph of the rhythm of mechanical production promises that nothing changes."¹⁰ Astonishingly, they were not speaking of the news. But that insight does prepare us for the realization that a periodical rhythm can erode social, cultural, and even political values while it reinforces a bureaucratic-economic establishment. Thus daily news is at the very bottom of what Daniel Bell called the "cultural contradictions of capitalism," in which compulsive and unsatisfying work is oddly paired with compulsive and unsatisfying indulgence.¹¹

Perhaps the most surprising scholarly failure was that of Jacques Ellul, who missed several opportunities to focus on periodical publication in his consideration of the triumph of technology. Ellul thinks of "technique" as the driving force of modern development, having replaced classical capitalism. But he is another who takes periodical news for granted—as something given in nature—and only complains of its propagandistic misuse. He calls the ordinary world of daily news "incoherent, absurd and irrational," but he does not see this as related to its periodicity, or treat it as a fault that cannot be fixed. So he gives no hint that periodicity is another of the dysfunctional characteristics of modern technology.¹²

This study will contribute an element that belongs in the theories of Ellul, Habermas, and Gouldner, but which has been too obvious to notice. On one level, it is a contribution to the history of capitalism. We shall see that the commodification of information was already "capitalistic"—an investment opportunity—at a time when book production was still organized as a craft.[13] But the study also contributes to the more purely technological view of cultural change. Indeed, the latter may be the more revealing perspective, since all classes are victims of the disoriented consciousness created by periodicity.

Literary critics come closer to recognizing the peculiar effects of periodicity. In his exposition of reader-response criticism, Wolfgang Iser states as a central insight that "indeterminacy is the fundamental precondition for reader participation." And his very first examples of this indeterminacy are news and serialized novels. Continuing news accounts, like the chapters of a thriller, break at points which create tension, and it is this tension that gets the reader involved. Iser notes that the novels that maintain their indeterminacy in this crude way, by serialization, do not reach the highest levels of art: "If we read them in book form, generally they will finish us before we finish them."[14] Serialized novels got a bad reputation as readers realized that there were subtler forms of literary tension. But newsmen have no alternative path to profits.

Marshall McLuhan was another who, despite his interest and insight into the technique and effects of media, gave no attention to periodicity.[15] He did note the newspapers' practice of juxtaposing multiple items. McLuhan thought that this was a defining feature of the news media and gave the news its powerfully convincing quality. Where books create a point of view, newspapers require readers to make an effort to assemble subjects and images. The variety or "mosaic" of the news—which reflects the "incongruity" or incoherence in life—forces us to respond.[16] McLuhan observed that this ambiguity was only "a superficial chaos which can lead to cosmic harmonies of a very high order." In fact, he credits it with creating "human solidarity."[17]

Roland Barthes took a more sardonic view of this incongruity when he described how even the tiniest news "filler" is structured. News items, however small, are never "simple," but include a juxtaposition or coincidence, like the toilet that fell on a car on the Pennsylvania Turnpike last week. "Life" may come at us as a lot of things to assemble, but news houses these incongruities within a familiar news world, so that news takes on some of the character of a nursery story.[18]

Contrary to what we have said of the decontextualizing effect of news, then, these literary critics show how "the news" begins to structure itself. Mass communications theorists, likewise, have always recognized the extent to which news is consciously planned and unconsciously standardized. One of them calls this "the news-frame's internally created consistency."[19] What they seem reluctant to face is the way in which daily news, having created the "intratextual" coherence required of all cosmologies, proceeds to destroy that coherence. In chapter 11 we shall take up their suggestion to see how far news deserves to be compared with a structuring "myth," or if it fails as a master text.

There is, to be sure, a contrived coherence in the continuing tale of the news, and one could parody its pinhole world paradigm.[20] But more serious psychic and social damage results from the fact that news *decontextualizes* everything it reports. This is how it can get us to pay to read about each plane crash in turn and make us mistake skyjackings for history.

It is the point of this book to show that nothing in the dynamics of this news world is new. A news consciousness did not begin with the mass circulation papers of the late nineteenth century, or with television. Even McLuhan's "electronic revolution" can be subsumed in the development of periodical news production. At the beginning, the periodical media may have served their purpose better, actually empowering their audience and creating a real, rather than a "pseudo-public," in Habermas's term. News treatment did not affect culture as drastically when its reports were used to start public discussion, rather than being consumed in private.[21] It did not have the same power to dissipate thinking when people read science, theology, poetry and economics for themselves, as well as news about them. But as we reduce our intake to little besides news, the distortions of decontextualization become more obvious. Seeing news in its original setting may help us recognize its tendencies even better than trying to analyze the media that have become our second nature.

To remind us of what to look for, we might began by asking what we would *expect* to be the result of publishing on a periodical schedule. How can a periodical make each issue important enough to insure its sale? How does it bring us back tomorrow? No doubt there is a wide difference between responsible journalistic method and true cynicism, with many gradations in between. But we may take the following as the structuring tendencies of daily publication, which responsible journalists must constantly work against.

Making today's product important means giving the news a forward spin, by suggesting what may be the *upshot* of today's event. This orients readers toward tomorrow's edition.

Making news periodical means pushing for change, to have more to report.

It means creating excitement—agreeable or otherwise. This might take the form of flattery, shock, worry, horror, puzzlement, blame. It needn't be pleasant to do the trick. At the time in which daily news first developed, people were also discovering snuff, which creates a sensation that would be intolerable if prolonged, but is only meant to be momentary.

It means presenting reports in terms of *facts*. Facts are knowledge in atomic form, not knowledge as part of a larger whole, which is wisdom. News stories must have a superficial appearance of completeness, of narrative closure, even in reporting endlessly developing subjects such as science.[22] Interim reports of criminal or political investigations become separate events, as the investigation itself becomes the story. Daily closure can cause us to lose track of more substantial conclusions.

Another way of saying this is that daily news means treating each day as equal, by producing an issue every day, keeping issues of relatively equal length, and charging the same whether the world turned a corner or not. We may term this the principle of the Absolute Present,[23] which is the secular rival of the Eternal in absorbing everything into itself.

Making today's product important also means relating everything possible to politics, which is the modern method of redress for the misfortunes which fill the news. Reporting on people suggests a necessity of doing something for them, and we are by now conditioned to connect this to political institutions. This may seem at variance with the notion that the news' main job is restraining political power. But, in fact, the news is forever suggesting that government is not doing *enough*. In this way the news has been a major force behind government growth, and the present symbiosis of news industry and government is only too apparent. Now that newspaper sales are declining, legislators in several countries are discussing subsidies, so that there will be continuing reports on their activities.

Making today's news important also means highlighting conflicts, which will insure further reports. Dividing society in this way is at odds with the putative function of the mass media in bonding society. Scholars have sometimes recognized that *conflict* can bind people, too, but some methods of doing this are not positive in their effect. Families can create such intense and conflictual bonding that they generate crippling neuroses, and there may be a social analogue in media practice.

Making today's product important means adopting anonymity, to give institutional or even societal authority to reports. The authority behind news comes from the scale of the corporation and the powerful symbolism of its logo. Naming authors would only raise doubts.

It means substituting social norms for social values in its reports. Norms *change* more rapidly than values and, to careless minds, seem to call values into question.

Related to this, it means using statistics to represent social reality. This, again, is for their brevity, and despite their tendency toward dubious dichotomies.

Finally, it means keeping reports short. For we tend to leave the longer stories for another time, or never.

There are numerous other features that are not perhaps *necessary* to news success, but might count as corollaries to these axioms. They likewise indicate how periodical production changes the relation between author and reader, and remind us of the media's dependency on their public. Selling today's and tomorrow's edition could also encourage editors to do the following.

Make it entertaining, if we can differentiate that from the simple rule of making it exciting. Concentrating on celebrities is an example of this impulse and just as profitable as concentrating on the powerful.

Emotionalize it, through caricatures, which don't only occur on the editorial page and are not always visual.

Keep it simple, in vocabulary and syntax as well as length, to make sure that newsreading does not become an effort.

Make "the news" a story in itself, commenting on the efforts made to bring us today's report or the difficulties that authorities or other groups are putting in the journalists' way.

Summarize books, of literature, history, theology, or philosophy, putting the rest of culture into play and making it all a matter of fashion.

Treat ideas as time bound. That is, give the *age* of ideas a logical significance, so that they need not be refuted, but will expire through neglect.

Once again, such practices may caricature the more responsible journalism of our time and of the seventeenth century. But they are the natural tendencies of periodical presentation, and we will want to see how many of them became evident in the first century of periodical publication.

The probable *effects* of all these tendencies upon consciousness, of course, give a point to our study, and we can make them explicit at the outset. For a start, we should consider that news can hardly help having what is called a "liberal bias," whether publishers are conscious of it or not. By definition periodical news is oriented toward change, toward the future, toward possibilities. It does not participate in the ritual suspension of time in which earlier cultures sounded the depths of human existence. The liberal emphasis is on liberty rather than on order, on testing authority rather than on honoring authority. Our reaction to the very suggestion of honoring authority is a measure of our present conditioning. It has become difficult to acknowledge the authority that must be inherent in community.

It follows that the notion of a conservative newspaper is a contradiction in terms. Periodicity is about movement, while conservatism is oriented toward order and solidarity. Those who publish daily or weekly papers will have accepted the idea that *change* is the really important feature of life and must live with their minds in the future. They might be actively reactionary, but hardly "conservative."

Of course, this is not to insinuate that conservatism is more desirable than liberalism. The point is that a healthy society needs both liberty and order, change and stability. It is not too much to say that the public needs more books than news to maintain its balance. A "news culture" will tilt steeply in the direction of change for its own sake and maintain a periodical tempo that is literally mindless.

Religion, though distinct from conservatism and sometimes at odds with it, inevitably finds itself at odds with periodical publication. At the Reformation, time was one of the first things to be secularized or divorced from its religious uses, and periodical news was one of the forms that the secularization of time took.[24] Periodicals gave a new urgency to the mundane. One can readily see that *news* of religion would be no way to bury things among the sacred foundations; rather the reverse. When religion makes the news, it has not been behaving itself. And, as we shall see, news discourse is a candidate to replace religion as our new master text.

One would expect the results of this to be far reaching. Anthropologically speaking, religion was involved in the beginnings of drama, art, philosophy, music, scholarship, political philosophy, and even modern science. Lacking such reference, the news will turn our attention toward artistic *trends*, which will impoverish the arts and the public.

The key to understanding the cultural change involved in a developing news consciousness has already been provided by literary critics such as Northrop Frye. Until the seventeenth century, Frye wrote, literature and religion operated in the language *appropriate* to those activities—myth and metaphor. "Myths" are, after all, what humans live by, and metaphors are what we live in. But now, as Frye observes, the phrase "metaphorical literalism" is jarring. Literal now means the plainest sense, not a metaphorical one. "Literal meaning" now insists on an expression of representational accuracy or correspondence. This language of fact was not even available until the seventeenth century when the scientific and historiographical revolutions created it, with its limitations.[25]

Frye did not mention that it was newspapers that spread the language of fact throughout culture. The very first English periodicals, the corantos of 1621, gave information a precise location in space and in time, they scrupulously identified its sources, and gave it a bogus closure in a developing reality. This is what we mean by fact. At that time, the factual diction inherent in periodicity was only a tiny part of a rich culture. It has hypertrophied to crowd out that culture.

The philosopher Susanne Langer discussed factual discourse from an even higher perspective. Facts do not exist in "nature," in her view, but are events as we construct or formulate them intellectually. Technically speaking, a fact is "an intellectually formulated event." A fact has the convenient property of being "something to which a proposition is applicable; and a proposition that is not applicable to any event or events is *false*." This leads to the hegemony of propositions—their ability to rule the Big Questions out of order. And it began in the seventeenth century, when Francis Bacon announced that "men should put their notions by, and attend solely to facts."[26] He pronounced that sentence at virtually the same time that the first corantos appeared, which produced a craze for facts.

In Langer's view, a turn toward the factual was a fateful change in human consciousness. "A society that has its mind fixed on religious symbols deals with facts in a purely practical spirit and disposes of them as fast as they arise." That is, events were absorbed into existing patterns of philosophical significance, or else dismissed. But after the scientific revolution there was "a new interest in facts, not as distracting interruptions to pure thought, but as its very sources and terminals." Langer thought that "great scientists were never distracted by the fact-finding rage; they knew from the first what they were doing. Their task was always to relate facts to each other." But the rest of society never achieved a balance: "Looking, measuring, analyzing things became something like sports in their own right."[27] While she does not mention news, it—more than anything—suggested that facts would speak for themselves.

Like Frye, Langer worried over the loss of a discourse in which the literal was the metaphorical and therefore the human. "The tendency to demand ever more signs to replace symbols at certain terminals of thought, more symbols to direct one to expect new signs, makes our lives more and more factual, . . . wedded to the march of mundane events, and beset by disconcerting surprises." Is it really human, she wonders, to regress from explaining to pointing?[28]

At the time that she wrote, Langer could not foresee how even our libraries would institutionalize the news approach to knowledge. Libraries are coming to be thought of as storage of "information" in bit form, catalogued for random access and assembly. Librarians used to try to assemble *texts* with a sense of their relationships; now they display data and help scholars with "information management." Data, in Langer's terms, are signs.[29] We have always heard that signs are what animals use, while symbols are more appropriate to humans. Our basic sense of human Being, once nourished by the arts, philosophy, science, play, may not be nourished by data about these things.

As for the effect of periodicity upon social consciousness, daily news makes it natural to regard society as an object of change and government as an instrument of change. Our mental image of government is likely to be of a busy legislature. Time was, when government was valued as an instrument of stability and imagined as a courtroom. While society needs a balance between these functions, news addiction will tip the playing field so far that politicians no longer feel the need to justify a call for "change."

Despite such concerns, we are bound to wonder how societies of a hundred million could possibly maintain any consciousness of themselves without the mass media, or carry on any version of democratic politics. Is it not the mass media that bind our impossibly large societies together? The recent discussion of "culture as text" may suggest other possibilities. There is much interest these days in how societies or cultures are maintained by participation in foundational texts of some kind. As Frye mentioned, individuals find their identity within the various tropes of their inherited literatures. The West's earlier culture texts were Judeo-Christian and classical. It is suggestive that the theologian Hans Frei dated what he called the eclipse of narrative participation in Scripture to around 1700, in England. That would coincide almost too neatly with the time when news discourse was triumphing over other texts.[30]

Periodical news has become our master text by undermining the reader's patience and driving out its competition. In light of all this, we need to consider whether it is possible for the "myth" of world news to function adequately as a cultural foundation. Fables and myths—not to speak of philosophies or even ideologies—may do these things much better. They don't deconstruct themselves, as daily news must.

Any functioning society depends upon something like a fundamental "myth," foundational "text," ideology, or metanarrative if it is to make any sense of experience or events. If we had to reappraise our perceptions afresh each morning we would never succeed in getting our bearings. If it were not for our culture's symbols we could not *think*. Whatever our suspicions of the hegemonic possibilities inherent in a cultural "text," something of the sort must be present as a basis for communication and human society.

Factual discourse, as it developed in news, science, and history, during the seventeenth century, would replace a fundamentally religious culture, whose text—even for illiterates—had been Scripture. A whole world of stories, metaphors, practices, values, and roles would cease to give meaning to the lives of English men and women, while new forms of being and thinking were forged in the press. The constellation of new meanings constitutes what a critic like Barthes would call a myth.[31] It is important to realize that the old "text" was being replaced not by "reality"—which has to be *processed* for thought—but by a different text. Mass communications theorists now frequently use the term "myth" for the cosmology—the intratextual consistency—of modern news. James Carey and those who take a "cultural" approach to the study of mass media think that they offer modern society what myth offered to earlier times. They enjoy the sardonic sound of this characterization. And they emphasize the way in which news organizes our worldview according to the implicit "stories" that shape the journalistic mind. Without the journalists' "news sense"—which amounts to implicit narrative archetypes—they could not "mend the holes" in a ragged reality.[32] This news "myth" even governs what gets chosen *as* news, out of the unimaginable variety out there.

There is some truth to this characterization of modern news as myth. If myth is defined as *a story about the whole world*, the place where one hears such stories nowadays is on the "evening news." But there is another sense in which the characterization of news as myth is profoundly wrong, in that the demands of periodicity undercut the mythic function.

It is true that foundational myths must be adjusted from time to time to give them the flexibility to deal with developments. But it is one thing for a society to make these adjustments to its outlook gradually and unconsciously, preserving the needed stability in thinking. It is quite another thing to have daily updates that insist on their novelty. And that is what periodical news does, whether the changes are significant or not. Through culture, through myth and traditional lore, societies feel that they have settled on what is important and sensible. If there is pressure to change, if the newest is always the most deserving of attention, if custom is by its nature suspect, we may come to think that there is nothing in that line with a claim to our loyalty. What it comes to is that the news industry's profits require a perception of change where there is none, or where the change is of their making.

In England, the inherent tendencies of periodical publication became apparent within the first years of the enterprise. Standard histories of journalism have ignored this, because they have not concentrated on the effects of the product upon readers. They have seen the history of news from the perspective of producers. So they have dealt with such matters as libel law, editorial objectivity, and censorship. The issue for us is not who controls the press, but how its daily tempo controls those who produce the news and those who consume it.

To anticipate some of our story, we will find that the character of the news enterprise suggested capitalistic investment almost immediately. This was not yet the case in book publishing and suggests a different relation to the market. Doubtless some newsmen started from a vision of informing the public, but many of the very earliest had purely economic motives. That bold claim rests on the many cases of early journalists who wrote for both sides in the seventeenth century's political controversies. At any rate, the second generation of journalists often put their papers up for sale to shareholders, whose attention was on profits. It was a common pattern by 1720.[33]

We also find that, two centuries before Joseph Pulitzer was credited with the discovery, these entrepreneurs recognized that periodical news could be an advertisement for one's advertisements. Some early editors were booksellers who wanted to plug their own books and block ads for their competitors and for circulating libraries. But others had simply learned that ads could provide most of their profit margin. So the news became wrapping for their advertisements—with all that this has meant for journalistic independence.[34]

It also occurred to the very earliest owners that maximizing daily sales demanded a show of impartiality—again, two centuries before some historians have supposed. When the *Daily Courant* began publication in 1702 the editor expressed what had become the standard line, that he would not "take upon him to give any Comments or Conjectures of his own, but will relate only Matter of Fact; supposing other People to have Sense enough to make Reflections for themselves."[35] Naturally, such impartiality was only extended to potential buyers—who needed to be flattered—while socially marginal groups were caricatured for the amusement of the larger part of the market.[36]

The last is a vital point. The dynamics of periodicity comes from the need to flatter readers, and this was recognized very early. Editors ostentatiously deferred to their customers' intelligence, knowledge, good judgment, and even asked for responses. Several papers consisted *primarily* of letters from readers, giving them the thrill of seeing themselves in print. And at a time when customers showed up at the printer's office to buy their copies, the first newspapers were a truly interactive medium.

Constant care was required to maintain this public, and this was often done by suggesting identities that readers could adopt. Journals created images by which readers could recognize themselves, sometimes by a club motif or an editorial *persona* like Mr. Spectator. These would increase in importance as the prototypical coffeehouse began to decline during the growing privatization of life in the eighteenth century. So a continuing participation in something like a public sphere was vicariously maintained through the newspapers, but only as a simulation of discussion.

Through the seventeenth century, as Habermas observed, newspapers spoke *to* this public and not *for* it. But later developments left less to chance, as papers began to *tell* readers what they thought. This was aided when the press adopted anonymity. At first, the news came with the name of a publisher who could be assumed to be writing it, or the byline of the foreign journal that was its source. By 1700 it was usual for papers to speak more directly, assuming the voice of society. Pamphlets and books could not achieve this authority so easily, since they could be refuted. A periodical can follow its reports with subtle corrections, so that its anonymous authority is institutional or even societal. In this way periodicals began to reverse the effect of the fixity of print, to which Jack Goody has drawn attention.[37] Periodicals were more slippery, harder to refute than books.

It will come as no surprise that sensationalism was an early development, when sales lagged. Addison complained that when the French wars ended, newspapers had to fall back on "the Marvellous," or miracles: "They are forced in a dead calm of affairs to ransack every element for proper amusements, and either to astonish their readers from time to time with a strange and wonderful sight, or be content to lose their custom[ers]."[38] A critic of the *Craftsman* accused that journal of having "to write something every now and then for which they hope to be sent for by a Messenger [from the Secretary of State], otherwise the Paper is supposed to have lost its poignancy [pointedness]."[39] As one historian notes, "The charge was made again and again . . . that many newspapers were not above actually inventing news."[40]

Controversies were created in order to amuse readers and steady sales. Edmund Curll is only the most famous of the hustlers who advertised publishing projects by starting quarrels. Rivals could attack him in other journals, at advertising rates if necessary.[41] Benjamin Franklin's brother James promoted his own *New-England Courant* by publishing an anonymous broadside attack on the paper.[42] The literary conflicts that resulted soon became as absorbing as literature itself. Public reaction to Pope's *Dunciad* indicates that those who were left out of Pope's attack were just as irate as those who were lampooned.[43] Periodicals were just the place to carry on the quarrels of literary celebrity, which threatened to eclipse an interest in literature itself.

Finally, by the 1720s newspapers had learned to keep the pot boiling by employing what we would call "reporters," who went looking for news rather than waiting for it to find its way to the printer. And thus the human race changed from news gatherers to news producers. At first, this was considered as disreputable as watering stock for market.[44] But once an editor has announced a schedule of publication, he is not going to issue a blank paper or charge less on a really slow news day. Henry Fielding put it metaphorically in speaking of his novels: "Such histories as these do, in reality, very much resemble a newspaper, which consists of just the same number of words whether there be any news in it or not. They may likewise be compared to a stagecoach, which performs constantly the same course [route], empty as well as full."[45] Fielding had been a journalist, one of those who wrote for both sides.[46]

For a brief period, seventeenth-century periodicals created a new kind of society, the informed public, which took charge of its own fate. Editors provided the ingredients for the coffeehouse discussion which generated an authentic public opinion. But very soon the media matured to the point that they could *provide* opinion, and discussion would become a spectator sport. It is difficult to imagine societies of hundreds of millions without such media, even if we suspect them of being pseudo-societies. But at the rate at which news consumption is falling, it is something to begin thinking about.

Daily news has had many liberating effects, for which it has received deserved applause. If this study views its periodical nature as a major source of social and cultural incoherence, it is because that is the part of the story that has not been considered before. And also because it is widely felt that we are not doing as well as the fish in our opening metaphor. For if periodicity is not our natural element we may be drowning in it.

TWO

Inventing Periodical
Publication, 1620–40

News may be one of humanity's oldest pleasures, but *daily* news is a comparatively recent invention. The time it took for publishers to master the technique
of regular, periodical news, and the false starts in the development of that idea, show
how curious a notion it is—natural though it may seem after three centuries. And
the shock registered by some of those publishers' better-educated contemporaries
reinforces the sense that a whole culture must change before regular, printed news
could seem a part of the natural order.

The itch to hear news did not begin with periodical publication or with printing. In its informal guise it must be one of humanity's characteristic traits and was
long surrounded with artistic conventions.[1] Throughout the sixteenth century irregularly printed news circulated in the form of ballads, satisfying a folkloric function—
the need for narratives of moralizing heroism, with all the joys of rhyme, rhythm,
melody, jokes, and ornamentation. Such professional news-tellers survived in France
as late as the revolution—long after the advent of newspapers—because some classes
of people preferred news with a certain style.[2]

The issue of "truth" in this early news is problematical. Many societies seem to
place the social value of communication over its factual accuracy, in a more obvious sense than we do ourselves. Traditional societies judge the importance of news
according to its source rather than its objective warrants, so word-of-mouth is still
favored in many countries that have news of both the personal and commercial vari-
eties. People look to village elders to interpret the news for them, in something of
the same way that we may prefer particular newsreaders whom we imagine that we
respect.[3]

Nor is breadth of coverage always a prime consideration in a situation of informal
and occasional news. Traditional societies are puzzled by those who want to hear

news that could never involve them. Farmers in the modern Near East think that those who listen to foreign broadcasts just worry needlessly. Ignorance of the outside world is not shameful in those circles; indeed, it is considered a virtue to mind one's own business. The impersonality of "world news" simply puzzles them, for they find it difficult to take in any news that is delivered in an impersonal manner, prefering to have somebody "tell" it. When it comes to using the radio, many of them prefer readings from the Koran over news broadcasts.[4] In short, there is less thirst for exoticism in the news than we might expect in such humdrum lives.

On the other hand, anthropologists are sometimes surprised at the speed with which news travels in primitive societies. And indeed, early modern governments were jealous of the freedom and velocity of oral news, which they wanted to stigmatize as gossip. Many of the earliest printed "relations" of news were the attempts of rulers to get their stories out before word-of-mouth versions carried the day.[5]

Printing presses had only existed in England for about ten years when Henry VII started, around 1486, the practice of publishing partisan diplomatic accounts. His publications were to counter rumors that might well have been more true. His government also produced "news," or announcements, in the form of occasional printed broadsides. By Queen Elizabeth's time, a century later, various groups besides the government were promoting their factional interests by timely and tendentious publication of news reports from abroad. It was not yet safe to comment directly on domestic affairs except in the form of ballads, but there were plenty of those: twenty-seven ballads have survived on the Northern Rising of 1569, nineteen on Mary Queen of Scots, thirty-two on the armada campaign, fifteen on the earthquake of 1580, and they were generous with their "editorial" reflections. Some of these ballads survived as art long after they ceased to be news.[6]

Early printed news could travel fast. Some Elizabethan broadside ballads appeared on the same day as the event, and the standard eight-page quarto newsbook might appear within two days. Some of the excitement is caught in Henry Radeclyffe's letter to his brother in 1569: "We have everydaye severall newes, and sometyme contraryes, and yet all put out as true."[7] We gather that even at that early date print did not necessarily confer authority on such accounts.

The term used for these news ballads was *novels*, like the French *nouvelle* or Spanish *novela*. It only suggested something new, and did not press the issue of fact versus fiction. News was anything that was not yet integrated into a larger history. But it still was expected to teach a lesson, and it did not need to be factually true or even new to do this.[8] As we shall see, it would be the periodical principle that forced the issue of truth.

There was an upper level of society that was contemptuous of news ballads. Abraham Holland in 1625 could not avoid comparisons with real literature.

A general folly reigneth and harsh Fate
Hath made the world itself insatiate,
It hugges these monsters and deformed things
Better then what Johnson or Drayton sings

As in North villages where every line
Of Plumpton Parke is held a work divine.
If o'er the chimney they some ballads have
Of Chevy Chase or of some branded slave
Hang'd at Tyborne, they their Matins make it
And Vespers too, and for the Bible take it.[9]

But for most ranks in society, apparently, neither news nor religion were matters on which critical standards were exercised. They both were valued for their expressive function and confirmation of assumptions, at a time before the taste for—or even the concept of—fact was fully developed.

For businessmen or diplomats, who had to be concerned with factual accuracy, one possibility was to subscribe to one of the written newsletter services. A scribe who supplied a subscriber had a continuing responsibility to his client and would take care to check his sources. Handwritten newsletters exist even for the reigns before Henry VII, in the time of the Wars of the Roses. Some of these may have originated with nervous governments.[10] But many countries had commercial news-writers—called *nouvellanten* in Germany—who supplied subscribers with a fairly steady stream of expensive news that might be of commercial value. The Fugger banking family in Austria is famous for the network of correspondents that it maintained at great expense.[11] Kings also found it worthwhile to subscribe to the services of commercial newswriters.

So a serial and factual news began as a luxury commodity, literally worth more than its weight in gold.[12] It was an information system based on scarcity, helping elites to maintain themselves by monopolizing political and commercial intelligence. Eventually, this system would be challenged by one of abundance. But as late as the mid eighteenth century, England's Parliament was still trying to keep its debates from being published. And in rustic Massachusetts, magistrates strangled the first colonial newspaper at its birth in 1690.[13] We must be reminded that even today there is a world of shadowy powers that is normally beyond the reports of the news industry.

But public, published news grew steadily through the sixteenth century. A quarter of all English publications from 1591 to 1594, for example, were devoted to current affairs. In the year 1590 alone there were thirty-eight English newsbooks concerning events in France, almost one a week devoted to that one country.[14] Such news "relations" strained to find a market, with titles that sound like headlines: *The Happiest Newes From Ireland That Ever Came to England. Since their first Rebellion. Being the True and Ekact Relation of a Great Overthrow given by the Earle of Clanrickards Company, Decemb. 20. being 500. foot and 100. horse, to the three great Rebels.* Such sensationalism was the result of an unorganized market for printed news (unlike the organized market for private newsletters). Printed news was chosen for its entertainment value and moral reflections, rather than its realism or utility.

Before 1600 there is no evidence that any attention was given to creating a regular schedule for *printed* news. The first hint of a commercial motive behind periodicity is found in the sixteenth-century almanacs that printed summaries of the previous year's events.[15] It took time to connect the newsletters' principle of regular intervals with the market for printed newsbooks. From 1590 to 1610 "relations" appeared in England, on average, about every two weeks, and they may, slowly, have created an expectation of a regular schedule.[16]

These newsbooks ran heavily to accounts of pageantry and crime, not unlike today.[17] In the absence of a habit of periodicity, publishers traded on sensationalism—witchcraft, monstrous births and strange animals, fire and weather, miraculous events and portents, and now and then a sporting event. Given the danger in dabbling in politics, it was safer to feed an appetite for wonder. So contemporaries had an excuse we no longer have for reporting unidentified flying objects—the angels in the sky above Silesia in 1593, two dragons fighting above Ghent in 1609, three suns above Cornwall in 1621, and storms of blood and brimstone.[18] The most constant interest was the Turkish threat to Central Europe, accounting for at least twenty-five hundred publications in sixteenth-century Europe and finding a market even in distant England.[19] It had all the ideological and apocalyptic resonance of the Cold War. Many of these newsbooks and news ballads were apparently written by amateurs, whose motives seem to have been religious rather than commercial.[20]

Around 1600 the notion of providing a constant flow of publications occurred to enterprising publishers in Germany. In 1594 the *Mercurius Gallobelgicus*, in Latin, began to appear semiannually from Cologne. It was to survive for decades, and copies found their way to England. Periodical newsbooks or newssheets then began to appear, in Strasbourg and Augsburg in 1609, Basel in 1610, Frankfurt and Vienna in 1615, then Hamburg (1616), Berlin (1617), Amsterdam (1618), and Antwerp (1620), edging ever closer to England. And these contained the features by which we define the newspaper—a standard and recognizable format and title, dates and serial numbers, variety of material, reports from various locations.[21]

One might date the birth of the modern world from this development. Serial and then periodical news was sufficiently different from books—even the "occasional" newsbooks—to suggest a new type of consciousness. What is important in periodical publication is not so much the information it contains, but the sense that regular customers have of being current with developments. Newspapers maintained contact with their audience, binding it together and giving it direction. Readers could be sure that hundreds of other people were reading exactly the same thing at exactly the same time. Such a "stream of perceptions and sentiments" created the stream of consciousness for a whole society.[22] In the words of one scholar, periodical news "does not so much inform as orient the public, giving each and all notice as to what is going on." It is not really intended to explain the connection between events as historians will try to do, but provides "facts" that will be the basis for discussion and generate what we know as public opinion.[23] And this public opinion, rather than traditional wisdom or learned philosophy, is the basis for a new kind of society.

The juxtaposition of multiple items was an essential feature of this news consciousness. Whereas books represent a "point of view," a collection of diverse accounts encourages the reader's participation in assembling the materials. This was the feature of news that got Marshall McLuhan's attention, rather than periodicity. The "mosaic" character of news convinces us of its essential truth, he thought, because we recognize it as a reflection of the variety and incongruity of life.[24] It might also be said that it tends to give stories an equivalence. Periodicity creates the impression that each day finds the world at a crossroads. Together, these two features subvert some of the defining characteristics of a traditional culture—the sense of wholeness, the assurance, and the pessimism.

Like the earlier newsletters, the focus of the earliest published serials was practical and commercial, with pricing, shipping, and diplomatic information uppermost. Accordingly, writers approached the news with an unaccustomed realism. One would expect this novel discourse to have a particular resonance with the mercantile class emerging in Northern Europe, which was independent, secular, and pragmatic.[25] Ballad news would seem intolerably silly to a commercial society bound together not by its arts, its history, or its religion so much as by its information. Discarding yesterday's newspaper symbolizes an orientation toward the factual and the future.

Scholars who discovered a "print revolution" maintained that print technology has the effect of isolating persons from each other and isolating ideas for sustained scrutiny. Oral culture was said to unite communities, whereas reading is a private act. Whereas orality has associations with religion (since God speaks rather than writes to his creatures), print creates skepticism, by fixing ideas long enough for refutation. These scholars contrast print culture with the "secondary orality" of the electronic media, with "its participatory mystique, its fostering of a communal sense, its concentration on the present moment . . . [which] forms hearers into a group, a true audience."[26]

They are forgetting that print does not necessarily mean books. Periodical publications also create a communal mind. They do not exist outside of time, as do books; indeed their periodical appearance defines the modern time dimension. And while it might be possible to refute a particular news report, there is no real way of refuting the periodical itself. Its next issue can slip out of difficulties with subtle corrections. Periodicals preserved a "secondary orality" for centuries before the advent of electronic media, and the effects on consciousness credited to television have a long prior development.

The serial newssheets appearing on the continent were particularly suited to a mercantile class and would insinuate its revolutionary consciousness through all of society. Not only did they carry the reports needed by men of business, they also represented a peculiarly capitalist form of information processing. Periodical publication reduced the financial risk to publishers by guaranteeing a steady return. It made possible a more rational scheduling of capital resources of the printing industry and required almost no creativity. And it was organized corporately from the very first, with opportunities for silent partners.[27] Of course, all publishing houses seek to publish on a regular basis. To that end, they might promote certain authors, whose works will be anticipated. But nothing in that line succeeded in creating a steady market like weekly, and eventually, daily news.

In December 1620 an English coranto was published in Amsterdam, translated from a Dutch original. This was Pieter van den Keere's single-sheet *Corrant out of Italy, Germany, etc.* Whether there were earlier ones may never be known, given the very fugitive character of these productions. At least fifteen more issues of this sheet appeared by the following September, which amounts to about one issue every other week. But the term varied from four to perhaps forty-six days, so that one would hesitate to call it periodical.[28] At the same time, an Englishman, Thomas Archer, was trying his hand at serial news, although none of his early papers have survived. He was imprisoned for "adding to his corantos," the implication being that it might have been acceptable simply to translate the foreign papers.

The term *coranto*, of course, refers to the "current" of information that was provided, the "stream" of consciousness that readers were entering. The first surviving coranto from among those produced in England is dated 24 September 1621, and called the *Corante, or newes from Italy, Germany, Hungarie, Spaine and France*, "printed for N. B." It was followed by at least seven more from the same source, translated from Dutch and German papers and allowed by license from the king's council. The title lines remained close to that original but varied in their spelling.[29]

Historians would like to know whether this "N. B." was Nathaniel Butter or Nicholas Bourne or perhaps both. As partners they came to dominate the coranto trade through the 1620s and 1630s. Butter's father had been a printer and published at least one newsy "relation," connected with the Armada. His widowed mother continued the business, publishing relations of the baptism of Prince Henry of Scotland and of a hailstorm in Kent. So it was natural for Nathaniel to set up in business with the publication of *Two most unnaturall and bloodie Murthers* as well as the account of the execution of the culprits. Of roughly two hundred books that he published before 1622, more than 40 percent were news tracts. Some of these were sensationalized chapbooks but others were sober diplomatic reportage. Nicholas Bourne published at least seventy-eight books and pamphlets before 1622, about half of which were news related. Both of the men produced as many religious works as newsbooks.[30]

Religion and the news started off together, in that period of high religious interest. The dominant news story at the advent of periodicity was the religious conflict that began in 1618 and raged in Germany for a generation. While the English government avoided involvement in the Thirty Years War, the English people were partial to the Protestant side. They took an apocalyptic view of its importance, as they had of the Turkish threat and would again in regard to England's Civil Wars. King James I, following Elizabeth's policy of staying clear of European conflicts, did not want to see a public opinion develop that would embroil him. But he was willing to allow so much news as could be found in translations of foreign originals.

As to format, Butter and Bourne showed a certain traditionalism in changing coranto news back toward a book form. Their Dutch model was the newssheet—a folio half-sheet printed front and back in double columns. It was a true "newspaper." Like the earlier "relations," the English corantos became quarto pamphlets of eight to twenty-four pages with a title page. Nor was the name of their initial series standardized, though it continued key words. Nor was it rigidly periodical. So there was not a clean break with past literature. Nevertheless, "coranto" or "continuation" was there to suggest the steady flow of information that was the essential element.[31] Reports typically employed the present tense ("The Hungarians continue . . .", "The Emperor sends . . .", "It is feared . . .") suggesting the need to stay tuned.[32] On the other hand, the hint of narrative closure required to justify another account tended to fragment experience; it made each installment a separate event. Thus, it would be easy to lose a sense of historical scale when each installment demanded equal attention.

For some reason the current of publication was soon interrupted, but the same publishers did produce unnumbered newsbooks through 1622, at the rate of about one per week. While these had very different titles, they were dated, unlike the news relations of earlier generations, and generally had some element in their titles as "More newes from . . ." or "The 30. of May weekly newes from . . ."[33] And each pamphlet contained more than one story, which made them different from a news "relation."

Other printers took notice of the new venture, and four other "stationers" (printers) joined Butter and Bourne in a specialty in printed news. In October 1622 this partnership resumed and monopolized coranto production in England until September 1624. The syndicate introduced serial numbering but were unable to achieve absolute regularity or a set day of issue. On two occasions, two issues appeared on one day, and once seventeen days went by. The problem, of course, was the English Channel and westerly winds. The printers could not count on the continental corantos arriving on schedule. But it appears that weekly publication was the goal, as was already standard on the continent; in the first year the partners produced fifty papers.[34] They did not make a fetish of regularity, and as historian Matthias Shaaber has observed, "When things failed to happen, the purveyors of news abroad simply laid down their pens, a wholesome custom no longer observed."[35]

Nor did the syndicate worry about an absolutely standard title. With an official monopoly, they did not need to worry about imitators. *A Relation of the late occurrents which have happened in Christendom* changed (the same day) to *A Continuation of the affairs of the Low-Countries and the Palatinate* and then to *A relation of the weekely occurences of newes, out of . . . .* Then it became *Weekely Newes* for a time, later *The newes of forraine partes. . . .* Finally, *The continuation of our weekly newes* became standard in 1624.

In 1624, the printer of this news began to be given as *Mercurius Britannicus*, doubtless inspired by the reputation of *Mercurius Gallobelgicus*. Thus appeared the sort of title that would become standard in later decades.[36] It has been supposed that this institutional title was a recognition of the advantage of anonymity, given the disrepute that journalism already experienced. For as we will see, criticism of newspapers is as old as the press itself; Ben Jonson would introduce a character named Nathaniel into his play satirizing the news, in honor of Butter.[37]

The periodical schedule was developing slowly. And the first twenty years of coranto publication also saw little development in the concept or the presentation of news. The English did run ahead of continental corantos in using their title page to list or even summarize the news inside. By 1623 these title pages had what amounted to the first headlines.[38] The news items themselves were often just one sentence in length, never more than a paragraph. Obviously, this was not long enough to be meaningful, except to steady customers. Items are introduced in a personal tone: "We understand by letters . . .", "They write from . . .", "It is generally thought . . .", and even "It is rumored . . ." The general warrant for truth was the fact that the content was "faithfully Collected and Translated out of the Originalls."

Unlike news ballads, corantos were supposed to be true in an historical sense, so vouching for those originals was sometimes acknowledged as a problem. *The Continuation of Our Weekly Newes* for 27 January 1625, for example, includes an aside warning that the news from the Turkish-Imperial negotiations might be a manipulation: "But I will leave this matter to your judgement, and deliver both the letters dated at Vienna the 1 of January." Some things are frankly listed as rumors while other reports are termed "certain," which may only have raised doubts.

Generally speaking, the warrant for truth was in the use—really the invention—of the unadorned, Baconian fact. "Because there is fraud in generalities," Butter observed, "we thought fit to acquaint you with each particular."[39] This would be the way to scientific certainty. Scholars of the older, humanist school might object that reports were too brief to be educational, but editors could counter that they were also too brief to be seriously misleading. It was up to readers to decide what the facts meant, to the consternation of the traditional knowledge elite. It was notorious that the latter had never agreed in their wisdom. Perhaps the new information atoms would be the building blocks of a more solid knowledge.

Not only did periodicity create a new consciousness of the issue of truth, there was also a new awareness of the scope of world affairs. In time, the geographical focus of news would narrow to include, and be dominated by, domestic items. But originally, news meant foreign news, and almost every coranto had reports from Rome, Venice, Naples, Milan, Savoy, Germany, France, Denmark, the Low Countries, "and divers other places of Christendom." They had the flavor of diplomatic dispatches or intelligence reports. Readers had to supply the perspective, for editors never bothered to define an English position with regard to the reports. "We," "they," or "the enemy" are the words used in the original, so that one must notice whether the account comes from Antwerp, Genoa, or Hamburg, to guess who was meant. "We" could be the Spanish, and "the enemy" could mean the English!

But this development of a broader and more realistic sense of the world and of its detail was soon undermined by efforts to make the news more personal and "coherent." Before the syndicate was formed, reports were simply translated and left unedited. They were organized by the source—that is, the gazette being quoted—rather than by the scene of the story. Reports were not given in any order of importance and were as dull as reality itself. Of course, even the most entertainingly-written newspapers are stale when they turn up years later. But these first attempts were stark, amounting to the details of troop movements, back and forth and back again. For generations who have been raised on the commercial news product, this kind of military intelligence would be an enormous letdown.

For whatever reason, the syndicate decided to give over the processing of news to an editor, who introduced style as well as order into the reports. He was Captain Thomas Gainsford—lawyer, traveler, veteran of the Irish wars, and nationalist pamphleteer.[40] Gainsford provided an editorial voice and a more personal style as he wove diverse accounts into continuous stories with an eye to reader interest. He even included news from the private letters of persons of various classes. The issue of 12 March 1624 contained the views of a private soldier, a burger of Brussels, and a London merchant. He also took it upon himself to comfort his readers through the stretches of bad news, exhorting them to trust in God.

Apparently, this raised questions about editorial bias, and Gainsford had to answer those who had already begun to criticize the news.

> I can assure you, There is not a line printed nor proposed to your view, but caries the credit of other Originalls . . . so that if they should faile there in true and exact discoueries, be not you too malignant against the Printer here, that is so far from any invention of his owne, that when he meetes with improbability or absurdity, hee leaves it quite out rather than hee will startle your patience, or draw you into suspition of the verity of the whole.[41]

Editors were already learning that a thing is not news if readers don't believe it, or won't buy it. Criticisms must have been general for Gainsford to answer them publicly, and they struck him as unfair.

> Gentle Readers; for I am sure you would faine be known by that Character, how comes it then to passe, that nothing can please you? For either custome is so predominant with you, or corruption of nature caries such a mast[e]ring hand; that you must be finding faults, though you know no cause. If we afford you plaine stuffe, you complaine of the phrase, and peradventure cry out, it is Non-sense; if we adde some exornation [embellishment], then are you curious to examine the method and coherence, and are forward in saying the sentences are not well adapted: if the newes bee forcible against the Emperour, you breake forth, it is impossible, and all is invention: if it tend to the dejection of the Country, you seeme to commiserate and wonder at the misfortune: if we talke of novelty indeed, you make a doubt of the verity: if wee onely tell you what we know, you throw away the booke, and breake out, there is nothing in it, or else it is but a repetition of the former weekes newes.

Like all journalists, he comforted himself with the idea that it was just the bad news that made readers blame the messenger.

On the other hand, it was clear to Gainsford that a news addiction had swept the country: "Both the Reader and the Printer of these Pamphlets, agree in their expectation of weekely Newes, so that if the Printer have not wherewithall to afford satisfaction, yet will the Reader come and aske every day for new Newes." And there was nothing that he wanted more than "every weeke to please or pleasure you and afford such novelty as the season affordeth us."[42] But readers must realize that they "must not looke for fighting every day, nor taking of Townes; but as they happen, you shall know."[43]

Editorial chattiness was not characteristic of the German, Dutch, or Italian corantos. Gainsford was an innovator in this respect, and when he died in late 1624 it appears that sales declined. The syndicate broke up and the use of *Mercurius Britannicus* was dropped. Even if there had been continuing efforts to make the news entertaining or palatable, the news from Germany was not encouraging. It may be that Butter and Bourne had concluded that the news industry could not expand beyond the size it had attained, so that employing an editor was a needless expense. Or they may have decided that the critics were telling them just to convey the necessary "intelligence" and not make it into something else.

At any rate, the birth of periodicity did not lead to steady growth. Their declining periodical continued to feature the heavy hitters—the emperor and pope, the Great Turk, and Bethlen Gabor, the only possible Protestant hope. There was plenty of world-shaking to report, for any who had the stomach for it. Headlines on the title page of the *Continuation of Our Weekly News* for 19 May 1625, for example, promised

> The warlike preparations of Bethlen Gabor, the Grand Signieur, and the Emperour; who prepareth to resist them.
>
> The proceedings of the Duke of Savoy, and the Constable Lesdigueres, and of the Marquesse DeCoeuvre.
>
> The agreement which is made betwixt the Generall Tilly and the States of the Land of Hessen.
>
> The Warlike exployts and enterprizes which have beene lately done in the Low Countries, and about Breda: With the late proceeding of both the Armies; and the taking of a Sconce.

But few issues could report decisive movement. Typical items in that issue, in their entirety, informed continuing readers that

> We understand from France, that the King of France caused yet many horse and foote to march towards Italy, and had sent many hundred crownes to the Constable Ladiguiere to pay his souldiers.
>
> The souldiers which are come from the Hanse-Townes and East-Land are all in very good apparell, and the most part of them have followed the warres [i.e., are veterans].
>
> The States Generall of the United Provinces sent lately great summes of money to our [sic] Leagers and they expect daily great store of money which is comming from France.
>
> The Marquis Spinola caused yet lately seaven or eight strong sconces to bee made with double contre-points, and furnished each of them with fower or five peeces of

Ordinance, besides great store of municion, whereby it appeareth, that hee will not as yet remoove his Campe which lyeth before Breda.

They had not yet learned to put a forward spin on reports, to create a news addiction.

Once in a great while Butter and Bourne stumbled upon a human interest story, involving someone too humble to have made it into diplomatic dispatches. The issue of 27 January 1625, for example, contains the account of an English recruit in the Dutch camp. When a Spaniard challenged anyone in the camp at Breda to single combat with dagger, rapier, and half-pike, a soldier from Reading had impulsively accepted the dare. On the day of the duel he attempted to back out, but both sides insisted, and though badly wounded he managed to kill the Spaniard in the contest with half-pikes. The Prince of Orange had rewarded him with a pension. It was the sort of thing that could have been done better in a ballad. In fact there was the same sort of ballad moralizing, as the correspondent invoked God to grant even greater victories "against the whole armies of our Enemies."

By 1628-29 the number of issues had dropped to an average of one every two weeks. The Protestant cause in Germany was collapsing, and false reports of Protestant successes had made the public suspicious of the news. In 1630 the rate was down to an issue every three weeks and Butter complained that he was losing money. He had hopes, however, that the arrival of the Swedes would "produce more action in Christendom then was this hundred yeares; and more Newes is like to come to our hands."[44]

He was a good prophet. In 1632 there was enough news for more than one issue a week. The earlier pretense of impartiality was dropped as Protestant forces under King Gustavus Adolphus began to prevail. Unfortunately the newsbook's open partisanship was at least part of the reason that the government decided, in October, to stop the business entirely. It seems that the Star Chamber's prohibition of further journalistic activity arose because of the objections of the Hapsburg ambassador in England, who did not like to see the papers trumpet the victories of the Swedes. Charles I was not unsympathetic to the newsmen and referred the matter to the further consideration of his secretaries of state. They were only willing to allow the publication—serial, though not periodical—of a history of the campaigns of Gustavus Adolphus, who had died on the battlefield only a month after coranto publication was halted.[45] Ballad news came back with a rush to fill the void.[46]

A certain amount of speculation is involved in deciding why periodical publication began when it did in England and why it failed to catch on more strongly. Of course, the continental example of periodical news inspired imitation and the vicissitudes of the religious conflict created interest. Also, England had a government that, whatever its deficiencies, was sufficiently self-assured to allow cautious experimentation.[47] But few in England were sufficiently involved in foreign trade to profit from such intelligence as was conveyed. And at two pence a week, the price of periodical news was too high to become a widespread habit. Production runs were probably around four hundred copies, at most. A generation later, with the establishment of coffee houses as the main venue for news consumption, one would use a multiplier in estimating the actual readership of that number of papers. But it is not clear that the corantos circulated widely before the industry declined and then disappeared.[48]

Nor is it clear exactly what elements in society read them. By the 1640s it is clear that competing papers were drawing literally all classes into the public for printed news. It would be reasonable to think that in the early 1630s the audience for the printed weekly was still essentially the group that Francis Osborne (b. 1593) remembered from his youth, who gathered daily at the Royal Exchange and Paul's Walk:

> It was the fashion of these times . . . for the principal gentry, lords, courtiers and men of all professions . . . to meet in Paul's Church by eleven and walk in the middle aisle till twelve, and after dinner from three to six, during which times some discoursed of business, others of news. Now in regard of the universal commerce there happened little that did not first and last arrive here . . . [49]

While diarists of the time were quite likely to record their newsreading habits, we do have some glimpses into the effect of the new medium. Periodical news seriously disturbed sensitive and reflective spirits. The insistent nature of periodicity registered on the nerves of those like the clergyman and scholar Robert Burton. In 1628 he complained in the revision of his *Anatomy of Melancholy* that

> I hear new news every day, and those ordinary rumours of war, plagues, fires, inundations, thefts, murders, massacres, meteors, comets, spectrums, prodigies, apparitions, of towns taken, cities besieged in France, Germany, Turkey, Persia, Poland, etc., daily musters and preparations, and such-like, which these tempestuous times afford, battles fought, so many men slain, monomachies, shipwrecks, piracies, and sea-fights, peace, leagues, stratagems, and fresh alarums.

Burton couldn't help wondering if there had ever been so much news to keep track of before, and doubted whether one could keep one's balance in such confusion.

> A vast confusion of vows, wishes, actions, edicts, petitions, lawsuits, pleas, laws, proclamations, complaints, grievances are daily brought to our ears. New books every day, pamphlets, currantoes, stories, whole catalogues of volumes of all sorts, new paradoxes, opinions, schisms, heresies, controversies in philosophy, religion, etc. Now come tidings of weddings, maskings, mummeries, entertainments, jubilees, embassies, tilts and tournaments, trophies, triumphs, revels, sports, plays.

To someone who had not grown up with periodical news and was not as jaded as we, it seemed impossible to ignore any of it.

> Then again, as in a new shifted scene, treasons, cheating tricks, robberies, enormous villainies in all kinds, funerals, burials, deaths of princes, new discoveries, expeditions: now comical, then tragical matters. Today we hear of new lords and officers created, tomorrow of some great men deposed, and then again of fresh honours conferred; one is let loose, another imprisoned; one purchaseth, another breaketh; he thrives, his neighbour turns bankrupt; now plenty, then again dearth and famine; one runs, another rides, wrangles, laughs, weeps, etc.

Trained in a Christian humanism, Burton apparently felt called on to render moral judgment, which was becoming impossible given the flood of news information: "Thus I daily hear, and such-like, both private and public news; amidst the gallantry and misery of the world—jollity, pride, perplexities and cares, simplicity and villainy; subtlety, knavery, candour and integrity, mutually mixed and offering themselves."[50] Burton was only grateful that he was able, amid all these distractions, to "rub on in complete privacy, . . . left to a solitary life and mine own domestic discontents."

Like the Renaissance scholar that he was, Burton would have liked to find that the ancients had faced the same thing; he feebly quoted Pliny to the effect that "we listen greedily, for men's ears are charmed with novelty."[51] But novelty may have been more charming when it had not come in such an unrelenting flow. There was no longer time to be reflective, when today's news drove out the previous news and forced the public along.

> One rumor is expelled by another; every day almost come new news unto our ears, as how the sun was eclipsed, meteors seen i' the air, monsters born, prodigies, how the Turks were overthrown in Persia, an earthquake in Helvetia, Calabria, Japan, or China, an inundation in Holland, a great plague in Constantinople, a fire at Prague, a dearth in Germany. . . . All which we do hear at first with a kind of admiration, detestation, consternation, but by and by they are buried in silence. . . . 'Tis heavy, ghastly, fearful news at first, in every man's mouth, table talk; but after a while who speaks or thinks of it?[52]

It seemed that the scholar had to make a choice, of keeping up with events as they were delivered in the weekly corantos, or of guarding one's solitude in the manner of the humanist scholar.

In Burton's comments we can see the devastation that a news consciousness wrought on older—and sophisticated—forms of thought. It was like coping with an addictive product of which the tribe had no previous experience. Like newborns, readers could not ignore the blooming, buzzing confusion around them, as is possible in our more blasé times. The whole world clamored for their attention, before the news industry had learned to screen reports with an eye to reader interest. As reports arrived from Constantinople and Japan, Burton thought it was his duty to take an interest in them all. They were the troubles of his world. Such lands might once have been mere curiosities, but now he was getting frequent letters from them.

There were complaints of the quality as well as the quantity of printed news. One can sympathize with the Reverend Christopher Foster, who prayed in 1632 for "the Saviour to inspire the curranto-makers with the spirit of truth."[53] But for Foster, too, news was not something that one could take or leave. Since it was going to be forcing itself past his defenses, he hoped at least that it was true.

Not everyone reacted negatively or apprehensively. Some welcomed the excitement of a regular supply of news. In 1631 Lady Barrington got a package from her nephew in London: "I have sent yow madam (because I harde yow once say yow loved forryne newes) a new boke, and could Mr Scott have stayed but an hour longer yow had received likewise the weekly currant. . . . [I will] send such newes unto yow weekly, unless I receive contradition."[54] Editors, of course, heard mostly from those who were excited by the prospect of news. In the days before newsbooks were hawked on the street, customers came to the shop for their copies. While there they might tell editors what they thought of the last issue. Gainsford remarked in one issue that "because the last Methode I used was acceptable unto you . . . I will proceed to give you the same satisfaction, which you your selves confesse, you received by the former."[55] The modern industry, which constantly polls readers to see if they are still interested, would envy such intimacy.

From the beginning, papers were an interactive medium, as customers made clear what kind of news they wanted. Editors learned to give the public satisfaction. Of course, this was implicit in the commercial rather than philosophical motives that dominated the industry. If philosophy had been organized capitalistically—in corporations—and retailed periodically, it would have had a different career in the seventeenth century.

What the playwright Ben Jonson could not forgive in the news business was that it was not a branch of philosophy. Jonson was not the closeted scholar that Burton was, but was even more offended by the idea of periodical news. His objection was not the tidal wave of reports, which gave Burton the sensation of drowning, so much as the insane notion of news as a business. And he thought other Englishmen would find their sentiments expressed in his rollicking play, *The Staple of News* (1625). "Staple," of course, refers to a wholesale emporium, and Jonson wanted to impress upon his audience that the news they gobbled so greedily was produced by the same kind of entrepreners who supplied them with adulterated lard. In short, the news industry was "a weekly cheat to draw money."

As he described it, news was a business that absolutely depended on the ephemerality of its product. Timeliness was everything; only that news had currency which was "fresh and new stamped" from the mint. Accordingly, an office had just been established in London, to collect

> all the news . . .
> And vent it as occasion serves. A place
> Of huge commerce it will be!

This news will be

> examined, and then registered,
> And so be issued under the seal of the Office,
> As Staple News, no other news be current.

This was an allusion, of course, to the fact that Butter and Bourne possessed a royal monopoly at the time. They might be counterfeiters, but their product had to pass as the informational coin of the realm. The office even employed four emissaries, who were

> *Men employed outward, that are sent abroad*
> *To fetch in the commodity. From all regions*
> *Where the best news are made.*

Here Jonson was actually anticipating a later development, when printers were not satisfied to pass along the reports that came their way, but used reporters to scare up enough news to make an issue. The use of what we now call reporters was long thought to be disreputable.

Jonson also introduces the "jeerers"—wits, or at least half-wits—whose job it was to make the news fun. They are still complained of today, of course, as those who lower the news by pandering to readers. It was all in the interests of making news enjoyable. And the fun was further increased by the fact that Jonson's newsmen included their own customers in news reports.

Jonson took notice of the question of whether news was more in character in written or in printed form. On the one hand it was argued that written news seemed more timely:

> *when news is printed,*
> *It leaves, sir, to be news. While 'tis but written,*
> *Though it be ne'er so false, it runs news still.*

But another character thought that printing added authority to reports, seeming to overcome its essentially ephemeral nature:

> *The very printing of them makes them news,*
> *That ha' not the heart to believe anything*
> *But what they see in print.*

To Jonson this is all beside the point, which is that there is no meaningful distinction between news and rumors. "Whether it were true or no, we gossips are bound to believe it an't be once out and afoot. How should we entertain the time else, or find ourselves in fashionable discourse for all companies?"

Jonson represented the culture of the English Renaissance in its creative mode, as Burton had represented its scholarly side. It wounded him to think that print was adding its authority to something so insubstantial as the news, and that the attention that might have been devoted to the great themes of the English stage should be squandered on gossip. He was not distressed by the burden of keeping up with a whole world of news, as Burton was. But he was appalled at the cheat of making knowledge a commercial product, and by the triviality of that product. He left his audience with an image of the clerks of the Staple filing the news alphabetically, so that a customer needing to entertain guests could buy sixpence worth of news of, say, the Dutch Anabaptists.[56]

The disgust of traditionalists was palpable. In 1631 Richard Brathwait reminded readers of what they had always thought of the older forms of news: "Stale ballad-newes, like stale fish," he observed, is "not for queasie stomacks." But at least ballads had the decency to disappear after brief circulation in the city and then the country.

Periodical news was a larger problem; the "Corranto coiner" runs a mint that never
ceases its counterfeiting of reality. Periodicity is only a new trick "to make his
reports more credible or (which he and his Stationer onely aymes at) more vendible."
For example, in order to bring readers back for the next issue, "he ever leaves some
passages doubtfull, as if they were some more intimate secrecies of state, clozing
his sentence abruptly—*with heerafter you shall hear more.* Which words, I conceive,
he onely useth as baites, to make the appetite of the Reader more eager in his next
weeks pursuit." Unfortunately, "the vulgar do admire him, holding his Novels oracu-
lar." And apparently there were plenty of these enthusiasts; they came to the printer's
shop on Monday before the Exchange opened, and on Tuesdays sent the corantos
on to friends in the country. "His Chymeras live not long; a weeke is the longest in
the Citie, and after their arrivall, little longer in the Countrey. Which past, they melt
like *Butter*, or match a pipe and so *Burne*."[57] But new issues would keep coming, to
the despair of the cultured.

Abraham Holland joined the chorus of contempt:

> *But to behold the wals*
> *Butter'd with weekley Newes compos'd in Pauls,*
> *By some* Decaied Captaine, *or those* Rooks,
> *Whose hungry braines compile prodigious* Books,
> *Of* Bethlem Gabors *preparations, and*
> *How termes betwixt him and th'*Emperor *stand:*
> *Of* Denmarke, Swede, Poland, *and of this and that,*
> *Their Wars, Jars, Stirs, and I wote not what:*
>
> *To see such* Batter *euerie weeke besmeare*
> *Each publick post, and Church dore, and to heare*
> *These* shamefull lies, *would make a man in spight*
> *Of Nature,* turne Satyrist, *and write*
> *Reuenging lines, against these* shamelesse men,
> *Who thus torment both* Paper, Presse, *and* Pen.[58]

The notion of a "book" not meant for the ages was offensive to the cultured. Print
and ephemerality did not belong together. Acknowledged authorship had aimed
at aesthetic or moral or philosophical elevation, whereas the newsbooks were
founded on exaggeration and venality. One historian goes so far as to say that to those
of Jonson's mind, the news revolution constituted a "basic threat to civilised
communication."[59]

The traditionalist view may have been fairly widespread in English society. In
the period between 1632 and 1638, during the government's prohibition, there were
only smuggled foreign corantos to read. People survived. And even after December
1638, when Butter and Bourne were again granted a royal patent to translate the news
from foreign corantos, the public's reception was unenthusiastic. The publishers
complained that "it is well known these Novels are well esteemed in all parts of the
World (but heere) by the more judicious, which we can impute to no other than the

discontinuance of them, and the uncertain days of publishing them."[60] They offered to reduce the price if more of the judicious in England would buy them; "if not, we shall be forced to put a period to the Presse, and leave every man to the pleasing of his own fansie, by a more uncertaine restrained way of private letters, or verball news, which cannot but suffer much alteration, according to the affection of the Relater."[61]

The first chapter in the history of periodical publication in England was about to come to a close. Bourne abandoned a sinking craft and Butter was alone in the business after 1638. He continued, simply translating the same three foreign papers for each of his issues, and battling the censors.[62] He was still thinking of innovations in format, however. There was now continuous pagination and signatures to aid any who wanted to bind back issues into a continuous history. And he developed a short caption title instead of the elaborate title page to save the rest of the first page for news.

But it was not innovations that revived journalism in England. Rather it was the revolutionary events of 1640–41 that created a new and perhaps different market. Butter's monopoly could not protect him from competition in reporting the news from the new Parliament. But when he ceased publication sometime late in 1642 no one had yet made a living publishing only news.[63]

The first two decades of periodical news was a false dawn. The basic techniques of periodicity had been learned, though it had not been possible to implement them fully. There were innovations in format, but these were not lasting. The geographical reach of the medium had been enormous, but would soon shrink to a national scale. A pioneering editor had shown some sense of how to build an audience, but he was not replaced. Opinion leaders scoffed at the entire effort, and the public for weekly news did not grow large enough to sustain the industry. The addiction for news was not sufficiently rooted before 1632 for it to revive six years later. And yet a new generation of editors, in 1641, seem to have had no doubt of the public acceptance of periodical news reporting when there was an occasion that demanded it.

Organizing a News Industry, 1640–60

So far, we have only seen periodical news as a commercial sideline among a handful of printers. That was to change when the monarchy lost control of England in 1641 and was too distracted to control the publication of domestic news. In the early 1640s, entrepreneurs competed to develop news production in a variety of ways. Elements with which we are familiar—partisanship, statistics, verbal caricature, editorials, humor, advertisements, and even pornography—soon became part of the formula for news success. Professionalization developed to the point that journalists could write effectively for opposing sides. And the success of the enterprise is evident in the size of their audience, which could not shake off its addiction for news even when left with only one, official newsbook.

The decade of the 1640s began with Nathaniel Butter's expiring foreign coranto, with ballads, and the old-style news "relations" that developed one story apiece as occasion offered. But what the English wanted in the hectic months of 1641 was no longer the events in Germany, but what was happening in London. In time, a new type of periodical appeared to keep them up to the minute, called the "diurnal." The word looks strange, until pronunciation shows it to be "journal" (like *giorno*, meaning daily). Diurnals were issued weekly, not daily, but weekly issues were divided into the news of each day's events. Initially, these publications had a slightly different task than the coranto, not giving facts so much as repeating texts—of speeches, proclamations, and so forth. For they were originially the news from a revolutionary Parliament.

In January 1643, when England was in full rebellion against its king, there was a further development when the first of the "Mercuries" began publication, indulging a partisan editorial voice. In that same month an "Intelligencer" appeared—a name previously given to newsletters and suggesting insider information. Given the confusion in the country and the unprecedented changes involved, it made some sense for these diurnals, mercuries, and intelligencers to advertise that they were "To Prevent Misinformation."[1] Print presented itself as a guarantee against rumor in a confused situation.

The situation was that military and monetary problems had forced the hapless Charles I to call on the ancient institution of Parliament that he, like his fellow monarchs in Europe, had been trying to do without. And the Parliament that convened had wrecked the royal administration. So there were no instruments for restraining publishers who were eager to make money from the public's excitement.

During most of 1641 gentlemen who could afford the expense had subscribed to handwritten, commercial newsletters informing them of events in Parliament. One of these was compiled by the scrivener Samuel Pecke, and on 29 November 1641 the first issue of Pecke's printed newsbook *The Heads of Severall Proceedings in this Present Parliament* appeared. It ran for the next three months, with some of the later issues being published by Butter. In December it was joined by three other "Diurnalls." By January 1642, there were sixteen newsbooks struggling to survive in London, and another three in Edinburgh. Ten of these were called "diurnalls" and another five were "true diurnalls." In time, another ten would appear with "perfect diurnall" as part of their titles. Parliament did not agree that they were true or perfect and decided to restrain this wild competition. The contradictions and extravagance of the diurnal reports were creating misinformation as well as preventing it— as in the sensationalizing of the Irish Massacres. So, as the temporary center of government, Parliament began to license some newsbooks and prohibit others. By April 1642 only two survived.[2]

The desire for printed news and for the profits from providing it could not be stopped that easily, however. One historian has counted 320 serials appearing between 1641 and 1655. The large majority, something around 84 percent, lasted for only one or a very few issues. But 33 of them went on for a year or more, showing a maturing of the industry.[3] The commotion in London and the country made regulation difficult, while that same confusion was the reason that news was so vital.

The key to commercial success and product loyalty, of course, was periodicity. And it was firmly established in the first few months. Publishers adopted the old weekly schedule and settled on a common day for these newsbooks to appear. Monday was chosen, so that newsbooks could be sent out from London with the weekly posts on Tuesday. Government posts had only been established in 1637, but Parliament saw more need for this communications network than the monarchy had. So a second weekly post was established in 1649, and a third in 1655—making a Tuesday, Thursday, and Saturday postal schedule.[4] Handwritten diurnals did not immediately disappear, but they were now at a disadvantage as to cost. What would have cost four or five shillings could go into a printed diurnal selling for a penny.[5] Newsletters carried more sensitive information, for those who could afford the difference, but the lower ranks could now get at least a peek into the nation's councils.

The printed diurnals followed Butter's format of an eight-page quarto news-book, with two of those pages wasted on the title page and its blank verso. Publishers aimed at neutrality and impersonality at first, because of a need to be cautious.[6] The caution was not only because of the fear of government oversight, but was also to please a public that was by no means agreed on the issues of the day. Historian Joseph Frank has observed that "occasional" pamphlets were more outspoken than periodicals in that day. The reason is obvious; periodicals want the same customers back next week and are trying to sell the next issue as well as the current one. Samuel Pecke put the issue a little differently when he expressed concern for his paper's reputation for accuracy, implying that his colorless impartiality was a guarantee of truth. His approach long provided one standard for the industry, suggesting that periodicals had to be more responsible than pamphleteers.[7]

The historian need not assume that the purpose of this early journalistic effort was to spread the truth. That is the impression given by accounts of these early years that concentrate on the problems journalists had with the authorities. It is true that governments and writers clashed, but that does not prove the writers' desire to spread the truth. Summing up his study of the mid-century press, Frank observed that "from the start most newspapers were set up and maintained to make money. In the seventeenth century, as in the twentieth, profits were usually more important than principle."[8] Newsbooks could not help being informative, to be sure, but the truth of their content was not as important as that there be something for sale every Monday. There may have been times when the government had the greater concern for the truth. Certainly it often had a greater knowledge of the truth.

When it appeared that partisanship might sell better than impartiality, periodicals explored that territory as well. After King Charles and his followers left his unruly capital, the London papers became more unrestrained in their comment. Royalists responded in kind.[9] And when Parliament began to divide internally, the different parties found papers that would promote their various principles. By that time Pecke's paper, called *A Perfect Diurnall of the Passages in Parliament*, was exceptional in maintaining a reputation for impartiality and accuracy. Some readers appreciated that; Pecke's journal remained a standard in the news field. It alone required two typesettings and presses, indicating the possibility of as many as 3,000 copies, while other papers might only print 250 to 500.[10] Other editors paid his paper the compliment of counterfeiting his title, his factotum (the decorative wood-cut around whatever letter began the issue), and eventually his elaborate woodcut logo, which showed the House of Commons in session. But there was no real point in copying his impartiality, since another "neutral" periodical would be redundant.[11]

We cannot afford to forget that journalism is a business rather than a profession. The search for profits made news publishers ingenious. Diurnals began appearing on other days of the week. No one attempted to publish more than one issue of the same paper, several times a week, since customers would have assumed it would repeat much former material. If an editor had more news to sell, he started a second paper with a different title. Several did just that, including Samuel Pecke, Daniel

Border, John Dillingham, Henry Walker, and Marchamont Nedham. They continued to give primary attention to their Monday papers, which remained the more popular ones. Not until the 1660s, with the monopolistic *London Gazette*, did a paper publish twice a week under the same name.[12]

Now that there was competition, one of its forms was in the amount of copy included. Corantos in the quarto newsbook format had sometimes not bothered to fill their space. But some of the diurnals went to two printed sheets, or sixteen pages. Economics (including the high price of paper) dictated that newsbooks give up the full title page to use a caption or head title. They could begin the news directly underneath—creating a "front page." They also began to reduce the size of their type and squeeze their margins. On the other hand, they might waste some space on an eye-catching woodcut flanking the title or a short news summary before the news began.[13]

Competition demanded the creation of brand loyalty, so standard titles were soon adopted, and the piratical mind of the time soon learned to copy the more successful papers. Printers imitated each other's titles, type, format, and even serial numbers, to get new papers started.[14] Parliament's regulations required newsbooks to carry the name of printer or publisher, to hold them responsible. Most gladly acquiesced, since this directed loyal customers to the right shop. But given the number of false printer/publisher "imprints" that bibliographers have identified in the early newsbooks, it is apparent that they were not all sold at their shops; some must already have been hawked on the streets. A false imprint would have sent customers to a competitor's shop, if that had been the main place of sale. So the "mercury women" we read about later must have made an early appearance on the London streets, giving news an increased presence in English life.[15] In this atmosphere of intense competition, the hour that a paper appeared on the streets assumed an enormous importance. So they appeared as early on Monday as possible, even though they had to contain the news from Saturday's parliamentary session. Royalists twitted the London printers for having toiled on the Sabbath.[16]

Sales were also encouraged by providing a continuous pagination so that customers would think to bind full sets as a sort of parliamentary history. It is clear that the printers themselves bound some back issues and sold them as histories.[17] Several editors expressed the idea that their newsbooks could be preserved as journals of record, preserving "to all posterity" the "true Memorials" of those epochal events. But those who had their copies bound would be disappointed at the failure of historians to use them for that purpose. Even some contemporaries sneered at such pretentions. John Rushworth, who licensed the press for Cromwell, published his now-famous collection of documents of the war years precisely to counter the false views and sheer fantasy of the newsbooks, which he feared would mislead historians.[18]

It was not long before periodicals were designed for particular niches in the market. *Mercurius Civicus* was especially a metropolitan paper, for those who wanted to follow local politics in London. The *Parliament Scout* was explicitly for a less

sophisticated audience of countrymen and the lower orders in London, and specialized in humanizing anecdotes. The *Moderate* was, despite its name, the first left-
wing newsbook, siding with the Levellers and becoming their party organ.[19] Nar-
rowing the audience in this way made it easier for editors to know how to create their
appeal.

In January 1643 a newsbook appeared that would electrify the nation and revo-
lutionize the industry. The king's entourage at Oxford founded the weekly *Mercurius
Aulicus* to counter the publicity that Parliament enjoyed in the many London periodicals. A king who had always disdained public opinion had finally concluded that
he needed to appeal to that public. Naturally, this required a different type of
periodical than one that only provided information. It became the first journal of
opinion. And its subject was very largely a consideration of the contents of other
newsbooks. So this first "mercury" gave the whole journalistic enterprise a new
self-consciousness.

The writing of *Mercurius Aulicus* fell largely to John Berkenhead, who realized
that he had to talk to—and not down to—the public. Berkenhead replaced the
pedantic, impersonal, Latinate prose of the first issues with a lively and even witty
style. This is surprising in a man who was a disciple, secretary, and confidant of the
authoritarian Archbishop Laud. Laud had always criticized Puritan preachers for
trying to find ways to appeal to an ignorant and fickle public opinion. Journalism
cannot have come easily to a man whom Laud had once employed as a government
censor. But Berkenhead proved good at it, and his activities represent a triumph of
popular authority over elite culture.

Berkenhead's modern biographer has remarked on the irony of the fact that "the
regime which had relied so heavily on suppression of news itself set about captur-
ing a nation-wide audience." The Royalists were playing with fire, for the demand
for news was part of the desire of the public "to assert itself in the life and government of the nation." The English monarchy had long recognized the danger here; it
was only desperation that drove it to appeal to popular opinion. There was still something a little superior in its attitude toward that public; Berkenhead spoke with disdain of the mob, taking readers into his confidence as if they were a superior group.
And in pioneering the use of wit—which was very much at the expense of others—
Aulicus began the use of journalism for the purpose of dividing the public in its
favor.[20] Otherwise known as rallying the troops.

The Royalists had no choice. In an earlier day, their propaganda would have been
conveyed in occasional pamphlets, when there was time to refine the presentation.
But a periodical format was of particular importance to the Royalist cause. Scattered
Royalist forces needed regular, encouraging reminders of the strength and superiority
of their cause. There were weeks when it was impossible to produce *Mercurius
Aulicus*, and morale did suffer as a result. In such instances Berkenhead pretended
that readers had only missed an issue, by jiggering the pagination and sheet signatures as if no gap existed. Once, when Parliamentary forces happened to seize a ship-

ment of five hundred copies, one of the Parliamentary journals gleefully estimated the effect of this mishap: "The grand newes is, *Mercurius Aulicus* was surprised on Wednesday last by the Militia of the City of London, a few onely escaped, and no fewer than five hundred lies were taken prisoners, it is thought as great a losse as befell his Majestie since the late losse at Gloucester."[21]

In his blatant public appeals, Berkenhead taught the industry the techniques of advocacy journalism—"the planted idea, the inadequately denied rumor, and the inside story." His use of "innuendo and smear"—to use the words of a sympathetic biographer—was new in the hitherto staid world of news reporting and eventually "it predominated over more sober material."[22] Whereas journalists had previously aimed at transparency, they now began to attract attention to themselves. This, too, had a marketing purpose in a periodical production. At times when events may slacken, discussing the news enterprise itself can fill up the scheduled space.

For example, Berkenhead began regularly calling attention to the contradictions in his rivals' reports. From June 1643, for about a year, *Aulicus* made it a regular feature to show the discrepancies among the parliamentary newsbooks. It touched a nerve. Parliamentary agents founded their own paper to answer *Aulicus* and devoted over half of its space to that purpose.[23] The nation was bemused as journalism became a story in itself. It would be twenty years before periodical news could again disguise itself in transparency.

Berkenhead was only in his twenties when he served as the king's journalist—twenty-nine when he lost his newsbook in 1645. His counterpart on Parliament's side was even younger when he showed even more clearly what the future of journalism held. The two men were quite different. Deep down, Berkenhead did not believe in journalism. To someone with his deep sense of the sacred, a journalistic obsession with the present, the mundane, and with conflict seemed to be a part of the sacrilegious character of his time. He admitted that he looked forward to the end of all newsbooks—which would have happened had the king's forces prevailed.[24]

Marchamont Nedham could not have been more different. Nothing could better demonstrate how rapidly professionalism developed in journalism—with all its "cynical" attributes—than the career of this most successful of seventeenth-century journalists. Nedham managed to take both sides in the civil war—and abuse both sides—and still be courted by them both because of his ability. Historians of journalism are severe in their denunciation of an individual who offered his pen to the highest bidder. For we find it hard to remember that journalism is not about sincerity. We might prefer that journalists be protohistorians or crypto-moral philosophers. But in fact they are writers, whose words are for sale.

After the appearance of *Mercurius Aulicus*, Parliament recognized the need to use the press to present its case more directly. This was a different thing from just allowing its proceedings to be printed; it meant a continuing dialogue with the Royalist position presented in *Aulicus*. So in August 1643 Parliament initiated such a project, which was misspelled *Mercurius Britanicus*. Marchamont Nedham, who remembered Berkenhead from their Oxford days, soon showed he was Parliament's ablest writer. He could adopt different voices in its columns—from pious, to ribald, to plain smart-alecky.[25]

Britanicus was a great encouragement to Parliamentary sympathizers after the wit and scorn they had suffered from Berkenhead. It soon outsold other "Parliamentary" journals. Stuffy moralists claimed that Nedham was taking bribes to promote certain persons' careers—writing what are now called "puffs." And he was bitterly lampooned by poets of the day, as Nathaniel Butter was, for debasing the profession of letters. John Taylor, George Wither, Francis Wortley attacked him in verse— compositions that have hardly stood the test of time as well as Nedham's prose. Upon reflection, the poets thought that torture and execution were the only adequate response for what he had done to intellectual life in England. The public reacted more favorably, and in return Nedham espoused the revolutionary position that *salus populi suprema lex*—the good of the people was the supreme law. He even had good things to say of John Lilburne, the radical, or "Leveller," champion.[26]

Between them, Berkenhead and Nedham began a revolution in English society and culture, by seeming to appeal to the public to judge the matters they reported. Periodical appearance implied that this judgment was not for a particular instance —as in the case of a pamphlet war—but would be continuous. At times, the journalists misjudged the public they led—or followed. For example, in the issue of 4 August 1645 Nedham stumbled badly. He laughed at the king's stutter. In something like a "Wanted" notice, he said that "if any man can bring any tale or tiding of a Wilfull King which hath gone astray these foure yeares from his Parliament, with a guilty Conscience, bloody Hands, a Heart full of broken Vowes and Protestations: If these marks be not sufficient, there is another in the mouth; for bid him speak, and you will soon know him: Then give notice to Britannicus, and you shall be well paid for your paines." In Nedham's defense it might be noted that Berkenhead had mocked the Speaker of the House's speech impediment a year earlier.[27] But Nedham's slip was unforgiveable to the upper classes in England, whatever they might have thought of Charles's rule. Caricature would eventually prove indispensible to journalism, but the audience was not ready for it yet. This instance brought the monarch down to the level of the common people, when public opinion still accorded the monarchy a sacred character. As Nedham's contemporary biographer, Anthony Wood, put it, he had sacrificed "the King himself, to the beast of many heads."

In the circumstances of 1645 the House of Lords took immediate action. It sent the printer and the censor to prison! Nedham himself only received a reprimand, and *Britanicus* missed only one issue. The Lords recognized that they needed the paper. Nedham just needed to be reminded of whom he had to please, besides the rabble. Accordingly, he was soon questioning the right of the people to petition Parliament with the intent of intimidating it.[28]

But Nedham could not keep from testing the journalistic limits, and one more mistake felled him. In May 1646 he called for a "strict account" from the king for all the blood shed in the Civil War—very close to the wording that Parliament itself would use in condemning Charles to death two years later. But the House of Lords again feared this was too inflammatory, and sent Nedham himself to jail—for two weeks. By the time Parliament was ready to use Nedham's terminology about Charles, he had changed sides and was writing for the king![29]

Nedham has proven an embarrassment to historians of journalism, who treat him as an aberration. Perhaps it would be better to think of him as a professional. Berkenhead and Nedham had "developed" the news in numerous ways. One historian lists, among others, the invention of "planted rumors, trial balloons, supposedly authentic gossip, destructive innuendoes, and blatantly political atrocity stories." As we begin to understand the media better we are more likely to acknowledge that news does, inescapably, represent particular points of view and will always have a tendency toward a propagandistic "spin." Nedham simply never had the illusions the rest of us are still struggling to outgrow.

Even the king, who was limited and old-fashioned in his views, understood that he could not always maintain a sense of honor in dealing with the public. So when Nedham tired of working for Parliament and thought he might be more appreciated in the royalist camp, the king accepted a suitably abject apology and hired him to freshen up his publications.[30]

Actually, the change made sense in terms of Nedham's own principles. If he had one abiding principle, it was anticlericalism. In this respect he was the opposite of Berkenhead, whose sense of the sacred basis of society made journalism uncongenial. Nedham had the more natural journalistic appreciation of freedom and movement. By 1646 the most frightening clericalists in England were no longer the bishops, but the parliamentarian Presbyterians. Nedham knew that if they ever came to dominate the whole country they would subject it to a religious discipline which he, personally, would find unendurable.

It is not clear that Nedham had any religious faith of his own. He could speak the language if he needed to. But he is one of very few contemporaries who cited Machiavelli and Hobbes with approval, and the issue of religious toleration seems to have been his one abiding concern. This was not out of a desire to protect his own religious practice, as it would have been for a Quaker at that time. Nor was it primarily from a sense of generosity to those who differed from him, a sensibility virtually nonexistent at that time. It was apparently out of a desire to protect his lack of a religious practice.[31] The lack of absolutist commitments and their attendant scruples is, of course, a professional advantage to journalists.

Nedham had decided by 1647 that the Royalist side was more likely to allow the toleration or laxity that would best suit him. For at that point it was not clear that Cromwell's more tolerant Independents would carry the day against the Presbyterians in Parliament. Nedham's anti-Presbyterian pamphlets ingratiated him with the king, so he was given a Royalist weekly to edit, the *Mercurius Pragmaticus*, in September 1647. Nedham's most recent biographer also thinks that at the age of twenty-seven he was bored by his success and attracted by the excitement of a new celebrity. So it may not even have mattered to him that the king's cause was collapsing.

Until some months beyond Charles's execution in 1649 the paper was the most successful of several Royalist newsbooks—due to Nedham's talents.[32]

One must wonder how his reputation for lack of principle affected the acceptance of his journal. In 1648 he was attacking the Levellers whom he had encouraged before, calling them the "dregs," "the rascal Multitude," "the mob," the "Prophane vulgar." They were now serving a different purpose for Nedham. He was treating them in the way that his new master, and his new subscribers, thought of them.[33] It is some indication of his reputation that in June 1649 the revolutionary Council of State arrested Nedham—and hired him to write for them again. This, mind you, was after he had called them all whoremasters and shit-britches. His new paper, *Mercurius Politicus*, would carry on through the whole of the 1650s. From 1655 on it was the only newsbook the government allowed.[34]

Not only was the public hooked on news, but government was as well. Periodical news management was important to Cromwell's triumphant Independents, who recognized that the media had created an arena in which discussion could be guided. They never trusted the rather narrow electorate, but they did hope to appeal to an even broader public through information. Leaking the government's views and plans to the public through news stories might be more effective than issuing proclamations.[35] The regime may also have valued the interactive character of the medium. Editorial offices heard back from readers and learned the reaction to their latest issue. So whether or not people "believed" the official newsbook, Nedham may have been valuable to the Protectorate.

Cromwell's Independents were in tune with Nedham on the important issue of religious liberty, but most of all they simply recognized his superior skill. He told the Council of State that he planned to write the new journal "in a jocular way," recognizing that "fancy . . . ever swayes the Scepter in Vulgar Judgement, much more than Reason." Apparently he did not expect these upright men to be offended at that sentiment. They gave him better sources than any previous news publication had enjoyed—government intelligence reports, two correspondents in Scotland, two more in Paris, one in the Hague. The newsbook cost twopence, twice as much as earlier papers, and with its monopoly on advertising income it made Nedham rich.[36]

When Nedham wanted to express ideas that he felt deeply about he did not use his periodical, but published anonymous pamphlets, thereby demonstrating the difference between journalism and philosophy. In order to use parts of his anonymous *The Case of the Commonwealth of England, Stated* in the editorials of *Mercurius Politicus*, he deleted the references to Machiavelli or even referred to him disparagingly. Going the other way, his pamphlets might ridicule his own newsbook for not being able to develop an argument, as when he referred to "that wondrous wise Republican called Mercurius Politicus (who served up the Politicks in Sippets)."[37] But there were limits to Nedham's facetiousness. His abiding anticlericalism encouraged him to develop a consistently Hobbsian political philosophy when no one else in England would do so.[38]

The size of the stage on which this journalistic drama was played out in the 1640s is somewhat conjectural. We do know that by September 1643 there were newsbooks issuing every day of the week (since *Aulicus* insisted on profaning the Puritans' Sabbath) and that in 1645 there were, on average, fourteen newsbooks for sale weekly in London. Their circulations seem small, at 500, 750, and 1,000 in most cases, and this hardly seems significant in a city of perhaps 400,000 and a nation of close to 5,750,000 at mid-century.[39]

But there are several factors to consider. Joseph Frank estimates that total weekly circulation in 1644 was about six thousand. He thinks this could be multiplied by a factor of perhaps ten to find the true readership, for in those days one did not throw something that cost a penny down at the next street corner.[40] Threepence would buy you a meal in a London tavern as late as the 1670s.[41] At a somewhat later date one of the free advertising papers in London estimated that each of its copies "cannot be supposed to be Read by less than Twenty times the Number of Persons."[42] Addison made the same boast of "twenty Readers to every Paper, which I look upon as a modest Computation" after only a week of operation of the *Spectator* (12 March 1711).

If the population of London, at about 400,000, were halved to eliminate the women, then halved again to eliminate those under sixteen, and halved again to eliminate adult male illiterates (by recent estimates), all 50,000 of those left might have seen a paper. Many of the women, children, and illiterates would have heard one read aloud. One cannot press such figures, but at least they suggest that Frank was being modest in estimating that half of the adult literate males in London formed the "audience" for printed news. Of course, there are also provincials to think of, who may have gotten pretty shopworn copies of the news. But this was rag content paper; the seventeenth-century copies that have survived till today will still exist when all of the pulp-printed papers of our own century have crumbled into dust.

We must also consider the possibility of a market in used papers. I know of no evidence on the resale of newspapers, but it is easier to imagine such a market than that readers would simply abandon papers after reading them. There was no possibility of recycling the paper itself for use as newsprint, for the technology for pulping and bleaching used paper was not developed until 1800.[43] Old paper would have had no commercial value except to wrap things in. Newsbooks might as well have been sold at a discount to those who could not afford them at the regular price. At best, the news in a newsbook was several days old when first issued, so their value would decline more slowly than today's newspapers. A secondhand market in news may have considerably extended the influence of the press.

Newsletters were also still part of the journalistic scene, helping to create a news consciousness. Many still favored them over printed news. For one thing, the authorities could not monitor them as easily as the newsbooks and so they included more sensitive information. For another, they sold by subscription, so that they did not have to stoop to tricks or exaggerations in order to maintain their sale. Historians have found them a more valuable record of events than printed newsbooks for this period. The continued sale of written news was a standing rebuke to periodical publishing well into the eighteenth century. The price the wealthy were willing to pay for insider information (at about £5 a year) implied the inferiority of the printed product.[44]

Like many industries, periodical publication did face some skepticism and consumer resistance. Contemporaries were quick to make a connection between printed news and distortion or falsehood. When diurnals had been operating for five months, the author of *A Presse full of Pamphlets* complained that selling printed news (to strangers) rather than writing it (to subscribers) had brought "things true and false to the presse." The House of Commons agreed, and in its order of January 1642 stipulated that nothing be printed without the name of the author, to hold printers responsible for what they published.[45] The argument that periodicity itself would insure responsibility, in the need to maintain a reputation for truthfulness, was not always convincing.

The criticisms of the news enterprise voiced in the time of the corantos continued unchanged into the Interregnum period. Journalism was viewed as an abortion of serious literature or philosophy by the poet John Cleveland—who had himself written for Nedham's Royalist *Mercurius Pragmaticus*.[46] "How should he record the issues of time, who himself is an Abortive," he asked in *A Character of a Diurnal-Maker* (1654), as if newsmen were historians who sold their wares half-baked. They are no more like historians than a "North Country Pedler" is like a London merchant. His parting taunt was that "the Turk should license Diurnals, because he prohibits Learning and Books."

Cleveland exhausted himself in heaping scorn on his fellow journalists, printing one pamphlet after another, calling them "the Quixotes of this Age" fighting the "Windmills of their owne heads." However insignificant their product, "to supply this smalness . . . they tug at the pen, like Slaves at the oare, a whole bank together."[47] When Nedham began his third paper—called *Mercurius Politics*—Cleveland remarked that he was taking the "mercury" cure a third time, for the promiscuity that was ailing him.[48] Such criticism found a very wide following; Cleveland's *Character of a London-Diurnal* (1647) saw at least seven editions. But it could count as evidence of England's fascination with the press, as well as of its exasperation.

Nobody at the time argued in favor of journalism in any philosophical sense. It used to puzzle historians that John Milton, the author of an eloquent appeal for freedom of publication in 1644, should have consented to censor newsbooks in 1651. But Fredrick Siebert, in considering the issue of press freedom, doubts that Milton ever thought of printed periodical news as a form of literature deserving of respect or legal protection. "Milton wanted freedom of discussion for serious-minded men who held honest, although differing opinion. He was not willing to extend this same freedom to men of lesser standing with less serious purposes. To him, both Roman Catholic literature and ephemeral journalism were beyond the pale."[49] In these terms,

Milton could have faulted periodicals either in the point of seriousness of purpose or of the sketchiness of argument.

Histories of journalism in the Interregnum typically devote most of their attention to this subject of censorship and press freedom. It is a central issue if one is primarily interested in what journalists intended. But what is interesting from our standpoint is what publishers actually provided, what people made of it, and how it may have affected them. And the point to be made is that once news had become a habit, all governments decided that it was best to encourage it. As a habit, news addiction could even be satisfied by the placebo of a managed press.

Since 1638 England has never been without periodical news. It was not always a free press but there were always papers to buy, keeping the news stream from becoming stagnant. Governments must have felt that if they could help frame public discussion they would not have to wonder quite so much what a restless people were whispering about. From October 1655 to March 1659 there was only Nedham's *Mercurius Politicus* (on Thursdays) and the *Publick Intelligencer* (on Mondays) for those for who could not live without news. It may have left readers unsatisfied, but it is worth repeating that Nedham charged twopence and still sold those periodicals.[50]

In the period of England's Civil Wars all the parties espoused the principle of a freer press when they were out of power and trying to get in. It was a useful tool against established authority. Once in power themselves, they may have felt they could not simply refuse to allow the circulation of news. This moral scruple, however, can only have been part of the story. All regimes felt the need of a connection with the populace, and this was now going through a conduit of periodical news. Arguments in favor of press freedom (for books, at least) changed from Milton's moral argument—that one *should* not control expression—to John Goodwin's practical argument that one *could* not control expression.[51] Periodical news had simply become a fact of life, a part of nature.

In 1660, at the restoration of the Stuart monarchy and the Church of England, the Royalists did not close down the press altogether, as Berkenhead might have preferred. Like Cromwell, they recognized that a periodical press was not only useful in opposition but also to the regime. For the public does not need a regular news production—for information or bonding—any more than authority needs the press for self-advertisement. Daily news became a habit for a sizeable share of the English population during the Civil Wars. The reading public learned that domestic news could be more absorbing than reports from the edges of Christendom. Editors developed authorial voices, targeted their market, and learned to live with competition. Distribution systems were exploited and production reached market saturation. Critics grew hoarse in condemning the news for being what it would always be, the flotsam on a churning sea. And governments had learned that a news consciousness was not necessarily an enemy of authority. Whether it would prove an enemy of traditional culture and society was another matter.

FOUR

Creating and Dividing the Audience, 1640–60

When the corantos delivered information from the edge of the known world it had not been difficult for government to break the news habit. Even when freed from restraint in 1638, the news industry, such as it was, did not revive. But things were different by the 1650s, after periodical news had held up a mirror to readers so that they could recognize themselves among the issues and the forces of the day. The Civil War created a need for periodical news that most times do not, and news gave the nation the means of facing the issues of social unity and social divisions. The effect, in dividing the nation, would linger into periods in which periodicals maintained the divisions, and when a communications revolution would produce a cultural revolution.

The sixteenth century had seen some progress toward the cultural unification of England. The religious debates of the Reformation constituted the first national debate. Elizabeth is often credited with having encouraged popular identification with the political nation. And in the early seventeenth century a preaching ministry, printed ballads, and an active theater set common standards. Periodical publication would put this "public opinion" into motion, with mixed results for the nation's unity.

The corantos of the 1620s and 1630s did not mirror their audience since they could only report foreign news. Besides merchants, that audience must have included many from the political classes who wanted to follow diplomatic developments. And given the nature of the European struggle that was reported, it must have extended to some whose interests were religious and who saw the world in terms more apocalyptic than political.

Lady Brilliana Harley's letters to her fourteen-year-old son in 1638 show that this varied audience might include women and children. Writing her son Edward at school, she rejoiced that "nowe the Curantes are lisened againe, you will wekely see theare relations." Later, in sending him a newsbook and a coranto she made the point more clearly: "I woould willingly have your mind keep awake in the knowledg of things abroode."[1] Young Edward Harley was, in time, the father of the first politician who fully accepted the place of journalism in political life, Robert Harley. A little later, the countess of Sussex was to complain to Sir Ralph Verney of the temporary suppression of the early diurnals in 1642: "I am sorry for it, for wee was glade to know what you dide" in Parliament.[2] By 1650, Marchamont Nedham envisioned society women as part of the fashionable audience for his fledgling *Mercurius Politicus*: "'Tis the talk of the Town who, and what this *Politicus* is. Those things called Fine Gentlemen, say he is a witty Fellow, because they do not understand him; yet they buy him, that he may be produced as a Complement [gift] to their Mistresses, when they are pump't to a Non plus."[3]

The corantos had never adopted this flippant tone. Rather, they showed a respect for the serious interests and intelligence of their readers, notwithstanding the satire of Jonson and others. Readers were encouraged to think of themselves as part of an information elite. No particular educational attainments were required, however; Latin was kept to a minimum. After an initial period of extreme caution, a partisan, Protestant agreement came to be taken for granted—as more conservative readers complained. Perhaps proprietors felt that it was better to lose that small part of the audience than to maintain an impartiality that no one felt.

The world of the diurnals was different. The nation was dividing, and newsbooks found themselves in economic competition. They had to settle for a fraction of the public, and to show it how to think of itself. Samuel Pecke maintained the tradition of a journal of record, and his various newsbooks attained the largest circulation of any. Readers must have valued them—most notably *A Perfect Diurnall of the Passages in Parliament* (1643–49)—for their sobriety, as it was their only notable feature. But customers could read him and then indulge more individual prejudices by reading his rivals.

An ideal of impartiality was never wholly lost during the Civil Wars. The *Scotish Dove*, for example, chose its name to suggest the innocence of that bird, which, in the first issue, was pictured flying above the contest between *Mercurius Aulicus* and *Mercurius Britanicus*. The editor implied a doubt whether impartiality would sell in 1643 when he wryly observed that "if men were as diligent to search out truth, as they are desirous to here Newes, our Dove may give light enough." Further indication of a cynicism about the public is betrayed in his expression of "wonder to see the stupidity of the common multitude of English people." But we may confidently presume that he made an exception in the case of his customers.[4] Many editors after him slipped into the same disparaging comments on the general public. It probably didn't register with most readers, who would assume they were exempted from the category by the fact of their reading a superior publication.

The *Parliament Scout* also chose its name with reference to the supposed desire of customers for impartial accuracy in the news, now that "the *Times* is the only study." The "Scout" who is alluded to symbolized the steadiness that that role demanded. Likewise, the *Moderate Intelligencer* began by declining "partiality" or "invective." All the writer meant was that he would blame the king's advisors rather than the king himself for his misbegotten policies. Still, he listened to his critics, including Royalists, and took time to counter complaints of partisanship.[5] So some customers, at least, thought they wanted impartiality.

Though he declined a partisan role, Pecke did help give definition to the news-reading public by measuring out the amount of news that would constitute their normal diet. As the former scrivener became more used to the printed medium, he crowded more news onto his eight-page sheet. Smaller type, narrower margins, and starting the news right below the title rather than on page three allowed the text of his newsbook to double and then triple—to about thirty-five hundred words. There it stopped growing, and throughout the next generation readers could assume that each week of the world's process would equal about that amount. Pecke never skipped a week or gave short measure, nor did he issue "extras" for especially exciting developments.

A limit on the amount of news registered for one day is part of our definition of the world. Daily news cannot deal in significance—by skipping days or issuing whole books on others, for instance. It is the contention of daily news (even when *printed* weekly as the diurnals did) that *each* day is significant. Perhaps all days are not equal in historical stature, but periodicals must suggest that they have an equal call on our attention. Journalists might admit that "history" is the only judge of the relative importance of different events, but insist that one must keep up with them all to be "informed." It is not their fault if the public has favored the excitement of news over the effort of reflection, or mistaken them for equivalent activities. Nobody in seventeenth-century England mistook these diurnals for a complete intellectual diet.

The audience for the first diurnals was expected to be men of affairs who were oriented toward the Parliamentary politics of the past week and could not wait for news from that front. They did not seem to require much news of the conflict that still raged on the continent, and it had not yet occurred to them that there need be periodic reports of religion, economics, science, or the arts. If the diurnals included stories from around the country, it was only because these were the reports received by Parliament, from its far-flung agents. So the question of what to include did not arise, nor the question of what editorial tone to take. There was also no problem about accuracy. Newsbooks did not have to vouch for the truth of their reports and could report later corrections without embarrassment. After all, they were only news printers and not news gatherers.

Likewise, diurnals did not need to appeal to their readers' agreement, and there was some hesitation in adopting an editorial voice in reporting from Parliament. But with the appearance of Berkenhead's *Mercurius Aulicus* and the other mercuries things began to change. Customers would be taught their own importance.

From his vantage point high on the Royalist side, Berkenhead could be contemptuous of Parliament in his reporting. He could also express his disdain for the timid London newsbooks that had been drawn toward a Parliamentary bias. He ridiculed

CREATING AND DIVIDING THE AUDIENCE, 1640–60 49

them, but he did not ridicule his readers. He did not even lecture them, but rather appealed to what they must already know or be able to judge. At most, he would chafe them for being taken in by ignorant and venal journalists. Whatever Berkenhead may actually have thought of his readers, he dignified them as sufficiently knowledgable and principled to use their own judgment.

Mercurius Aulicus was on sufficiently easy terms with its audience that it could humor them, something uncommon before. It implied an equality between consumers and the king's own representatives. The tone was appropriate to a conversation among equals, somewhat above the general public: "The world hath long enough beene abused with falsehoods: And there's a weekly cheat put out to nourish the abuse amongst the people, and make them pay for their seducement."[6] But the people were about to get something very different and more lively: "This day there came a Drum [envoy] to Court about the exchange of Prisoners, sent from no worse a man then the great Captain Ven, who having a command in the Castle of Windsor, conceives he may capitulate on equall terms with the Lord of the Castle. So soone hath he forgotten that he was lately called *a base rascally broken [bankrupt] Citizen* by the Earle of Peterborough."[7] There was a bounce to this prose that had never been seen in earlier periodicals, which still presented themselves as histories. While Berkenhead would soon be sneering at the homey phrases and downright vulgarity that began to invade the London press, in fact he had encouraged it. It was all in the interests of winning friends for his side, which was the side of all honest Englishmen.

By the second month of operation, Berkenhead recklessly drew attention to another matter that had been complained of since the days of the corantos—the discrepancies between rival reports. These had been treated before as evidence of incompetence; he raised the issue of deliberate deception, and invited readers to be the judge. Such criticisms of the London newsbooks became a major part of his mission. By June 1643 he was saving his last page or more for a list of the false reports found in the London papers, accompanied by his wry comments. By August these lists had grown to twenty-odd items, and in the 24 February 1644 issue it reached forty-five. It must have made an impression, even on those who did not believe everything he reported from Oxford. If the media were above the politicians, readers were above even the media.

Criticism of the London papers brought retalitation. We have seen that *Mercurius Britanicus* was founded to counter every move of *Aulicus*. Its approach was also jocular, its epitaph upon Berkenhead being "here lies Mercurius Aulicus, and there lies Mercurius Aulicus." Jocularity, of course, is an appeal to the reader's sense of what is fitting. Nor did Nedham care whether readers took him seriously: "Why should not the Common-Wealth have a Fool, as well as the King had?" Around the court, comedy was always "the ready Road to Preferment and a Ladies Chamber." In fact Nedham expressed the fear that he would not be thought humorous enough, "because I make neither Rimes nor Faces, for Fidlers pay, like the Royal Mercuries." And so he descended to the bathroom humor that would characterize much of Interregnum journalism: Aulicus "tells us in his last page, [that] he hath turned his back on us, so I begin there." He loved to report the activities of the Groom of the Stool, that archaic office that priggish historians long took to be a misprint for Groom of the Stole.

Readers had never been treated this way by news journals. And thus the natural tendency of a news industry to appeal to and flatter its customers was hastened by the partisan character of the times. Nedham had to rally the forces on Parliament's side in what was still a close contest. What shocked his readers—as we noted in the previous chapter—was that his sarcasm did not even spare Berkenhead's masters. "They write from Oxford, her Majestie wept, that the King wasted his Army so before Gloucester, and would not rather hasten for London and Kent. The Citizens may see her Majestie weepes not that they are ruined, but that they are not ruined soone enough."[8] In days gone by, the people of England could celebrate the holiday inversion of social and religious standards in inebriated rituals. Now this inversion climbed the social scale into a culture of print. Medieval peasants had known that this was all a game and that when they woke up groggy the next day they would be back at the bottom. Readers of the news may have forgotten their place, as disrespect became a constant theme.

Even the execution of the king, in January 1649, did not sober the new journalism. With the less dignified Prince Charles, Nedham had a broader target for his wit: The prince's Scottish supporters wanted to "make him worship their grand Idol [Presbyterianism] as his only Diana, and prove himself more affectionate to her than ever he was to any of his mothers maids of Honor, when he lay in France." They "intend to present him more Propositions than yet he is aware of; which if he refuse, then down go his Breeches; for they'l handle him without Mittens, as old Buchanan did his grandfather."[9]

All this was infectious. Even comparatively staid newsbooks such as the *Moderate Intelligencer* got into the habit of opening with some cute sally: "Here's fruit of a green Army. What, every week a Town or a Victory, Sir Thomas? Did the Royall party ever imagine they should be thus chased from Field to Field, from hold to hold, by such a stripling?"[10] Most of the journals at least took up the habit of offering a prefatory paragraph to set the mood for the week's news—introducing the editorial element.

John Cleveland's many lampoons on the craze for news especially played on these groveling efforts to please the customers. It requires something of an effort for moderns to think of this as a fault, so accustomed we are to the association of news and entertainment. But for Cleveland, news was a pretense to history, which had always been thought of as a branch of moral philosophy. In his *The Character of a Moderate Intelligencer* he likened newsmen to astrologers, who told their customers what was about to happen, and made sure that the prediction was a welcome one.[11] It was not until Cromwell's iron rule and the Restoration's equally authoritarian government that steps would be taken to reestablish the credibility of English journalism, by removing the audience from the center of journalistic attention.

Of course, Berkenhead was not one of nature's democrats; he would rather have lectured these masses. And occasionally he revealed his more severe side. Most notably this took the form of using what we would now call "statistics"—like cold water on a giddy inebriate. *Aulicus* made a point of having accurate figures, to counter the skepticism created by his attacks on rival papers. Numbers are natural to the transcendent perspective of periodical news, creating some sense of proper scale, but the early diurnals had been careless with their figures. Even Pecke had given preposterous numbers for troop strength and casualties: "It was credibly reported the Lord Generall had neare 50000."[12] His next issue topped that with a claim that forty thousand foreign Papists had been raised for the Royalist side and would be followed by fifty thousand more. Some newsbooks had no figures which were not good and round—twenty thousand, one thousand, five hundred. Berkenhead sensed that Englishmen no longer lived in a mythological world and would appreciate his more scientific tone. Though he rounded most of his figures to the nearest hundred, at least he qualified them as almost, about, above, and such. And he constantly attacked the other newsbooks for their childish carelessness in this respect.

All this made for a certain awkwardness on *Aulicus*'s darkest day, just after it had announced a Royalist victory at Marston Moor! Berkenhead had reported what was, in fact, the greatest defeat of the king's forces, as a "total rout" of the Parliamentarians. In the next issue (13 July 1644)—hidden on page eight—Berkenhead gave further "particulars," which readers would have "had last weeke, if the Rebels on the way would have suffered any Messenger to bring us a true Relation." And, in an effort to blow smoke in readers' eyes, he immediately turned to the casualty figures, as if that made a difference in assessing this catastrophe. It appeared that there was a difference of over twenty-four hundred between Royalist and rebel claims, as well as further discrepancies among the London newsbooks.[13]

If statistics showed a respect for the reader's intelligence, they did not aid social realism as much as one may assume. Statistics abstract particular elements of a situation, which is often the most that busy readers can absorb. But this has a dehumanizing effect, in two respects. First, figures tend toward a fixation on power. The news has always been too brief to develop arguments, and what is left is power—who has got the votes or the troops. It was the situation in England in 1643; the time for argument was over and it was time to count the forces deployed. London newsbooks had offered estimates of the divisions within English society.[14] Berkenhead needed to counter their exaggerations and modestly called his statistics "a particular that deserves mention." It is hardly surprising that he "fiddled" his figures as well. His biographer even speculates that he may have misled men into volunteering for the Royalist forces from the mistaken reports of their strength.[15]

Second, statistics are a form of caricature when they—inevitably—reify and exaggerate social divisions. There were not just two sides in the Civil Wars, as Berkenhead suggested, but a myriad of positions. This was only one of the ways in which he encouraged social caricature. Knowing that he would not appeal to all sides, and being satisfied to rally his own party, he ridiculed those elements in English society who would not be part of his audience. Religion and class offered the most promising terms for his satire, or both together: "We had before [the wars] some cobling Preachers, but never heard till now of a Preaching Cobler."[16] He liked to picture the Parliamentary faction as Jews, referring to their covenants and righteous remnants, their rabbis, levites, patriarchs, and "the tribe of Pennington." After describing the visit of some Jewish pawnbrokers to London to buy up plunder taken from Royalists, *Aulicus* reflected, "What pity 'tis the Turke lives no neerer to us, that as we are beholding to the Jewes for money, so with that money we might wage their Janizaries for the defence and maintenance of the perishing Gospell."[17]

Caricature does nothing to improve the tenor of social or political life. It could be said that the London newsbooks initiated such slurs by stigmatizing the court party as Papists and "cavaliers." The latter term seems innocuous to us, with even a touch of glamor to it, but at the time it had a sinister sound, more like that conveyed by *caballero*, rustler, or bandit. When Berkenhead joined in, his caricature was more resourceful and probably more conscious. His biographer thinks it was central to his outlook: "Berkenhead was a caricaturist, seeking out the distinguishing tell-tale detail, preferable physical, which could be so exaggerated as to make the victim ridiculous or repulsive." Cromwell's nose was a favorite, as well as Sir Samuel Luke's hunchback, Speaker William Lenthall's stammer, and John Sedgewick's missing thumb. "The strain of crude sensationalism ran through Royalists satire down to the Restoration and after."[18]

English court culture in the period before the Civil Wars had also been characterized by wit, and wit always has a target. But the more satirical and wounding wit of Charles II's court never recaptured the decorum and effortless superiority of that earlier period. And the Restoration practice of choosing its targets from among pariah groups got a big boost in the journalism of the Interregnum.[19] It was part of the pandering to one's customers that is our theme.

The roots of English caricature go back to the 1590s—far from the court—in Robert Greene's "coney-catching" pamphlets, with their grotesque animal and diabolic imagery.[20] Mid-century newsbooks spread this tradition over the whole of English culture. Parliamentary periodicals like the *Spie*, the *Scotish Dove*, and especially *Mercurius Britanicus* responded to *Aulicus* with an answering ridicule. Royalists treated the results as only an embarrassment, protesting that Puritan wit was oxymoronic. Wit, after all, was the province of the aristocracy and the university educated; others could only exhibit a low buffoonery.[21] The accusation was itself a caricature.

Berkenhead did not abandon this level of attack after the Royalist cause collapsed and *Aulicus* disappeared in 1646. He continued the satire in fugitive pamphlets. He was so taken with his ballad about the sodomizing of a Presbyterian elder's maid by her dog that he kept recycling it even after the Restoration, and it was featured in a print as late as the 1680s. The point, apparently, was that the Puritans' instincts were coarse, unnatural, and uncivilized.[22] Royalist instincts were not in question. This from the man whom Charles I—to reward him for editing *Aulicus*—had made Reader in Moral Philosophy at Oxford.[23]

In the brief revival of Royalist newsbooks in 1648, Berkenhead's new *Mercurius Bellicus* and the others had very little news that they had the heart to report. As a result, their newsbooks became little more than comic papers. And in the difficult years of Cromwell's rule, a nonperiodical pamphlet literature of the "satiric comedy of manners" was all that survived of Royalist journalism. In this way caricature was kept alive until the Restoration.[24]

Visual caricature would not be ready for use in periodicals until a century later. *Mercurius Civicus*, a paper especially directed to London metropolitan concerns, pioneered the use of woodcuts, beginning in May 1643, and including them in most issues. But they were so crude that the same cut was used for different people, like the cuts that graced the news ballads. Other newsbooks were not inspired to follow suit, or to develop them as cartoons.

Invective, ridicule, statistical division and caricature suggest that the idea that the periodical media provide the bonding within modern societies is not the whole story. Mass media are likely to bond certain elements in opposition to others. Historians have remarked on the extent to which Parliament's official rhetoric stressed consensus and concealed conflict.[25] But Parliament's journalists needed to caricature their enemies as Papists in order to maintain a superordinate loyalty among their diverse followers. And Royalists needed to create division between Parliament and the Scots, or between Parliament and London, or the factions within Parliament, or Parliament and its own army, or finally, between factions within the army.

In the end, Royalist journalists did not succeed in stopping the consolidation of the regime. But when the Restoration came, England was a different country, having created groups of the politically, religiously, and culturally disenfranchised and driven them into internal exile. It was partly a legacy of journalistic rhetoric. Rather than continue to demonize them, the Restoration media would simply make those groups invisible.

On the other hand, there is no reason to doubt the common assumption that printed news helped bring elite and common cultures together. A taste for printed news undoubtedly encouraged the growth of literacy of a certain sort. Of course, reading for ephemeral information was a different thing than reading for literary appreciation, philosophy, or scholarship, and the new readers may not have crossed over into that culture. But in later chapters we will see that a different sort of literature altogether—the novel—would be created for the news mentality. In time, of course, this "news-novel discourse" would tend to unify culture across classes, by driving competing literary forms from the field.

Despite what we have said of the disdain of elites for printed news, there is evidence that even they were beginning to depend on what they viewed as a plebian product. The Royalist earl of Hamilton exhibited the old, superior attitude when he wrote sarcastically to a fellow nobleman of putting their enemies off their track: "For newes I shall referr them to the copious intelligencers of this age."[26] But Adam Eyre, of the minor Yorkshire gentry, reported spending up to sixpence for a diurnal in his remote area.[27] The Parliamentarian General Edmund Ludlow was proud to have his letter refusing to surrender Wardour Castle turn up in *Aulicus*.[28]

Readers often had no choice but to depend on diurnals if they wanted to keep up with the swirling developments. Poor Brian Duppa, bishop of Salisbury, frequently complained of having to get his news from the loathed diurnals, after the Royalist press was silenced.[29] As the earl of Leicester fell from favor with both Parliament and the king, he derived more and more of his diary from the diurnals. He mentioned ten different newsbooks, including those by Pecke and Nedham, and sometimes cited three papers in support of a particular fact. The Leveller paper, the *Moderate*, horrified him with its "endeavours to invite the people to overthrow all propriety [property], as the original cause of sin; and by that to destroy all government, magistracy, honesty, civility, and humanity. It passeth every weeke for one of the Parlement's writers, and it is a wonder that it hath bin so long suffered."[30] But this did not stop him from reading it regularly.

This class may have begun reading the published newsbooks more for their viewpoint than for any information they contained. But by the end of the century the highest figures in government were not ashamed to depend on the papers in any area but their particular expertise. The duke of Marlborough even read them for military and diplomatic intelligence![31] So in the course of time, periodicals would form a bridge between classes. But as we shall see, this was often to the cost of high culture.

There was one place—the advertisements—in which all readers could have come together. These were a development of the Interregnum and provided, well into the eighteenth century, most of the "human interest" to be found in printed news. Advertising was not at first associated with periodicals, but found its natural home there. Initially, the plan was to create registry offices for the posting of ads, which would bring buyers and sellers together. A patent to that end was granted in 1611 covering the city of London, but the attempt failed within the year. Another patent was granted in 1637, but before an office could be opened it had occurred to people to submit their advertisements to newsbooks, as had been done a couple of times in corantos.[32] No longer did one need to remember what one needed, to look for it; periodicals would suggest to readers what they might want.

Book notices began to appear in 1646, and *Aulicus* and *Britanicus* promoted books they approved whether or not they were paid to do so.[33] By 1649 it was common to see notices of books (most frequently), medicines, lost and found goods, requests for information about stolen goods, and runaway servants or relatives. The charge to the advertiser was normally sixpence, but the most respected papers like Pecke's *Perfect Diurnall* could ask twice that. Some charged extra for using bold type.[34]

By 1652 readers were complaining about the number of ads that crowded their news.[35] But they did not disappear so long as journals could sell the space. When Nedham found himself with a monopoly of the news, he raised advertising rates by a factor of five, to two shillings sixpence. And he started a weekly advertiser, the *Publick Adviser*, in May 1657, listing shipping and stagecoach schedules, real estate and horses for sale, money to be lent, and services of all kinds—nurses, valets, doctors, tutors. Coffee (on 26 May) and chocolate (16 June) got their first exposure in its pages. It was new products, especially, that were advertised, reinforcing the association of periodicity with novelty.[36] Nedham's initiative was followed in the Restoration by the *City Mercury, Merchant's Remembrancer*, and others, to be considered later.[37] In those years of a managed press, ads added a touch of realism to newssheets that might otherwise have risen above the public reach.

But through all this time there were some who did not care for journalistic realism. There was not only a level of English society that thought itself above the news, but also a level that could not keep up an interest in public affairs, and wanted something more down-to-earth. For them, publishers offered periodical pornography. It happened under the very nose of a regime that historians long characterized as "Puritan." Several periodicals existed for no other reason than to pander to this taste. Why they needed to be periodical is a mystery, except that the habit of periodicity had gone that far down the social scale.

Cromwell's censor, John Rushworth, licensed year after year of John Crouch's scabrous publications—*Mercurius Democritus, Laughing Mercury, Man in the Moon, Mercurius Bellonius, Mercurius Fumigosus*—which enjoyed fairly long runs. Crouch might begin with a half-page of news, but would follow with seven and a half pages of the "Nocturnal News," consisting of cuckolded husbands, rapes, unnatural acts, farts, excrement, and pubic hair. If an example is needed, there is the story from *Mercurius Fumigosus* (4 July 1655) of the man whose girl friend

> would put her wedding Ring upon his middle finger before, which she most willingly did; but his finger presently after swelled so bigge that he not onely lost his nails, but in all haste was forced to send for the Barber Chyrurgeon, who at first resolved it must be cut off, but applying some mollifying and assuaging Plaisters, he (as good luck was) got it off, to the great ease of the poor man whose precious thing he vowed should never more ware Wedding Ring.[38]

Some of the serious press decided it must join the fun, and so the readers of *A Perfect Account of the Daily Intelligence* (24 January 1654) got smut without benefit of humor:

> At Cobham in Kent, a woman jealous of her husband, sent for the suspected female, and having drunk freely with her, she at last demanded of her, if she would have her nose cut off, or her bearing part; and immediately she and her maidservant fell to work, and exercised [sic] that part of her body which they thought had most offended. Not long after her husband came home, and demanding what there was to eat, she reply'd, that she had got him the best bit which he loved in the world, and so presented him with that most ungrateful object.[39]

Crouch had many imitators, like *Mercurius Infernus, Mercurius Jocosus*, and *Mercurius Cinicus*, which were so tiresomely nasty that no paper today would print their content. Apparently, the regime saw no danger in such matter, and may have welcomed it for its lack of political content. It satisfied the habit of periodicity, at least. But it was one way in which periodicals helped to maintain a separation of high and low culture.

In the late 1640s, with the Royalists' cause collapsing and no news they felt like recounting, their mercuries filled up with jocularity. It is painful to see Berkenhead starting up *Mercurius Bellicus* in late 1647 in this style: "But what's the Newes? The Newes is; That Sir Thomas doth now begin to act, like a true Generalissimo, and rally the holy Saints into a better posture of warre. The only way to reduce 'um into a compleat New Modell is to cut 'um of the simples in the Foreheads; and slash out their Wherligig'd whimseyes out of their Factious Noddles."[40] England was re-turning to its starting point, when news had meant ballads. As the regime consoli-dated its power, many customers saw little point in buying the factual and political reports of the diurnals and mercuries. Readership declined with only one newsbook circulating.

For those who were still under the spell of periodical journalism, the excesses of satire and smut seemed to call for a reconstruction. Sobriety may have looked re-freshing after the Interregnum binge. At any rate, it began to reestablish itself even before the Restoration. Nedham, who had reentered journalism in 1650 in such rol-licking fashion, became quite subdued in 1655 when his was the only newsbook licensed by the regime. His content reverted to that of the old coranto, with foreign news and government announcements.[41] No editorializing survived; it was unbecom-ing the dignity of an official paper. Its Restoration successor, the *London Gazette*, was even frostier, as we are about to see. But contrary to the expectations of the authorities and the judgment of historians, the dynamics of periodicity would insure that the public would recapture even that managed media.

Periodical publication had created a sufficient following that governments dared not close the business down entirely. Newsbooks were one of the few innovations that survived the Restoration, if only in a limited form. And the *Gazette* would find that it could not entirely suppress domestic news and England's social divisions, despite a determination to provide only official and objective fact. For the mercu-ries had succeeded in introducing the English to themselves. They had never before seen themselves in a motion picture rather than a portrait, and they never got over the experience.

FIVE

Developing Despite Monopoly, 1660–80

Histories of English journalism pass rapidly over the period 1655–95 as a dead spot, the era of a managed press when the promise of midcentury experiments went unrealized. The perspective of those historians, of course, is that of the journalists—what they were trying to do and what they were kept from doing.[1] From that viewpoint it was a frustrating period. Our perspective is that of readers—what they paid money for and read week after week through those decades, and how it shaped their thinking. Our evidence is in the papers historians dismiss as censored and therefore illegitimate. What is impressive is how the dynamics of periodicity broke through constraints, to maintain a news consciousness.

We have not concentrated so much on the journalists' putative concern to inform their public as on their desire to market their product. And even official newspapers must be sold, in order to have the desired effect. The period of the English Restoration gives us a chance to test the theory that the demands of periodicity can overcome the intentions of editors. The development of the *London Gazette* shows how subtle those pressures can be. Observing this process may affect the way we think about the press, even in totalitarian countries.

By October 1655 Oliver Cromwell was in a position to eliminate all periodicals, as Charles I's government had done in 1632. He chose instead to continue to allow Nedham's *Publick Intelligencer* on Mondays, along with a Thursday edition called *Mercurius Politicus*. It had not yet occurred to anyone to issue the same title more than once in a week, and there was a large degree of overlap. All other unlicensed, licensed, and official newsbooks disappeared. We have already noted how this responsibility sobered Nedham and how his news drifted back toward coranto fare, being extracts from foreign newsletters. Nedham's editorializing, which had once furnished much of the nation's entertainment, simply disappeared.

57

Power does not seek publicity, and the regime was successfully consolidating its power. Little politics was afoot, so the news was robbed of its main domestic content. The original function of the diurnals in keeping a watch on Parliament, and of the mercuries in taking sides on the issues, had vanished. Journalistic morale must have fallen, if one can judge from a decline in the standard of production. Nedham's newsbook presents a very jumbled appearance, with as many as four different sizes and styles of type in the same edition, including "black-letter" ("gothic") for government pronouncements. Advertisements were interspersed among the news reports.

But before we waste too much sympathy on the newsmen, we should remind ourselves that it was not only governments that saw monopoly as an ideal at this time. Members of the Company of Stationers of London—the printers' gild—were always eager to protect their patent monopolies. Monopolies had been one of the supposed grievances against early Stuart rule, but only among those who did not enjoy them.[2] Nedham had simply achieved the dream of any editor, of having the field to himself. Despite his minimal effort in gathering and producing his news, it is estimated that he was selling something over a thousand copies of each paper, at twopence. People paid nearly as much for *managed* news, that is, as for the day's dinner in a tavern (at threepence).[3]

The problem with monopolies is that they can be taken away and given to another. This happened when Cromwell died and General George Monck took charge of restoring the traditional institutions of government. Nedham was fired in April 1660, and in October his nemesis, Berkenhead, was made censor of the press.[4] In the meantime there was a little flurry of freedom, in which the country saw its first daily newsbook, *A Perfect Diurnal or The daily Proceedings in Parliament*.[5] But Monck soon returned to the policy of allowing only a single, censored periodical.

Much as England's rulers might have liked to, it was no longer feasible simply to do away with periodical news altogether. We will see that Roger L'Estrange suggested this possibility to Charles II's government, but the motion died for lack of a second. While histories may give the impression that there is a long gap in the development of the press, there was a section of the public that demanded periodical news and was willing to pay for it. Beyond that, this was the time in which the institution of the coffeehouse spread through London and the country, with the primary purpose of discussing the news. The news they discussed came largely from official sources, including official newsletters. We may well wonder what it was about this news that could retain their interest.

The man whom Monck chose to run the nation's news industry, Henry Muddiman, continued past practices. The titles he chose for his journals differed as little as possible from Nedham's. Monday's was called the *Parliamentary Intelligencer* and Thursday's was *Mercurius Publicus*. Twice a week was what the country was used to and so that schedule was continued. Thus Muddiman kept the amount of news provided from becoming an issue. The format and appearance of his newsbooks was similar to Nedham's, and there were the very same advertisements. Like Nedham, he had no reports of parliamentary proceedings. The House of Commons, which had sanctioned the publication of its activities in 1641 when it was the challenger, prohibited such reports now that it was the establishment.[6]

What was the point of a periodical press, then? Muddiman's job, as supervised by Berkenhead, was to lower the political temperature, narrow the range of debate, and spread a healing balm on England. It was, very consciously, to help bond a divided society, whereas earlier newsbooks had often been intended to divide society. Muddiman's publication filled up with foreign news, proclamations, loyal addresses to the new monarch, announcements of honors and appointments, and ads. It is amusing to see news of the Restoration of the monarchy itself tucked in at the end of the issue of 31 May 1660. The type for the story become smaller and smaller in order to squeeze it all in, rather than to shorten the banal reports that had been set earlier to lead off the issue.

Muddiman's newsbooks did not exhibit the vindictiveness that the Royalists otherwise displayed during the Restoration.[7] Indeed he went out of his way to avoid the unpleasantness of the times, as in the issue of *Mercurius Publicus* for 10 January 1661. It began with an announcement of the birth of a son to the king's brother James, who might someday inherit the throne. This was followed by a description of the queen's trip, which involved the king's sister, "the Beauteous Princess Henrietta." And then there was the sad news of the funeral of the king's sister Mary, Princess of Orange. It continued with foreign news, ads for toothpaste, notice of stolen sheep and a forger, and finally we learn that there had been a armed uprising in London!

After remembering to mention this disturbance, Muddiman told the story without rancor or alarm. Readers were assured that everything was under control, that "the Nobility and Gentry" had assumed their proper duties and "the people" of London stood staunchly behind the government forces. In following issues Muddiman even minimized the percentage of the sectaries who got involved in Venner's Rising, and described some of them as of greater humanity than their principles would suggest. At worst they were viewed as confused rather than diabolical, in the grip of manias unleashed in the Civil Wars, inspired by persons long departed.

This is remarkable, coming from the same sources as *Mercurius Aulicus*. And indeed, this vision of a harmonious society—of able and kindly leaders, loyal subjects, and pitiable deviants—was too artificial to be sustained in a periodical. The conscious effort to use the newsbooks for bonding society was too contrived to seem quite natural. For example, the next issue, which had to report the mopping up of sympathetic risings elsewhere in England, actually started with the report of the consecration of four new bishops—unconvincingly presented as the answer to England's domestic unrest. All this fit in with Charles II's attempt to convince Parliament of the desirability of a religious toleration toward such Dissenters. But Berkenhead wanted to take a harder line than this and leaned on Muddiman to slant the reports of *Mercurius Publicus* against Dissenters. One acquaintance said that Berkenhead seemed to think that the country could be governed by newsbooks.[8]

But there was an even higher level of government with a responsibility for the management of news, and the motivation there was more typical of the industry than were Muddiman or Berkenhead. The two secretaries of state ran the government's intelligence system, and it was thought natural for them to oversee the dissemination as well as the collection of information. Their profits from the enterprise came to dominate their thinking, rather than ideological purpose. And the secretaries began to change the official journalists carelessly, for mercenary reasons rather than with regard to skill or ideology. There were rapid transfers of the post from Muddiman to Roger L'Estrange, back to Muddiman, then to the nonentities Charles Perrot and Robert Yard, always with an eye to the secretaries' cut of the profits. They knew that the country needed a sufficient supply of news, but did not think it mattered how the news went out. During the Civil War, Berkenhead had a lot of help in producing news—which was thought to be worth whole regiments; now he was surprised to find that the king did not bother to read his government's paper.[9]

One would hesitate to argue with the secretaries if they were taking the view that journalism is not good at propaganda. They continued to allow Muddiman to run their information network. Continuing as the government's official newswriter, he sent insider newsletters to about two hundred foreign and domestic correspondents, who were to return news from their areas for his next edition.[10] But when it came to producing news, the secretaries seemed to realize that reports were not to end discussion, as would be the point of propaganda, but were to start discussion. They only wanted to decide which faraway topics would be discussed. This would continue to be the government's attitude during the coming decades with the *London Gazette*. So while Muddiman was a far better journalist than his successors, his supervisors put the enterprise in the hands of higher bidders.

They began with a misstep, however, when they called on Roger L'Estrange to produce the official newsbook. L'Estrange is treated by historians as if he represented the antithesis of any true notion of news. And there is a sense in which he got into the machinery in order to wreck it and treated his journalistic activities as a part of his role as censor, or Surveyor of the Press. Despite the motto of his newsbook, *The Intelligencer*, which read "Published for the Satisfaction and Information of the People," his first issue was brutally candid in disabusing readers of any hopes they may have had: "Supposing the Press in Order; the People in their right Wits, and Newes, or No Newes, to be the Question; A Publick Mercury should never have My Vote; because I think it makes the Multitude too Familiar with the Actions and Counsels of their Superiours; too Pragmatical and Censorious, and gives them, not only an Itch, but a kind of Colourable Right and License, to be Meddling with the Government." Still, like Berkenhead, he thought that there were times when a periodical propaganda organ might do some good.

> All which (supposing as before supposed) does not yet hinder, but that in This Juncture, a Paper of . . . Quality may be both Safe and Expedient: Truly if I should say, Necessary, perhaps the Case would bear it, for certainly, there is not anything, which

at This Instant more Imports his Majestie's Service, and the Publick, then to Re-
deem the Vulgar from their Former Mistakes, and Delusions, and to preserve them
from the like for the time to come: to both which purposes, the prudent Menage
[management] of a Gazette may Contribute in a very high Degree.

Where he differed from Berkenhead is in the level at which he proposed to meet the
public. *Mercurius Aulicus* was a tribute to the public's humor and good judgment,
whereas L'Estrange hoped to manage society by dumbing down his style. He made
no effort to conceal his designs. Having thrown his readers in with the "multitude"
and the "vulgar," L'Estrange proceeded to tell how he intended to manipulate them.
Since news is "(in truth) a good part of most mens study and Business; 'tis none of
the worst wayes of Address to the Genius and Humour of the Common People; whose
Affections are much more capable of being tuned, and wrought upon, by convenient
Hints, and Touches, in the Shape, and Ayre of a Pamphlet, then by the strongest
Reasons, and best Notions imaginable, under any other, and more Sober Form whatsoever." The contrast which L'Estrange makes between pamphlets and reason im-
plies that no thinking person would read news for enlightenment.

Finally, he repeats the usual claim that his reports were to prevent misinformation. That was the crux of the issue. Since there would be news, willy-nilly, it might
as well be official news, which was now assumed to mean periodical news. As
for the frequency required, "Once a week may do the business (for I intend to utter
[issue] my News by weight, and not by Measure)," but he left open the possibility
of two issues a week. He did not intend to have the pamphlet sold "about the Streets
by Mercuries and Hawkers"—who were too likely to spread seditious materials too—
and must have planned to make customers come to the printer's shop.[11] All of this
seemed calculated to destroy any authentic news enterprise.

Sir Robert Moray wrote a friend that, like Berkenhead before him, L'Estrange
"thinks the kingdome is to be governed as it seemes by newes bookes."[12] His talents
fell short of the challenge. When Samuel Pepys saw his first issue of *The Newes*
(L'Estrange's Thursday edition) on 4 September 1663 he commented sourly that he
had been to "Westminster-hall and there bought the first news-books of Lestrange's
writing, he beginning this week; and makes methink but a small beginning."[13]

L'Estrange made few changes in the format of the news—the better to lull customers to sleep. His titles followed the familiar pattern, with the *Intelligencer* on
Mondays alternating with the *Newes* on Thursdays. By reducing their size from sixteen to eight pages (from two sheets to one) he kept his pledge of reducing the news
by half. Beyond that, type became larger and spaces opened up between paragraphs.
The price stayed at twopence, and people paid it.

But they grumbled. The news habit involved a certain weekly minimum of
words, and readers were not getting it. When L'Estrange again threatened to go to
just one issue a week they grumbled even more, and he backed off.[14] What is surprising in all this is that, however historians of journalism may disparage this managed press, many contemporaries only complained that they wanted *more* of it. Even-

tually complaints like Pepys's—of the staleness and short supply of news—got back to the government, and L'Estrange went back to sixteen pages in June 1665.[15]

What public opinion had to work on was one or two paragraphs of domestic news, with usually a report from the court about honors bestowed or the king's trips. A typical issue of the *Newes* (7 January 1663) was satisfied with the report of a comet that could be seen in daytime, notice of Sir William Petty's invention of a double-hulled boat, and the account of a schoolteacher who committed suicide. The rest was foreign news, including the situation at Vienna where the Turks were still threatening. Many stories were as short as the following (from Paris): "The Swisse that are in the Service of his Majesty have made a Proffer, for a very reasonable Summe of Mony, to clear Paris both of Dirt, and Thieves."[16] Like the corantos of old, L'Estrange did not editorialize or even translate them out of the form they took in the foreign report: "His Majesty," in a report from Paris, meant the king of France. When one read, from Vienna, of "our forces," it meant the Imperial army. Journalistic discipline kept the ethnocentric impulse at bay.

Unlike Muddiman, L'Estrange did raise concerns about the political threats that swarmed in his imagination—the thirty Quakers found meeting near Southampton, and the show trials of plotters. He was eager to report the executions of the seditious, the disgrace and deaths of nonconforming ministers, the activities of the government in sniffing out the sects. More usually, he had only a disaster to occupy him for a week, as of the accident to a ferry in Wales which took ninety-four lives, "all ordinary Country people, except one Gentleman with his Servant." The most curious account may have been of a feral child found living with bears in Poland.[17]

Human interest was largely sustained by the advertisements, which were often as good as gossip.

> At the Miter near the West-end of St Pauls is to be seen a rare Collection of Curiosityes much resorted to, and admired by Persons of great Learning and Quality: among which a Choyce Egyptian Mummy, with Hieroglyphicks; the Ant-Bear of Brast; a Remora; a Torpedo; the huge Thigh-bone of a Gyant, a Moon Fish, a Tropick Bird, etc.[18]

> An excellent Engine of a new Invention is now perfected and erected by vertue of a Grant from his Sacred Majesty, which without either Wind or Water, grinds all sorts of Corn, and may be seen at the Falcon Wharfe on the Bankside, where it is so employed. It is excellent also for Sugar Canes, draining of Mines, Colepits, or Fennes; for improvement of Lands where Water-mills hinder the use of the water; for sawing of Timber, beating of Hemp, making of Paper or Powder; and it will raise Hammers for all sorts of Iron-works. Whoever desires to see the working of it may repair to the Falcon aforesaid, and whoever desires to set up such an Engine, let him apply himself to the House of Col. Henry Chester in Butcher-Hall Lane near Christ-Church London, or over against Poulterers Hall.[19]

Book ads were the most frequent—for plays, travel accounts, sermons, almanacs, experimental reports, dictionaries and histories—often with titles long enough to give away the plot. The modicum of political news amounted to no more than lists of the acts passed in the latest session of Parliament.

Despite his eagerness to support an oppressive Parliament and administration, L'Estrange's tenure was not secure. A slip by his printer, who called the Catholic duke of York "His Holiness" rather than "His Highness," caused some glee among the public. But apparently it was L'Estrange's coverage of the Dutch War of 1665 that caused his dismissal. Once he left out the duke's courageous encounter with Admiral Opdam and gave too much credit instead to the earl of Sandwich. That, coupled with the obvious reluctance with which he performed his duties opened the way for those who wanted—again for mercenary reasons—to issue a journal directly out of the secretary of state's office. They used the fact that the public wanted a greater knowledge of (foreign) affairs to justify grabbing his office.[20] After all, what good was a government periodical that people didn't read?

And so a government that did not dare prohibit all periodical news actually founded England's first newspaper (as opposed to newsbook). Its task still was to direct the nation's conversation and only had to ignore what was better left out. When Pepys saw his first issue of the *Oxford* (later the *London*) *Gazette* on 22 November 1665, printed on its unfolded halfsheet, he declared it "very pretty, full of news, and no folly in it."[21] One might suppose that this meant that it was a larger journal than the one it had replaced. But in fact it was about the same length (twenty-six hundred words), closely printed front and back in double column, and appeared twice a week. Nor had it changed toward a domestic focus. The difference Pepys noticed must have been in the greater care taken with its presentation. With its neater type, economical format, chaste title line, and objective tone, it seemed a more mature production. It represented England's first use of the term "gazette," which in Paris and Amsterdam suggested authority.[22] And it was imitated by all subsequent news publications in England.

Pepys was, of course, contrasting it with the "folly" of L'Estrange's newsbooks, which were an insult to readers' intelligence.[23] We should pause to note, however, that he had read L'Estrange's news closely. It is hard to imagine anyone saving all the back copies of the *Intelligencer* and the *Newes*, but Pepys had done so, and had them bound for reference purposes. This was despite knowing of examples of absolute untruth, as when Lord Buckhurst's lying account of his murder of a tanner was printed as the truth.[24] Pepys's diary rarely recorded his seeing a newspaper, but the habit was becoming ingrained at a time when historians are loath to admit that newspapers really existed in England.

The *Gazette* was popular, as intended. Simultaneous typesettings were required from the beginning, even though there was no necessity to rush to beat any competition onto the streets. Multiple settings had not been necessary for the earlier official newsbooks. Sometimes three typesettings (i.e., three presses) were required for the *Gazette*.[25] This did not mean there were no complaints; by the end of 1667 the government was aware of some unhappiness over the lack of domestic news.[26] Some things might be suppressed and, as Elias Ashmole speculated, "the Gazett news, is not like to bee all true, some of it will seem purposely inserted." But that did not mean it was just made up. And as his friend William Lilly the astrologer wrote, a prophecy reported in the *Gazette* "will pass all over England if not the whole world," so great was its reputation.[27]

There was good reason for this reputation. One of the features of the news developing under conditions of government management was the journalistic taste for the factual. It suited a reticent regime. Despite L'Estrange's debasement of news coinage, Muddiman's newsletters had maintained a standard for reliability, and the *London Gazette*'s return to austerity helped to consolidate England's commitment to "facts." Historians and philosophers of science have given much attention to the development of an empirical philosophy. By the end of the seventeenth century John Locke could sum up a development that Francis Bacon had begun.[28] The contribution of periodical news to a factual discourse—so dominant in our "information age"—has gone largely unnoticed.

In the 1620s, just as the English corantos were beginning, Bacon was presenting the idea of a fact in "natural philosophy" or science. In this, he made use of the concept as used by his own profession, the law. Facts were not taken for granted in a court, but had to be established. They were not the province of experts, but were identified by common people—on juries. While judges were experts in matters of law, laymen determined matters of fact. There were rules for the delimitation of facts, which Bacon saw would have to be established for philosophy as well: "Those however who aspire not to guess and divine, but to discover and know; who propose not to devise mimic and fabulous worlds of their own, but to examine and dissect the nature of this very world itself; must go to facts themselves for everything."[29] This has remained the goal of scientists ever since, who may express it as simply as Bertrand Russell did: "I mean by a 'fact' something which is there, whether anybody thinks so or not."[30]

So far as I have seen, journalists did not cite Bacon for their practice in presenting information in the form of facts, even though they could have adopted the quote above as their watchword. But the requirements of periodical publication provide a sufficient explanation of the development of the concept of the fact, and doubtless represent a parallel development. Bacon remarked that many reports should be set down "with a qualifying note, such as 'it is reported,' 'they relate,' 'I have heard from a person of credit,' and the like." But that was natural to journalists from the beginning. Some such qualification is part of every other coranto news item.[31]

The contribution of periodical news toward the popular reception—as opposed to the production—of facts was unquestionably more important than anything the scientists did. From the time of the corantos, news reports had to be kept brief and to the point. They had a specific locus in time and in geography. None of the stories were general in their reference, in the manner of myth, romance, or even ballad news. The particular perspective on each fact was also specified; the source of reports was scrupulously identified, as from the *Haarlem Courant*. And of course, no news would be reported that was perfectly pointless; each report had some kind of closure despite the sense of a developing reality. (This last characteristic suggests a paradox; the news needs to convince readers of a relative finality in today's episode, even while inviting them back for tomorrow's continuation.) The combination of these features—specificity of place, time, and perspective, and a self-contained particularity—is what the philosophers would mean by a fact. They were the "particulars" that Bacon described as "circumscribed by place and time."[32]

Periodical publication encouraged all these features more than occasional news production would. That is because corantos had to revisit the same reality next week and every week. Periodical news constantly brought readers back to a mundane world, while other kinds of literature might—with sufficient skill—imperceptibly escape into worlds of their own creation.

Diurnals followed the factual habit started in the 1620s, except that they generally did not identify their sources. Initially, the source was assumed to be Parliament. The mercuries were even more vague about their sources, except when they had to correct earlier reports—which happened often. Correcting past misstatements itself reminded the public of the goal of factual accuracy, suggesting the journalist's desire to get it right. And since journalists were not yet taking responsibility for gathering the news, but only for printing it, there was little embarrassment at these corrections.

Correcting mistakes did not call the *idea* of facts into question. Indeed, it may have given readers more confidence in news discourse, by contrast with other rhetorics. But news had one characteristic that did depreciate individual facts. In the news, facts crowd in on one another and displace each other. An account of a great victory would be followed by news of continuing difficulties. Each day's news deflated the news of the day before. That is what justifies a continuous supply and a periodical schedule. Facts were not something to build on, as it turned out, but were replaced. It is the essence of news discourse and is why it is better suited to unimportant subjects.

The *Gazette* was not the first journal to be self-conscious about its factuality. In June 1643 a mercury had appeared under the title *The Parliament Scout*. The name suggested something new in journalism—the necessity of making an effort to search out and discover the news. Before this, printers gave no suggestion of how news found its way to their shops. But with the country now swarming with military scouts and spies, it occurred to journalists that a similar effort was needed to find out what was really going on in a confusing situation.[33] In January 1644 the name *Spie* was first used for a periodical. The editor announced that he "intends to shew you fair play (viz. nothing but truth) by discovering the usuall cheats in the great game of the Kingdome." For that, he would have to go undercover.[34] At that time Berkenhead was actually using reports from Royalist spies in compiling his news.[35] The *Faithfull Scout, Citys Scout, Impartial Scout, Armies Scout, National Scout*, and *Loyall Scout*, continued this theme of the *discovery* of facts as well as their transmission.

A profession of factual accuracy and objectivity became the facile claim of all journalists in the seventeenth century. Of the periodicals begun then, more than forty contained the word "perfect" in their titles, twenty-seven more the word "true," seventeen "moderate," nine "faithful," while others were "exact," "impartial," "certain," and "particular."[36] We may take it that editors expected the public to appreciate their efforts toward a more "particular" knowledge.

Not everyone was ready for the challenge of the factual. In the midst of the news revolution there is the strange appearance of pornographic mercuries. This showed that there was still a taste for ballad-style "news" or "nouvelles," which had only a vague placement within the factual grid. And while it might be argued that the development of the literary novel confirmed the cultural favor shown to factual expression, the novelists subverted that discourse by synthesizing their facts. But, to be sure, it had not occurred to authors to place literary action in the most familiar surroundings until those surroundings were *made* literarily familiar in newspaper accounts.[37]

An appreciation of facts naturally bound the news to another enthusiasm of the time—science. Facts, lists, and numbers were frequently used in the periodical news, in the form of casualty assessments, "bills of mortality," current price tables, lists of bankrupts—which would have been a blemish within any previous literature. The use of facts as news can be seen in its purest form in the weekly publication that lacked a title line but is known as the "London Bills of Mortality." Printed since 1603 by the Worshipful Company of the Parish Clerks of London, the Bills of Mortality reported the deaths in the city and its environs.

No one has ever seen this publication as a form of journalism. But John Graunt, who first made a statistical study of their contents, wrote in 1662 of their use as a newspaper of sorts: "Most of them who constantly took in [i.e., bought] the weekly Bills of Mortality, made little other use of them, then to look at the foot, how the Burials increased or decreased; And, among the Casualties, what had happened rare, and extraordinary in the week currant: so as they might take the same as a Text to talk upon, in the next Company." In other words, readers used the bills as ordinary news, to have something striking to talk about. Gentlemen watched to see if a plague outbreak meant that they should leave the city for their estates. Tradesmen calculated how it might affect their business.[38] Others were just interested to learn of the sad reality of their neighbors' lives. There was a lot to be gleaned, if one were stuck with nothing else to read. Contemporary diarists—the Essex parson Ralph Josselin, the Cambridge alderman Samuel Newton, the London lawyer John Greene—copied those figures into their diaries.[39] People were still doing so in the eighteenth century, and the provincial papers of that day often made the London Bills a regular feature.[40]

The only full sentence printed in the Bills was the week's "assize of bread": "A penny wheaten loaf to contain eleven and a half ounces, and three half-penny white loaves the same weight." Otherwise, it was just numbers, but the numbers represented one's neighbors. On this halfsheet publication the deaths were first distributed among the 130 metropolitan parishes, so that one could get a more particular sense of the various neighborhoods. Then they were broken down by the cause of death—abortive, aged, apoplexie, ague, blasted, bleeding, flux, burnt, calenture, cancer, gangrene, fistula, canker, thrush, childbed, cough, collick, consumption, tiffick, convulsion, "mother," distracted, dropsie, drowned, executed, and so on, to vomiting, winds, wormes. Some categories amounted to little more than a shrug: "suddenly," "grief," "found." Then the total of the above was divided according to sex, as were the numbers born (i.e., christened) in that week. Finally, the increase or decrease from the previous week was noted.

This told a lot about the community. One can imaginatively project oneself into the desperate worlds of these many sufferers and their families. In the 1660s people paid four shillings a year for a subscription, for news that was nobody's "business." And there were enough subscribers that it required two settings of type, keeping two presses busy.[41]

After the plague year of 1665 Graunt published the collected bills of that year, in their original state but bound together, creating a history of that holocaust.[42] But one may doubt that his subsequent reduction of this "data" to scientific generality would have been as interesting to the general public as the weekly reports, which reminded them of people they knew. As we have said, true statistics are only an abstraction and represent a loss of realism. But seeing the raw numbers on a weekly basis doubtless did something to establish the new factual discourse. For we are told that readers argued over the accuracy of the mortality figures, as if it were important to get them right.[43]

Periodicity gave a point to facts, since it made them part of various series and overcame their isolation. The periodically printed bills of entry (like the daily *London, imported*), commodity price lists (like the weekly *Proctor's Price-Courant*), stock price and exchange rate currents (like the twice-weekly *Course of the Exchange*), marine lists (like the thrice weekly *Lloyd's News*), and advertisers (like the weekly *City Mercury* and *Merchant's Remembrancer*) would all serve to encourage discussion of a world of mundane factuality.[44] There was much food for thought in their lists (from customs records) of what various London merchants were exporting and importing and from where.[45] If nowadays this sounds like dry stuff, it only shows how dependent we are on journalists to entertain us. In the Restoration, readers were forced to use their imaginations, and the makings of a *Wall Street Journal* were available in those weekly publications.

Readers who could find topics for discussion in bills of mortality and bills of entry would have had little trouble using the official *London Gazette* for this purpose, skimpy as it seems to us. Its development as a popular medium was slow, but the important fact is that it developed at all.

The first thing to notice in the crisp new journal is its deep authorial anonymity. All trace of personality has been removed. Corantos and mercuries had been required to reveal some of their identity in their imprint. Nedham, Muddiman, and L'Estrange were real, live journalists, known by name, who happened to have a connection to the government. Now that the news was written by government clerks, it did not behoove them to remind readers of the fact. By an odd psychology, anonymity gave their reports greater credibility.

One of the ironies of human nature is that we are more likely to believe what is published anonymously. E. M. Forster put this nicely back in 1925:

> It seems paradoxical that an article should impress us more if it is unsigned than if it is signed. But it does, owing to the weakness of our psychology. Anonymous statements have, as we have seen, a universal air about them. Absolute truth, the collected wisdom of the universe, seems to be speaking, not the feeble voice of a man. Journalists have taken advantage of this. If everything in a paper were signed, it would lose its all-pervading influence on our minds. It actually serves up a mixture of true facts, false facts, and comment, and serves it unsigned. Modern journalism is therefore a pernicious caricature of literature. It has usurped that divine tendency toward anonymity.[46]

The voice of the *Gazette* aspired to be the voice of society, rather than just the voice of government. And we shall see that it escaped the unpopularity of the reigns it served.

The government's intention was to produce something like a coranto, with predominantly foreign news in chunks of one paragraph. And this was not the insubstantial fare of L'Estrange's *Intelligencer*. The reader's familiar world was supposed to include, for example, the city of Leghorn in Italy.

> Jan. 16. On the 12 instant the Tunis Merchant arrived here, coming from Algier in 11 daies, who adviseth that an Algier Ship had burnt the Charity of Hamburgh, bound hither from Archangel, with 106 packs of Hides, etc. He saies farther, that the Algier Men had sunck a Dunkerke Fregot with 300 Soldiers coming from Spaine and Naples, and several Dutch and French. The Peace which the French have concluded with Tunis, is reported here with much dishonour to the French; and the Italians understand it so, the humor of Tunis being chiefly to follow Trade, in which they found themselves so much debarred, that they were in consultation to deliver up the French Captives gratis; and indeed they might have been brought to any termes, had the French not been so forward to patch up a Peace with them. Since Genoua made their Agreement with the Grand Signor for Traffique, they are endevouring to make all sorts of Cloth to send for Smyrna and Constantinople. The Grand Duke hath for some time been deteined by an Imposthume at Florence, from whence he is weekly expected, with the Court at Pisa.[47]

The *Gazette* maintained the perspective of the foreign source, so that a report from Deventer begins, "We expect the return of our Ambassador from England daily."[48] This continued during England's wars with the Dutch, which means, for instance, that jubilation over Dutch victories was not translated into the language of English gloom.

Obviously, the government's editors were very far from pandering to their readers' prejudices. In that connection, historians make much of the fact that domestic news was weirdly missing. To be sure, the paper for 3 September 1666 did include a notice that "about two a clock this morning a sudden and lamentable Fire brake out in this City," and went on briefly to tell how the king and his brother went in person to help stop it, with "several Companies of His Guards." But the next issue actually apologized for taking the space to give "this short, but true Account" of the greatest domestic catastrophe in London's history. The *Gazette*'s official view calmly discounted the suspicions directed at Dutch or French aliens, and concluded that "the whole was an effect of an unhappy chance, or to speak better, the heavy hand of God upon us for our sins, shewing us the terrour of his Judgment in thus raising the fire, and immediately after his miraculous and never enough to be acknowledged Mercy in putting a stop to it when we were in the last despair." The next issue (September 13) had only one mention of the Great Fire, in announcing a national fast day. Perhaps the government hoped that this severe objectivity would appeal to—and create—sophisticated readers.

And yet, domestic news did break through. The *Gazette* was, after all, an official journal of record. So there were executions to report, although these and the crimes involved were not described. News of the royal family was at first considered safe and perhaps it was included in order to set the right tone for society. Readers began to read of their comings and goings—where the queen was vacationing, how the duke of York's campaign was faring—until they felt like neighbors. Unfortunately, the royal family had some fairly raffish friends, who sometimes could not be kept out of the paper. Notices of criminals and runaways occasionally included the duke of Buckingham. Lord Morley-and-Monteagle's trial for killing Henry Hastings in a duel was reported, along with what many thought was the disgraceful commutation of his sentence.[49]

As remote and cool as all this may seem to historians, contemporaries actually taunted the *Gazette* for pandering to its audience. The play *Tarugo's Wiles* included a burlesque reading of a "gazette" to an enthralled audience in a coffeehouse.[50] It may only be our jaded tastes that keeps us from sensing its entertainment value. For instance, the gathering at *Tarugo's* coffeehouse were concerned about the ads—parodied as spring-saddles for hemorrhoid victims and a book on sex by the Dry-Nurse to the Society of Philosophical Demonstrators.[51]

In 1671, after resisting advertisements for six years, the *Gazette* started accepting what we would call "personals." This would prove another thin edge of entry for domestic news. The reasons for the change of policy are unknown, but they may have had more to do with the desire of the paper to ingratiate itself with the public than the few extra pounds income involved. Ads for commercial interests would have paid better than personals, after all. In any event, the queen herself helped initiate the development, appealing for the return of a lost spaniel with liver-colored spots and furry feet (21 September 1671). Notices of cheats and runaway servants, stolen horses and lost dogs, kidnapped children and misplaced "notebooks" (purses) brought the public into the official world of news.

These appeals were given in enough detail to start discussion around the parish pump: "A swarthy man, middle stature, black haird, twenty two years of age, his name John Worfdale, went away from his Friends (being Mellancholly Distracted) about two months since; Whoever can give notice of him to Mr. John Sharp, at the Queens head in Fleetstreet, Millener; or to Mr. Worfdale's at Satabbelford in Leicestershire, shall be well rewarded for their pains." (6 August 1674) The promised rewards by themselves would have involved the audience in a way that most news does not.

> Christopher Gibbons, Doctor in Musick, and principal Organist to His Majesty in private and publick, had stoln out of his house, which is in New Street, betwixt the Ambry and Orchard street in Westminster, the 26th of June, between 9 and 12 in the Morning, a Silver Tanckard, to the value of near Seven pounds, with the marks of CGE on the handle: the reward for any that can give tidings of the same to the said Mr. Gibbons is Two pounds. (6 July 1671)

Soon every issue contained at least one reward notice, making the *Gazette* an investment of sorts. Listing the winning numbers in the lotteries also encouraged audience interest.[52]

One can readily see how fiction could grow out of such notices: "A Considerable Estate in Land, is by the death of Vincent Fowler, late of Thealby in the Parish of Burton upon Stather in Lincolnshire, fallen to Robert Fowler his Son, who is desired (if living) to repair or send to Mr. George Rayner at Ganesburgh in Lincolnshire, or to Mr. Kellet of Staple Inn, London, for better satisfaction." (1 January 1694) This was the very stuff of Victorian novels, with all the suspicion of a trick to catch young Robert.

> On Wednesday the second of August, there went away from his Masters house the Blew-Bell in Milk-Street London, a young man by name John Kirke, about eighteen years of age, with a considerable summ in Guiny Gold [guineas]; in a short brown hair Peruke, he is indifferent tall and very slender, being thin fac'd, hollow ey'd, and of a pale complexion; in a saddish coloured stuff suit with silver buttons: if any Person can apprehend and secure him, and send word whereof to Mr Thomas Kirke in Milk-street aforesaid, shall have ten pounds for their pains. (21 August 1671)

Gossips could have begun with the fact that the blackguard John must have been related to Thomas.

The detail of these reports exceeded anything found in the foreign news, sharpening that sense of fact natural to journalism. And in time, more commercial ads appeared, especially of new books but also of auctions—of jewels, plate, furniture, libraries, and real estate. For wealthy families to hold auctions would initiate a little celebrity news, to go along with the crimes and mysteries embodied in the ads.

All in all, there was not that much difference between one's neighbors and the royal family, which was always losing things. Immediately after the coronation of James II (4 May 1685), for example: "Lost at Their Majesties Coronation the Button [knob] of His Majesties Scepter, set about with 24 small Diamonds, three Rubies and three Emeraulds: A Pendant Pearl from His Majesties Gown about 9 Carrets of 30 common grains, and about 16 great Links of a Gold chain. Whoever gives notice thereof to the Officers of Her Majesties Jewel-House, shall be well rewarded." Apparently the dignity of a coronation did not allow one to chase down the things that kept falling off the regalia, or even to count the links one has trodden underfoot. The palace also had to report the loss of some of "His Majesties Plate" at the Coronation Banquet, to the extent of six spoons, five forks, and two salts. Whoever "found" those was also promised a reward (30 April 1685).

Whether it meant to or not, the government was using its paper to reach out to its subjects. And those subjects also found a way to use the paper to reach the government. Here we are speaking of the creative use of the "Loyal Address," for purposes of political advantage, commercial rivalry, social and religious complaint, and local boosterism.

There had been loyal addresses in the papers of the Interregnum period. In the fateful spring of 1660 General Monck was the recipient of "humble addresses" of encouragement and advice, published in Muddiman's *Parliamentary Intelligence*. The restored monarchy did not give them much attention thereafter, until the hysteria of the Popish Plot, discussed in our next chapter. But these addresses began to show up in the pages of the *Gazette* in 1681, congratulating the king on the decision to abandon his obstreperous parliaments. One may assume that these addresses, or some of them, had been solicited by the editors. If so, they came to regret it.[53]

A classic text would be something like the following, from 25 August 1681:

> The humble Address of your Majesties most Loyal and Obedient Subjects, the Grand Jury of the County of Northampton, at the Assizes there held the 12th day of July, 1681.
>
> Most Gracious Soverign.
> We Your Majesties said Dutiful and Loyal Subjects, do with all Humility, give your Majesty our most hearty and unfeigned Thanks for Your Majesties most Gracious Declaration of the 8th of April last, and of those Instances of Your Royal Goodness and Condescensions therein expressed; and more especially for Your Princely Resolution, in preserving the Succession of the Crown in its due and legal course of Descent, in humble and thankful acknowledgment whereof, and sense of our Duty, we presume humbly to give Your Majesty an assurance, that we will sacrifice our Lives and Fortunes in the preservation of Your Majesties Sacred Person (whom God long preserve) the Protestant Religion, Monarchical Government, and the Succession, as now established by the Laws of this Your Kingdom, against all Opposers whatsoever. And we humbly beseech God to give Your Majesty a long and happy Reign, and that we may never want [i.e., lack] one of Your Royal Line, so long as the World endures, to sit in the Throne and Rule over us.

It did not take long for such petitioners to realize that they could mix this groveling with expressions of concern for things other than the monarchy. Loyal subjects could express their anxieties in print, moving the laws, or Parliament, or Protestantism, or certain liberties, up or down the scale of their avowed concerns. Soon, these addresses came to resemble letters to the editor on the issues of the day. Thus, what had been encouraged as advertisements of the nation's devotion got away from the editors, who found themselves broadcasting the ideas of their customers.

The basic loyal address continued to be of use in various rivalries, as where the Royal African Company beat the East India Company into print, or the bishop and clergy of Hereford became the first diocese to record their allegiance, or the University of Oxford, the Sussex Militia, the province of Maryland, the apprentices of Westminster, or the lawyers of the Middle Temple outdid their various rivals in expressions of political piety. Since no county or borough could afford to be left behind, the *Gazette* often had to expand its space for such addresses to four pages, and sometimes it could only list the names of those groups who had been heard from.

Whether the impressionable James II was actually misled by these professions would bear considering. Some in the political classes did pay attention to such expressions, at a time when the *Gazette* was the nation's main communications medium. A correspondent of Henry Sidney, envoy to the Hague, sent him a *Gazette* to let him see the counties' reaction to a royal prohibition of seditious petitions.[54]

Commercial and religious rivalry also found expression by variations on the loyal address. Craft gilds used them to advertise, and to disparage foreigners and interlopers who were invading their trades. A poignant example of their use came when groups of Dissenters thanked James for his Declaration of Indulgence—announcing religious toleration—and used the occasion to describe the cruel treatment they had suffered. The address of the "Loyal Subjects of the County of Essex, Dissenting from the Church of England" (25 July 1687) hinted that Parliament should enact the policy in a statute and urged reluctant courts to be scrupulous in enforcing it. Nowhere else could the nonconformists have reached such an audience with their appeal.

Anglican Tories like those of the Borough of Eye in Sussex could not wait to respond, however, with an implied criticism of James's policy (8 August 1687):

> Although we resolve that the Loyalty of our Lives shall be one continued Address of Duty to Your Sacred Majesty; yet since we find that many who have been lately Indulged, have published their [blurred] acknowledgments, we cannot be satisfied that any offer a more vigorous Duty from the sens of their Liberty, than we from that of our Security, or that what Your Majesty hath now done for them, should be more Solemnized, than what You have always done for us. We of the Church of England must ever be solicitous to deserve that indelible Character, which Your Most Gracious Majesty hath given of our strict Adherence to the Crown. And we hope a Sacred Emulation for Your Service, shall be the use that all Your Subjects will make of Your Favours. In that contest only, Great Sir, shall You hear of us of this Corporation, Praying for Your Honour and Your Health. And we do assure your Majesty, that if Your Glory, or Your Safety shall require, our Lives, and our Estates, shall be offered at Your Feet.

Ignoring this protest, James used the *Gazette* on 26 April 1688 to reissue the provocative Indulgence, with the following reflection: "Ever since We granted this Indulgence, We have made it Our principal Care to see it preserved without distinction; as We are encouraged to do daily by Multitudes of Addresses, and many other Assurances We receive from Our Subjects ... the Effects of which We doubt not but the [elections to the] next Parliament will plainly shew." A week later came the fateful order to read the Indulgence, which marks the beginning of the end for the Stuart dynasty. The part that the government's own newspaper played in the episode would bear consideration.

After the Revolution of 1688 there were, naturally, addresses to the new monarchs from England's ever-loyal subjects. But the practice soon went out of fashion. There may have been some embarrassment about the same groups' earlier declarations to James. Also, after the revolution there were more frequent elections, which meant that political opinion could be expressed more straightforwardly. Within the *Gazette*, local pride then took the form of reports of how the proclamation of the new monarchs had been handled in the various towns of England. This, again, revived a practice begun by the newsbooks of the Restoration. Subjects were eager to see themselves in print, and even the *Gazette* found it impossible to make communication a one-way street.

A managed press did not work out exactly as planned. Its cool objectivity may have helped lower the political temperature of the nation. The quick resolution of the Revolution of 1688 showed that the country could keep its head during a crisis, making a vivid contrast with the terrible upheaval of the 1640s. But censorship did not keep the public from making its voice heard, thanks to the government's love of flattery and magistrates' love of the limelight. And it did not keep the public from seeing its interests, reflected as advertisements, begin to crowd out the news of the world. While the government of England may have wanted only a news mechanism, it created a news medium.

It is interesting to note that those who have studied the periodical press in the Soviet Union report some of the same development. Despite an openly avowed purpose of indoctrination, *Pravda* received as many as 360,000 letters a year (1,000 per day) and *Izvestia* even more in the 1960s. The *New York Times* at that time got about 50,000 per year. Many of those letters were written to get the Soviet government's attention, protesting the lack of bureaucratic response. However cynical intellectuals might have been about the papers' policies in publishing letters, a great many persons thought they had found a way to use "their" media. We may also note that audience surveys showed that Soviet readers were far more interested in international than in domestic news. This suggests that it may be a mistake to assume that readers of the corantos and the *Gazette* would have preferred domestic news, just because we do.[55]

No doubt there are differences between the ways that readers make use of periodical media in controlled and in free societies. But this does not necessarily mean that a managed press will only be resented as meaningless. Soviet readers commonly subscribed to not just one, but three or even four papers—national, local, occupational, sport—as well as magazines. Surveys indicated that the average reader of just one of these papers spent forty minutes a day on it. Total circulation in the nation was 170,000,000 copies in 1976, as compared to 103,000,000 copies in the United States. When readers became aware of inaccuracies in local papers their reaction, just as in the United States, was to turn to the central press as more reliable, rather than to distrust all papers equally.[56] All in all, it is a mistake to assume that the revulsion of intellectuals against the Soviet press was any more characteristic than the revulsion of intellectuals against the news industry in this country.

Despite a determination to monopolize news production and to limit it to the most factually objective reporting, periodical publication continued to develop some of its inherent tendencies during the Restoration. The public saw itself in the *Gazette*'s personals, despite the government's efforts to keep news from leading to reflection. By a shrewd use of Loyal Addresses the public reached out to its leaders, disturbing their dreams of absolutism. And despite government efforts to use the media as a bonding influence, the public continued to use it to register its divisions. To complete the picture of an emerging public opinion in the teeth of authority and news constraint, however, we must examine another development of the Restoration, the emergence of the coffeehouse as a periodical medium in its own right.

SIX

The Coffeehouse as a
Periodical Medium,
1660–80

Rather than imagine that periodical news is primarily to provide information about the world, it is possible to see its job as starting the discussion necessary to create an authentic public opinion. If one takes that view, it would follow that accurate or important information—always problematical—is not absolutely necessary to its purpose. Its function could be well served even at a time when the news industry was at low tide, which was certainly the case during Restoration England. In the 1670s, with little more than the official *London Gazette*, the highbrow *Philosophical Transactions*, the skeletal London Bills of Mortality, and occasional political pamphlets to discuss, there was a vital cultural life and a rising political debate—all because of the opportunity to discuss things in periodic visits to one's favorite coffeehouse. One did not have to visit every day, any more than one had to see a paper every day, to be shaped by the news consciousness fostered in those surroundings.

Whatever its deficiencies as information, news is the normal way to initiate conversation, whether it is periodical or not. Its value is in focusing society's attention, as sociologist Robert E. Park explained in his classic description, "News as a Form of Knowledge" (1940): "Once discussion has started, the event under discussion soon ceases to be news, and, as interpretations of an event differ, discussions turn from the news to the issues it raises. The clash of opinions and sentiments which discussion invariably evokes usually terminates in some sort of consensus or collective opinion—what we call public opinion. It is upon the *interpretation* of present events, i.e. news, that public opinion rests."[1] Not the news, but the discussion of the news, creates public opinion. When one consumes the news product in private, as is the rule today, it may be mistaken for something rather different. The news becomes a final statement and may be taken for a more or less adequate—if brief—account of history, social issues, and so on. When that happens, public opinion may not develop and commentators assume an unchallenged power.

Communion in the news operates at a level deeper than the conceptual. The excitement that surrounds news creates human bonding. Park likened this to certain signals that animals use to create "contagious excitement," a kind of "communication" that leads to a sense of togetherness and a kind of "understanding."[2] When this becomes a regular thing, he says, one has an exciteable herd.

Although he took a more critical view of these effects than Park, Alvin Gouldner agreed in pointing out the essential contribution that news discourse had in the functioning of society: "The development of a public in bourgeois society clearly entailed the interaction of growing news, printing media and technologies, and a cleared, safe space within which *face-to-face talk* about news and its meaning could occur."[3] His emphasis on face-to-face interchange is significant. News is best when it stimulates discussion and does not merely simulate it.

Jürgen Habermas's treatment of communication makes better sense if seen in these terms. We have already noticed that he passed over the fact that an information *industry* constitutes one of the economic and administrative "structures" that encroach on the public sphere of free and rational communication. He did not indicate that the commercial nature of periodicity itself made it part of the economic structure, and part of a "strategic" (manipulative) interchange rather than a "communicative" (rational) one. It is hard to see how a news industry could, by its nature, be part of his "lifeworld" of honest communication.[4] But in an early work, Habermas described the "golden age" of the English coffeehouse—which he put at 1680–1730—as a time when a general discussion of literature and philosophy was mixed with "consequential" affairs like religion and politics to further real communication. The counsels of state and church were quite properly "problematized." And the mixing of classes in this institution meant that the regulars at a coffeehouse were like "representatives" of a new cultural electorate. For a time, and to the benefit of the public weal, the existence of the coffeehouse resisted the increasing privatization toward which bourgeois culture was moving.

Unfortunately, as Habermas pointed out, its early promise in maintaining a vibrant public opinion was not to be fulfilled. Rather, bourgeois society would move from debating culture to consuming culture.[5] This happened when (if not because) periodicals began to provide discussion as well as information, so that discussion has become another of our professionalized, spectator sports.

The institution of the coffeehouse in the late 1650s and 1660s constituted something of a social revolution. To show just how remarkable it was at its beginning, Steven Pincus has compared it with the seventeenth-century tavern. The tavern was thought of as a place where one came to find companionship, conviviality, approval; one went to the coffeehouse for stimulation and debate. Tavern politics was a matter of drinking healths to one's leaders, while the coffeehouse was a forum for political criticism. Contemporary comment showed that taverns were considered to be Tory while coffeehouses were Whig, inevitably representing a challenge to authority. Taverns were dark and libidinous; coffeehouses had to be well-lit and tended to dry one out. Taverns encouraged inebriation, while one went to coffeehouses to sober up, as several pamphlets testified.[6] So coffeehouses marked a new stage in England's history, allowing society to be bonded through discussion, rather than through ostentatious devotion to tradition.

Coffeehouses came in with a rush under Cromwell's Protectorate, which may have had something to do with the decline of newsbooks then. By 1663 there were eighty-two within London, clustered near the Royal Exchange. Some of them were large establishments, like Garraways, which was assessed on 16 hearths under the Hearth Tax. By 1700 there were five hundred whose names are known, perhaps nearly as many as taverns.[7] And they quickly spread to other towns—Edinburgh, Glasgow, Dublin, Oxford, Cambridge, York, Bristol, Exeter, Tunbridge Wells, Nottingham, Preston, Plymouth, Dorchester, Harwich, Yarmouth, High Wycombe, King's Lynn, Warwick, Sheffield, Ipswitch, Chester, Northampton, for a start.[8] In 1673 a contemporary declared that coffeehouses had spread to "most cities and eminent Towns throughout the Nation."[9]

The excitement must have been intense. Contemporary accounts describe customers bursting in demanding "What News have you?", or more elaborately, "Your Servant, Sir, what News from Tripoly?/ Do the Weeks Pamphlets in their Works agree?"[10] One coffeehouse was said to have a parrot who would prompt patrons by squawking, "Where's the news."[11] And there is ample evidence that all classes were represented, which was a matter for surprised comment among contemporaries.[12] The play *Tarugo's Wiles* was only being realistic in introducing a baker and a barber to the coffeehouse scene, to mix with the students, merchants, and even gentlemen there. For it was not an expensive habit except in terms of the time spent; one could stay two or three hours for no more than the penny for the first "dish" of coffee.[13] Women might enter, since swearing and gambling were frowned upon.[14] The Puritans had approved all this sobriety, economy, egalitarianism, and discussion, as part of their countercultural orientation, and it had their blessing as it first began to spread.

But the radicalism of the coffeehouse went far beyond anything Puritans had envisioned. There was a definite exoticism in the Turkish associations that many coffeehouses affected. Bryant Lillywhite's register of London coffeehouses lists sixty-two that had Turk in their names, eight that used Black Boy or Blackamoor, and another dozen that mentioned Saracen, Sultan, Smyrna, or Africa.[15] Contemporary references constantly allude to the outlandishness of coffee and coffee drinking, and spoke facetiously of the black brew as demonic. They made much of the un-English and un-Christian character of such establishments. The play *Knavery in All Trades: Or, The Coffee-House* (1664) casts a comic but unappealing Turk as the coffeehouse owner, and there is mock horror concerning a Turkish invasion and conversion to Islam, connected with news of the continuing struggle in the Balkans.[16] *The Maiden's Complaint Against Coffee* (1663) used coffee's blackness to suggest a number of disturbing images—of hell, Negroes, Africa, and heresy.[17] Conservative critics of coffeehouse wrangling and the obsession with news could draw from a deep well of prejudice.

Anthony Wood was not charmed by coffeehouse exoticism and was depressed at its distracting effect in a university town. Conversation at Oxford was turning from "solid and serious learning" to mere news, and Wood blamed it on the introduction of coffeehouses there, beginning in 1650. "Nothing but news and the affairs of Christendome is discoursed of and that also generally at coffee houses." There may have been something sinister in the fact that the first two coffeehouses in Oxford were opened by Jews.[18] But the larger point is that printed news and coffeehouse excitement was a threat to traditional academic culture.

The same was reported from Cambridge by Sir Roger North, who described the 1670s and 1680s:

> They had only the public Gazette, till Kirk [the coffeehouse owner] got a written news letter circulated by one Muddiman. But now the case is much altered; for it is become a Custom, after Chapel, to repair to one or the other of the Coffee Houses (for there are diverse), where Hours are spent in talking, and less profitable reading of News Papers, of which swarms are continually supplied from London [during the Exclusion Controversy]. And the Scholars are so Greedy after News (which is none of their business) that they neglect all for it; which is a vast Loss of Time grown out of a pure Novelty, for who can apply close to a Subject with his Head full of the Din of a Coffee-house?[19]

Others without this devotion to academic sobriety simply objected to the sordid circumstances of this scene, and the alien habits that were tolerated: "You may go into a Coffee-house and see a Table of an Acre long covered with nothing but Tobacco-pipes and Pamphlets, and all the seats full of Mortals leaning upon their Elbowes, licking in Tobacco, Lyes, and Lac'd Coffee, and studying for Arguments to revile one another."[20] Coffeehouse sociability was not well integrated into domestic life. None of the "heathenish" drinks they served—coffee, tea, chocolate, "sherbet" (lemonade)—had ever been seen in England before the 1650s.[21] No one drank them at home. The easiest way to dismiss the whole scene was to treat the craze for coffee as a pretense, given how badly it tasted:

> *A loathsome Potion, not yet understood,*
> *Syrrop of Soot, or Essence of old Shooes,*
> *Dasht with Diurnals, and the Books of News.*[22]

Not only was it "ugly in colour and tast" but it had a "drying" effect on men's sex drive. Critics warned that it was making men so excitable and effeminate that they now "out-babble women."[23]

The strangeness of the coffeehouse was symbolic of the strangeness of the activity that went on there—the regular, incessant, almost institutionalized discussion of the nation's and the world's news. It was not only the government that found this intolerable: Traditionalists objected that "every little Fellow in a Chamlet-Cloak takes upon him to transpose Affairs both in Church and State, to shew reasons against Acts of Parliament, and to condemn the Decrees of General Councils." The coffee-house atheist, who "holds his Gospel from the Apostle of Malmesbury [Hobbes] . . . is so refractory to Divinity that Morality itself cannot hold him. . . . Whatever is sacred or serious he seeks to render Ridiculous."[24] In making everything political, cultural foundations were becoming subject to negotiation.

It was not only political and religious truth that would suffer from rough and constant handling. Scholarship would evaporate in the fumes of the coffeehouse; anyone who presents his views "in the terms of Aristotle, or argues by Book, is lookt on to want terms and reason of his own." All questions were to be started anew, with no guide but one's native wit. Which meant that important questions would never be concluded, any more than one can reach port "without a pilot or rules of navigation."[25]

But it was the connection of news with politics that was most disturbing. In 1673 a serious proposal to the government to close the coffeehouses complained of those who "sit half a day, and discourse with all companies that come in of State matters, talking of news and broaching of lies, arraigning the judgments and discretion of their governors, censuring all their actions, and insinuating into the ears of the people a prejudice against them."[26]

In a comedy of 1681, a customer enters a coffeehouse and asks "Which is the treason table?"[27] Sir Roger North complained that some coffeehouses had "tables for irreligion, like the Rota for politics."[28] Another complained that "every carman and porter is now a statesman; and indeed the coffee-houses are good for nothing else. It was not thus when we drank nothing but sack and claret, or English beer and ale."[29] Not all such complaints were facetious.

It was not ridiculous to think that a news-driven democracy would eventually become shallow and its culture debased. And it would be a mistake to think that all of English society was chafing to become involved in such discussion. Many had learned from the mid-century revolution that the world could indeed come apart when society threw over respect for monarchy and church. Some commentators took comfort in the fact that coffeehouse discussion was self-defeating, as the arguments of the "gazette-philosophers" canceled each other out. After all, each coffeehouse amounted to "a congress of old Rome and of new, of Turkey, Geneva, and Amsterdam." Critics sneered that the idlers who crowded them could argue about anything: "The Society hath been divided about the manner of the creeping of a Louse"—perhaps a reference to the early meetings of the Royal Society.[30]

Traditional society craved agreement and could not imagine it coming out of the tumult of a coffeehouse. It seemed to conservatives that coffeehouses depended on *disagreement* to the point that the company would have to disband if they ever found that they agreed. Some thought that discussion would drain the life out of all topics, for the same thing that would sound profound to the fuddled fellowship of the tavern, in the coffeehouse would begin to seem "first familiar, then contempt-ible." So they could take comfort in the thought that coffeehouses would never be a danger to the government, since the company would never be able to agree on a plot or a constitution.[31]

It may be hard for us to see any merit in these complaints, conditioned as we are to believe in uninhibited discussion. But the critics rightly recognized the anti-intellectual mood of Restoration society. Polite society was being encouraged to think that the intellectual elites had failed. Since the latter had not managed to conclude philosophy, science, theology, what was to keep the public from settling matters according to reason? The question, of course, is whether this "Reason" represented anything more solid than the prejudices of coffeehouse society in a particular coun-try at a particular time.

In retrospect, we can see some gain in the intellectual revolution of the period. Such anti-intellectualism may have been necessary where a decadent humanism showed a greater concern for words than ideas, where theology was overrationalized, where science had taken the wrong path. But culture may suffer by keeping all ques-tions constantly in play, and deferring to a coffeehouse jury will not result in solid advances in philosophy, the arts, theology, or science. Nor is diplomatic wisdom found in proportion to the extent of the debate; democracies are not proverbial for wisdom in managing their foreign affairs. It is different in domestic politics. Discus-sion is always necessary on social and political questions, where popular consent is the critical element in resolving problems.

Of the various branches of learning, only science was well served by its clubs and periodicals. Modern science has been described as a "conversation,"[32] and it was natural that it should create its own club organization and publications. The fa-mous *Royal Society of London for the Promotion of Natural Knowledge*, chartered in 1662, had antecedents in weekly gatherings in taverns.[33] Even after instituting its formal meetings, members of the society liked to continue their discussion in coffeehouses like the Grecian, the Crown in Threadneedle Street, and Garraways.[34] The society's main business, aside from hearing of its members' experiments, was to respond to the news from scientists abroad. That correspondence became so large and technical that the society's secretary, Henry Oldenburg, decided to print the most important items—monthly—so that members and others could feel that they were keeping abreast of developments. And thus the *Philosophical Transactions* was born in 1665, which, despite some lapses, continues to this day. The Royal Society did not authorize this publication; it was a private venture of Oldenburg's and con-tinued to be unofficial until 1753.[35] But it helped greatly in giving shape to modern science.

The scientific clubs and periodicals were very different from those we have seen. The formal meetings of the Royal Society were far from being the free-for-all of a coffeehouse. Discussion was based on a formal paper, a demonstration, or correspon-dence from England or abroad. Speakers had to be recognized by the presiding officer. Still, this made a marked contrast with the academic disputations of university science, with its elaborated rules and unintelligible vocabulary. John Locke complained of the persistence of the old approach to science in the universities of the 1680s. Meanwhile, as Thomas Hobbes declared, leadership in science was "remov'd from Oxford and Cambridge to Gresham-College in London [where the Royal Society held its meetings], and to be learn'd out of their Gazets."[36]

The *Transactions* are an instance of communication within an elite, rather than for the general enlightenment of the public. Within the new, alternative scientific elite, periodicals built a real community, more authentic than that served by newspapers. They extended the community internationally and issued calls for help in larger projects. The *Transactions* contained readers' submissions, helping to establish reputations and a hierarchy within the enterprise.

Given the incremental understanding of scientific advance popularized by Bacon, periodicity was essential to the enterprise. Scientific academies were proliferating and were eager to read what others were doing.[37] Active members who wanted credit for their contributions found periodical publication useful in dating their claims to discoveries. Unlike other periodicals, each issue was not meant to make the last one obsolete. In fact, in 1667 Oldenburg began to reprint the collected issues for those who had just gotten in on the game. From the beginning, the reprinted volumes were indexed. In 1689 a cumulative index of the nine most prominant European intellectual periodicals appeared in Holland, including the English *Memoirs for the Ingenious* as well as the *Transactions*.[38] So the *Philosophical Transactions* were more a repository than a periodical.

The first issue, for 6 March 1665, was a 16-page quarto, containing ten articles. The first three of these were on astronomy, showing the excitement of using telescopes. One article was from Italy, another from France, and the third was "Mr. Hook's" claim to a prior observation of the rotation of Jupiter, dated to the previous May. Robert Boyle then issued a prospectus on projected experiments at low temperatures and offered a description of a monstrous calf. Others reported on a peculiar lead ore from Germany, the medicinal use of bolar earths, an account of whale fishing off Bermuda "By a Seaman," and the use of pendulum watches in navigation, by "Major Holmes." Finally there was an obituary of M. de Fermat. The sense is of a small and intimate community—"the Commonwealth of Learning," it is called—with friends overseas who might be mourned as relatives.

This sense is reinforced in the second issue (3 April 1665), when the same correspondent from Rome responded to M. Auzout's discussion of cometary orbits in the previous issue. That submission was immediately followed by Auzout's response from Paris! Such an exchange demonstrates an efficient mail service and eager editors. There was some asperity on both sides, as they sought to enlist the testimony of friends in dating discoveries from a time before the periodical existed. This April issue also reported on astronomical observations from two months earlier, carried a correction to Boyle's description of the calf, and included an engraved plate with two figures representing a mercury mine near Venice. Like all periodicals, it stuck close to facts and argued over them. Lists of errata became a regular feature, including corrections of the plates. It all seems exactly suited to the philosophical enterprise, involving polite disagreement and the humility of honest scholarship.

In one notable respect the *Philosophical Transactions* resembled all other periodicals in England. Unlike the natural philosophy of previous generations, the new science appeared in English, for those who would have found Latin too taxing. This created some problems, as when Hooke had to point out that one source of Auzout's confusion was his insufficient knowledge of English.[39] But the suppression of Latin—and the enlargement of the audience—was one of the things that made the journal so important. When it began to offer book synopses, these were usually of works in Latin, for a grateful public. It also excerpted articles from its French counterpart, the *Journal des Sçavans*.

Just as the newsbooks brought the public into the political discussion, so the *Transactions* opened science to help from those outside the elite. They printed contributions from amateurs, who might tell how they killed rattlesnakes in Virginia. It printed appeals (to "Sea-men") for help in gathering data on navigation and agriculture, listing the questions of greatest interest. At Hooke's suggestion, the editor called on readers for work on inventions that would sharpen the senses of hearing, smelling, tasting, and touching as much as optical glasses had the sense of sight. And he ended one of his book summaries with an appeal to readers to "prosecute the same by further experiment, either to confirm what this Author has stated, if true, or to reveal if he be mistaken."[40]

One can carry this sort of thing too far, if readers begin to suppose that one opinion is as good as another. That was often the way science would appear in later literary periodicals. But the *Philosophical Transactions* was a "refereed" journal from the beginning, building a foundation for scholarship. It has been said that if all other scientific publications of that first century of modern science were missing, one could reconstruct the scientific activity of the time on the basis of the *Transactions* alone.[41] It was translated, reprinted, abridged, and abstracted all over Europe.[42]

Unfortunately, the *Transactions* was not a commercial success. The price of either sixpence or a shilling did not cover the cost of the paper used for the three hundred copies sold.[43] Foreign sales and the sixty copies the society bought for its own use did not always make accounts balance, and Oldenburg complained of the money he lost.[44] When he died in 1677 the journal lapsed, allowing other experiments in scientific publication, which we will note in due course.

In the case of science, the dynamics of periodical gatherings and periodical publication did not subvert the enterprise. A more formal discipline was involved than was observed in the coffeehouse. Science was understood to be a cumulative endeavor, in which today's report does not usually supercede yesterday's but rather builds on it. More usually, the news industry depends on forgetfulness if it is to hold reader interest. An instance of the discontinuous nature of periodical reality was noted by Samuel Pepys in a diary entry for 13 December 1666. Pepys was struck by his own forgetfulness when someone reminded him of a report in the *London Gazette* of 29 April 1666 that predicted a great fire on September 3—the very day of the destruction of London. Pepys could find nobody else who remembered having read it and had to consult his file of back issues to confirm the claim.[45]

This might not worry us, who no longer depend on memory, but it was part of what concerned traditionalist critics. In the late 1660s Samuel Butler had not got over the sense that anything that reached print ought to have enduring value. Among his "Characters" he describes a "News-Monger" as one who dealt in a "perishable Commodity, that will not keep: for if it be not fresh it lies upon his Hands, and will yield nothing. True or False is all one to him; for Novelty being the Grace of both, a Truth grows stale as soon as a Lye." Readers no longer responded to wisdom so much as to the breathless intensity of the journalist: "He would willingly bear his Share in any public Calamity, to have the Pleasure of hearing and telling it."[46] In the coffeehouse there was the pleasure of telling sensational news, if not of selling it.

Finally, as coffeehouses amplified the periodical news, another institution of the Restoration heightened the impact of coffeehouses. That was the independent Penny Post that began in London in 1680. That date quite properly suggests a connection with the commotion surrounding the Popish Plot and the campaign to exclude the Catholic James from the succession. The official posts had never proved a very satisfactory method of communication. The government felt free to open letters and keep track of its subjects, and people knew this.[47] Perhaps it was the opportunity for surveillance that had induced the state to allow public access to its communication system in the first place. During the 1640s some private postal services had developed, but stronger governments had reestablished the postal monopoly.[48]

In 1680 came the possibility of more confidential communications. William Dockwra was allowed to set up a private penny post in London and Westminster. Previously, Londoners had gone to the General Letter Office to pick up their letters. The Penny Post delivered them to the addressee, within the hour—meaning four or five deliveries a day. Or, very often, it would deliver them to a designated coffeehouse, as a kind of "box number."[49]

So the new post increased the velocity of information above even a daily schedule. And its political significance was not lost on the government. The Penny Post was vital to the Whig conspirators of those years, connecting their various coffeehouse headquarters and transporting the independent newspapers that were reemerging in that period. Dockwra listed seven coffeehouses as receiving stations for his system.[50] By 1682 the authorities were able to take the Penny Post out of Dockwra's hands, incorporating it into the general mail service. The new post thereby lost its brief political importance. But it continued to deliver to coffeehouse addresses, and thereby maintained the faster tempo of information exchange.[51]

During the 1660s and 1670s coffeehouses were surely deficient in the amount of information supporting discussion. In our next chapter it will become clear how much work had to be done to assemble the scanty materials available. But it will also become clear how intense was the public participation in this activity. Habermas is not alone, however, in noting a decline in the institution of the coffeehouse already in the early eighteenth century. We may guess at some of the reasons. Press licensing ended in 1695 and newspapers multiplied, allowing one to consume the news in private. The General Post Office was trusted more widely after the revolution, when the government began to appoint two postmasters—one Whig and one Tory—to insure that the position was not used politically.[52] The gin shops that spread throughout the metropolis must have taken off some part of the trade. Tea and coffee began to be drunk at home, and houses were numbered so that mail was not picked up at a coffeehouse address. And private subscription clubs, embodying the club motif of the essay periodicals, became one of the characteristic features of eighteenth century society. Some of these had originated in coffeehouse fellowship.[53]

Beyond this, England's politics became less truly revolutionary. In part, this was due to the contribution of coffeehouses and a few dog-eared newspapers toward bringing down the old regime. It is ironic that the more fully developed newspapers of the next century would have no such successes, despite the political din they created. One must wonder whether it was the very maturity of those later papers that worked against their political impact, as readers became satisfied to watch the world rather than participate in it.

SEVEN

Periodicity and Press Freedom, 1670–90

W e are used to thinking of the press as an instrument that can be turned on government to create pressure for change. But whence comes the pressure that is needed to win press freedom where it had not existed? To all appearances, the restored Stuart monarchy had succeeded in strangling the infant press. It may seem paradoxical to look at the controlled press itself as part of the explanation for the Revolution of 1688 and its associated changes. And yet the bare existence of periodical publication and of coffeehouse periodicity generated a public opinion that helped win press freedom and liberate the political classes from an unacceptable dynasty. Even the official *London Gazette* inadvertantly helped in this process. It all has to do with events in the late 1670s and early 1680s that historians call the Popish Plot and Exclusion Controversy.

Taking stock of the situation after 1660, we recall that only one newspaper was allowed, and eventually that it issued directly from a government office. In 1665 the *London Gazette* was joined by the *Philosophical Transactions*, and there were other publications that kept up the habit of weekly appearance, even if only in an obscene vein. Beginning in March 1676 and running for a year and a half, *Poor Robin's Intelligence* was heir to John Crouch's pornographic periodicals. Not as grossly obscene as Crouch, it could better be described as ribald, and in fact, knew enough to refer to Rabelais.[1] Why it needed to appear periodically is a mystery, unless it has to do with profits. But it must have been profitable to run so long, and the copies that survive look like they have passed through hundreds of hands. One almost feels sorry for the licenser, Roger L'Estrange, who had to read each one carefully to make sure it could not be taken as political comment.

The coffeehouse "news" would have included the daily broadside list of imports, *London, imported* (starting in 1660), the weekly strip publication *Prices of Merchan-*

dise in London (from 1667), and a quarterly list of all the new books, *Mercurius Librarius* (1668). From the late 1660s onward there were also weekly advertisers, printed and distributed free, like *Mercurius Civicus, London Mercury, Weekly Advertisements*, and several that went under the title *City Mercury*. They may seem dull to us, but it was one of these that asserted that each copy "cannot be supposed to be Read by less than Twenty times the Number of Persons."[2] They included lists of those scheduled to be publicly executed and the numbers of those to be branded ("burnt in the hand"), transported, and whipped. And they made the most of the human interest to be gleaned from the Bills of Mortality:

> The chief Diseases and Casualties of this week were the drowning of Two, One at St. Mary Magdalen Bermondsy, and another accidentally in a Sawpit at Hackney. Three killed by the Fall of a Ladder at Christ Church; Another accidentally by a wound in's mouth with a Tobacco pipe; and an Infant by a Fall out of a window at St. Clement Danes; One accidentally scalded to death, in a Distillers Fat [vat] at St. Olave Southwark; 50 of Consumptions; 54 of Convulsions; 58 of Feavers; but 18 of the Flux and small Pox, and (God be praised) of the Plague none.

Even real estate ads might create some gossip, particularly if they described the upper end of the market:

> At Acton, the Back part of the Town, is a very convenient House, containing 4 Rooms on a Floor, with good Cellerage, Barn, Stable, Coach-house, Brew-house, Larder, Milk-house, etc., upon which above 100 L. had been laid out within one year, being the House which was the late Lord Chief Justice Hale's, together with a Garden containing an Acre and a half, Walled in, and excellently planted with Choice Fruit, all in their prime, a Tarras Walk, with 2 Banquetting-Houses newly painted, and a fine Row of Elms in the Garden, to be Lett by Lease, or any term from 2 years to 20 years. Enquire of Mr. Burrastone at the Examiners Office in Chancery Lane.[3]

Readers who exercised their imagination could turn such stuff into news and keep the habit of periodicity alive through decades in which the government thought it had matters firmly in hand. Those of a political or conspiratorial turn of mind might imagine that they saw the government's hand hidden in the detail of these publications, and it would only take the spark of coffeehouse conversation to turn such information into debate.

Also important in this process were the periodical newsletters that resumed furtively in the Restoration.[4] Their current cost of perhaps four pounds per year plus postage could easily be absorbed by the coffeehouses that subscribed. So they had a following far beyond their modest production figures, which were in the low hundreds. It has been said that one copy of a newsletter generally served a whole countryside.[5] In them, readers typically received about eight hundred words of mostly foreign news with each of the week's three posts.[6] Coffeehouses sometimes took in foreign newsletters or papers as well, which might carry better intelligence of England than of their own countries.[7] For a time during the coming commotion someone even published a translation of the *Haerlem Courant* in London.

To be sure, the public's addiction for periodical news was not being satisfied by such fare. Even at Whitehall—the center of affairs—Henry Saville complained to Viscount Halifax that "there is no news from abroad newer or privater than the Gazette," and again "there is nothing come of more moment than you may learn in the Gazette."[8] The earl of Sunderland marveled that Sir William Temple knew only what appeared in the *Gazette* of a recent diplomatic exchange. And when the diplomat Henry Sidney wanted to punish Sir Leoline Jenkins, he did so by sending him only the printed gazettes from the Hague.[9]

Samuel Butler, in a character sketch of the "Intelligencer" or newswriter, alluded to "remote Country Virtuosos [literati], who finding themselves unsatisfied with the Brevity of the Gazette desire to have Exceedings of News, besides their ordinary Commons [diet]. To furnish those he [the newswriter] frequents Clubs and Coffee-Houses, the Markets of News."[10] Henry More, the Cambridge philosopher, fit this picture, complaining to Lady Conway that the weekly "journall" is "as much newes as I am ordinarily furnished with." Lady Conway, like other women, may have benefited more from the printed news than their menfolk, if they were bypassed by other channels of information. Lady Sutherland, for instance, referring to the *Gazette* as if everyone read it, did not complain of its brevity.[11]

But even such deficient media as existed, when played against the coffeehouse sounding board, proved disturbing to an authoritarian government. Political tensions increased during the 1670s as many began to see Parliament itself more as a tool of the regime than a champion of the public. This "Pensioner Parliament" had been sitting, on and off, since 1661, and represented a position that was coming to seem reactionary. So in 1675–77 there was a flurry of unlicensed "libels" calling for new elections, and the authorities identified the source of this unwelcome agitation as the coffeehouses and moved to close them down.

A proclamation issued on 29 December 1675 declared that the government would close all the coffeehouses of the whole realm, just as it had closed down the independent newspapers. Its charge was that "Idle and Disaffected persons" were attracted to them, and that "Tradesmen and others" who could not afford the time away from "their Lawful Callings and Affairs" were hearing a swirl of "false, malitious and scandalous Reports . . . to the Disturbance of the Peace and Quiet of the Realm." Nothing was said of taverns. The proclamation was sneaked in at the end of the *Gazette* (of 27 December), as if to minimize its importance.[12]

The government immediately began to have second thoughts. In the words of the Tory Roger North, the "coffee-men" petitioned the king and "promised to be wonderful good for the future." But North sadly thought that the real reason for the government's retreat was that it feared that "a convulsion and discontent would unavoidably follow."[13] That proclamation was ignominiously withdrawn before it was to go into operation (on January 10), by a face-saving proclamation "clarifying" the first.[14] By the new proclamation, coffeehouse keepers were required to prevent scandalous papers from being taken in or read on the premises and to give information of any libelous reports that circulated there.

Coffeehouses had proved that they were part of the English constitution. Or as we now say, the news industry was recognized as the fourth branch of government. When the sensational Popish Plot broke in the late summer of 1678, there were no printed periodicals that could spread that story. But the institution of the coffeehouse made it possible to turn that episode into the first media-driven investigation.

On 6 September 1678, after attempts to approach the king and his chief ministers, a strange figure named Titus Oates gave a deposition before a justice of the peace that alleged a high-level Catholic conspiracy to murder the king and seize the state. Such an event would put the king's brother James, the grimly Catholic duke of York, on the throne. Oates was a man of a very checkered past and the king realized that there were gaping holes in his story, but the historical memory of the English public taught them that Catholics were capable of anything. And when that very justice, Sir Edmund Berry Godfrey, was found murdered a month later it increased the sense of a conspiracy penetrating high into the government. Other things turned up which the slippery Oates wove into his story; new details sprouted every week. The wonder of it is that the government was not able to face down such a charlatan, for he was backed by a public opinion based on nothing more than the threadbare media we have mentioned and pamphlets. Despite the government's doubts, the "Popish Plot" grew into the kind of witch-hunt in which denials themselves were treated as proof of involvement.

Before July 1679, there were no opposition papers to encourage the hysteria of the Plot. But one could still consider it media-driven, when including coffeehouses in our definition. One should note the words of a Secretary of State, Henry Coventry, that "we are without news but what the coffee houses *make*."[15] As Steven Pincus has observed, during the whole agitation to exclude James from inheriting the throne, "each political move that was made, and some that were not, were revealed, debated, celebrated and vilified in the coffee houses."[16] The earl of Shaftesbury, the diminutive but fearless leader of the Whig opposition, tuned the coffeehouses to resound to rumors designed for all who came in to ask "What News?"

Shaftesbury realized that a constant supply of news—however questionable—could be a force for political change. His pamphlets acquired a serial nature by being provided to the coffeehouses. For what was important—which the coffeehouse habit provided—was that readers felt that they were not missing anything. Even though pamphlets appeared at a rate of several per day, readers could feel "informed" enough to trust their understanding of the issues and act upon that knowledge. The government soon began sending out its agents to spread stories of Presbyterian plots in the same setting.[17]

So the common claim that the Plot, the Exclusion campaign, and the Whig party created English public opinion is a little wide of the mark.[18] Public opinion already existed because of the bare existence of periodical media, and the Whigs seized it while the government was still hoping it could be ignored. As the plot broke, the machinery of opinion increased. The Penny Post, begun in 1680, immediately proved its value to these intelligencers and journalists. Giles Hancock's Whig newsletters probably went out in over a hundred copies.[19] He soon had rivals, and coffeehouses were paying four or five shillings a week for the opposition newsletters.[20] The Privy Council duly arrested the writer of the first unofficial newsletter in April 1679, but found it increasingly difficult to protect Muddiman's monopoly.

The Privy Council tried suppressing newsletters by an order of December 1679, which forbade coffeehouses to receive them.[21] This could be justified simply as a regulation of trade if one took the view that newsletters were vending a false or fraudulent product. And even historians concur in that view, calling the Whig papers "notoriously untruthful." For example, when Muddiman reported fires in the city he attributed them to some accidental cause, while the Whig newsmongers attributed them all to the Papists."[22]

About the same time, as the government hurriedly dissolved the old Parliament, it discovered that the Press Licensing Act had not been renewed. It came as a shock to the king to find that it was perfectly legal to print newspapers again, without government license.[23] The crown responded with a proclamation of 31 October 1679 that promised to punish any "Books and Pamphlets whatsoever, being Libels against the Government, or against any Publick or Private Person." But by way of enforcement, the government could only enlist hawkers to reveal the publishers of these libels and promised to share fines with others who could give such information.

There had always been a term to the Licensing Act, and it had been renewed before. The lapse in 1679 was inadvertant, but the excited state of public opinion made it impossible even to debate a reinstatement. So England was without a statute for controlling the press until 1685. Royal judges tried to fill the gap by ruling that the monarch had an inherent, or "prerogative," power over the press. It was self-evident to them that he had the right to "prohibit the Printing and Publishing of all News-Books and Pamphlets of News whatsoever . . . as manifestly tending to the Breach of the Peace, and disturbance of the Kingdom."[24] That is, it was self-evident or "manifest" to the mind of that time that printed, periodical news tended to political disturbance.

Proclamations were difficult to enforce yet continued to appear. One dated 17 May 1680 acknowledged that "it is of great Importance to the State, That all News Printed and Published to the People, as well concerning Foreign as Domestick Affairs, should be agreeable to Truth, or at least Warranted by good Intelligence, that the minds of his Majesties Subjects may not be disturbed or amused by Lyes or vain Reports, which are many times raised on purpose to Scandalize the Government." It therefore prohibited all unlicensed newsbooks or pamphlets, on the authority of the declaration "by all His Majesties Judges unanimously" that "malicious Reports . . . would in a short time endanger the Peace of the Kingdom." But in the absence of statutory power over the press, the government fell back on common-law prosecutions for seditious libel. These followed from the theory that the king was the source of all law and any censure might damage his authority. When the popular excitement over the plot began to die down and the government found juries that would convict, prosecutions for seditious libel became common.[25] Only in 1683, with the

aid of a newly elected Tory city government in London, could the unlicensed newspapers and newsletters finally be swept away.

Eventually, the government created media of its own to counter those of the
opposition. And when it sponsored a pamphlet campaign to answer Shaftesbury's
writers, they hired none other than Marchamont Nedham, who came out of retire-
ment to produce five anonymous pamphlets. Having changed sides once again, he
found himself opposing Shaftesbury, who ought to have been his libertarian soul
mate. Actually, it is encouraging to see Nedham accuse Shaftesbury of being a turn-
coat—someone prepared to "shift principles like shirts"—for it shows that the public, at least, still had enough principle to be moved by an appeal to honor. Nedham
attacked Shaftesbury's republican ideas, which had come straight out of his own
political philosophy. And for good measure he made fun of journalists, who die away
like flies when there is no trouble to report: "There's nothing revives them in the
Interval, like some unlucky Mischief befal'n the Court."[26] In fact, they had greatly
increased the mischief at the court.

Historians of the Popish Plot have denied that the media contributed to the panic,
on the grounds that the *London Gazette* ignored it and that other newspapers appeared
after it was raging. J. P. Kenyon, indeed, suggests that it was precisely the absence
of printed news that allowed unfounded rumors to cause so much commotion. Leaving aside the question of whether published rumors are superior to spoken ones, this
ignores several factors that were operating from the beginning—the coffeehouse as
an oral medium, the newsletters, and the use that the Whigs made of the *Gazette*
itself.[27]

Four years is a long time to maintain what historians always describe as a "hysteria." It could not have lasted that long without constant, unrelenting efforts to keep
it in the forefront of public attention. In the end, the news periodicals could not sustain the effort; losing vital allies in the Whig sheriffs and juries of London and in the
House of Commons cleared the way for prosecutions of the Whig journalists. But
until then, the antics of Shaftesbury—presenting the duke of York to the Middlesex
grand jury as a popish recusant and the king's mistress as a prostitute—only make
sense in the context of a powerful public opinion created by a very rudimentary
press.[28]

Kenyon and others also offer too simple a picture of the *London Gazette* during
these years. Of course it tried to stay above the fray, hoping to maintain a good example for the happier, more settled times ahead. Other Tory newspapers were started
in 1679 to carry the fight into the trenches. But one can see, in the *Gazette*'s content,
ways in which periodicity subverted the best editorial intentions.

Titus Oates's deposition before Godfrey was presented to the council on
28 September 1678. On 21 October the *Gazette* carried out its official responsibility
of publishing a proclamation for the discovery of the murderers. It offered no larger
context for the announcement. The next two issues contained no mention of any plot,
but on 31 October the paper published the proclamation of a national fast that spelled

things out. Eight of the next nine issues published proclamations or other official announcements that seem designed for no other purpose than to raise questions in the public mind.

And of course they were precisely for this purpose. All of these proclamations are described as issuing in response to petitions from Parliament. In short, the opposition leaders knew that the *Gazette* could not refuse to print official proclamations, and they had found a way of forcing the government to issue them. Sales of the *Gazette* climbed to a new high of seven thousand.[29]

Shaftesbury's party may have been glad to have the *Gazette* treating the matter so tersely. The paper's obvious reluctance indicated to the public that something was wrong at the top. After Parliament was dissolved, news of the plot was weirdly missing from the *Gazette*. This would not have gone unnoticed, especially when the paper advertised books by the "discoverers" of the plot, like Oates's collaborator Ezekiel Tonge's translation of *The Jesuits Morals*, and *A Sermon at the Funeral of Sir Edmundberry Godfrey* (16 December 1678). Such ads might be the only reminder of the plot in a particular issue.

So for several months there was something related to the plot in roughly every other number of the *Gazette*—that is, once a week. The paper did not have to carry comment in order to encourage speculation. Indeed, the less comment, the greater the speculation.

By August 1679 the *Gazette* began to take notice of the opposition newspapers that were appearing. On 11 August it reported that the London city government had ordered the suppression of all hawkers of "seditious Books, scurrilous Pamphlets, and scandalous printed papers," especially around Cornhill Street and the Royal Exchange. Thus it even told people where to go if they were curious. On 18 December it began to correct the misstatements appearing in the *Domestick Intelligence*, which would become a continuing job. It also announced the interrogation of several writers of "false and seditious News-Letters" and gave the names of coffeehouses involved, providing free advertising for their wares.

In chapter 5 we noticed government efforts to make the *Gazette* a more "popular" medium, to insure that people would actually read it. These features were now used against it. On 12 January 1680 several politically involved individuals inserted a "personal" to announce that they would demand a trial to clear themselves. And on 15 January the *Gazette* itself published a letter complaining of "a very gross Mistake" in one of its own political reports. Probably this was only because one of the Whig papers had likewise pointed out the mistake.[30] When the *Gazette* printed this letter it also justified itself: "This Mistake, which had its rise from those that affirmed they saw those Two Gentlemen, was however not so great an one as theirs who gave out that the King returned a most gracious Answer." An aloof posture was cracking as periodicals competed for the public's faith.

When the tide began to turn in 1681, the *Gazette* began to print the loyal addresses we described earlier, which oddly helped to create a more truly public sphere. They were a direct Tory response to the Whig petitions published in the new Whig news-papers and show how hard it is for periodical media to keep from being drawn into controversy.

After an absence of twenty-five years, it took some time for the opposition news-papers to learn the trade. The first of them, the *Weekly Pacquet of Advice from Rome, or, The History of Popery* (3 December 1678), was despite its sarcastic title a mild and scholarly effort to serialize the history of the Reformation. This, of course, was to remind Englishmen of what was at stake in Europe's continuing religious struggle. At first it contained no news of the plot or of anything else, so that its periodical form simply seems a way to make a lengthy book affordable. But in accordance with its periodical nature it began to develop a current focus. The last two pages of its old-fashioned, eight-page newsbook format became a humorous appendix called the *Popish Courant*. This was a parody report of a global Catholic conspiracy from the center of that enterprise, and in this weekly caricature the periodical became timely.

Every other opposition newspaper that emerged was, oddly enough, a clone of the *London Gazette*—halfsheets printed front and back in double columns, with a head title above a dateline. Thus, the new Whig papers did not try to reject the ap-pearance of "managed" news by reviving the material form of an earlier and freer journalism. It is evidence of the success of the government in creating a respected institution.

In July 1679, three papers were begun to keep up interest in the plot. Benjamin Harris's *Domestick Intelligence, or News Both From City and Country* (9 July 1679) was the only one of these first entries to survive. It had to change its name several times (eventually the *True Protestant (Domestick) Intelligence*) to keep ahead of Tory journals that tried to confuse the public by copying the name.

Harris was joined by others, after it appeared that it was safe and profitable to enter the trade. Some of the papers, like the *English Currant, Or, Advice Domestick and Forreign* (8 September 1679) and the *English Gazette* (22 December 1680), pre-tended to be corantos and only sneaked domestic rumors in among the foreign reports. Others, like the *London Mercury* (6 April 1682) professed to be "impartial . . . always avoiding Reflections both on Church and State, publick Transactions, and particular Persons." That is, they might report on these, but without "reflecting" or editorializing. But some, like Harris's paper and *Smith's Protestant Intelligence: Domestick and Foreign* (1 February 1681), fearlessly ran the domestic reports first and obviously wanted to put heat on the government.

Everything became grist for the Whig mill; Harris reported the famous assault on John Dryden (a Catholic) in Covent Garden as "some Feminine [i.e., cowardly], if not Popish vengeance."[31] Their papers only ran foreign news that could be related to the supposed global Catholic conspiracy. And all the papers thought it safe to print the Whig petitions to Parliament, which became a propaganda form and induced the Tories to counter with their own appeals to public opinion.[32]

Even *Mercurius Librarius*, the booksellers's quarterly catalogue, helped drive the plot. In 1679 it no longer needed L'Estrange's license and promptly began listing all the plot-related publications. Since, as one contemporary said, it "goes all over England," it could do much to widen the political public.[33] Coffeehouses made these catalogues available to their customers, who might be too bashful to go into a bookshop without knowing what they wanted.[34]

Finally, a newly elected and more radical House of Commons once again authorized the publication of the *Votes of the House of Commons*, which began to appear on 30 October 1680. This amounted to a small halfsheet containing the status of bills, the king's speeches, and the kind of orders and resolutions that went into the House of Commons' Journal. It appeared daily when Parliament was meeting, and is said to have sold in the thousands.[35] Whig Parliamentarians attempted to use it as a forum for their own propaganda, as in the issue of 1 November 1680 when they had it "Ordered, that the same Committee do inspect the Journals of the Lords House of the Two last Parliaments, and make a Report of their Lordships Proceedings relating to the Horrid Popish Plot." The Whigs insisted on the inclusion of addresses to the king and the articles of impeachment against his officers and judges. Editorial reflection was unnecessary when any tableful of coffeehouse customers could exercise their own wits on such information and speculate as to what they weren't being told.

The Tories cannot have liked what they were forced to do next. The comments of Roger North, Roger L'Estrange, and others make it clear that many of them would have preferred suppressing the newspapers to answering them, but that was not yet in their power. So Tory papers began to appear. By 26 August 1679 their *Domestick Intelligence: or News both from City and Country* was appearing, to confuse those who thought they were getting Harris's Whig news. This, however, was by Nathaniel Thompson, whose approach was not to attack the plot news so much as to ignore it and try to immerse his audience in foreign news and domestic irrelevancies. There was much small-scale reporting of family quarrels, announcements of coming events, and doubting comments on other periodicals.

L'Estrange would later denounce Thompson for publishing Catholic and Whig books as well as producing his loyal counterfeit. Like others, he never understood that accusing a journalist of being "a mercenary fellow" was beside the point.[36]

Nowadays it is L'Estrange's honorable Royalism that needs explaining. Whatever we may think of his politics, he devoted his long lifetime to trying to disseminate the truth about the government. And it was painfully ironic when he was forced into journalism in order to reach his audience. With very little encouragement from that government L'Estrange felt a need to counter the Whig periodical campaign. So on 13 April 1681, as competition drove *Gazette* sales below four thousand, L'Estrange launched the *Observator, in Dialogue*.[37] It ran until 1687, which was several years after all the Whig papers had been silenced and after he had exposed all the lies of the plot-mongers and brought Oates to justice. When some within the Tory camp asked that it be closed down—along with the other newspapers, for inflaming opinion—L'Estrange explained that it was not a newspaper; it didn't have any news in it.[38]

L'Estrange published the *Observator* periodically because that was the form that now created public opinion. He also published pamphlets in the government's cause and seemed happier when he had the space necessary to develop an entire argument. Awkward as his dialogue form was—the second issue beginning, "To go on where we left. . . . You were speaking of Indignities offer'd to the Church"—one might almost suspect that L'Estrange intended to wear out his countrymen's taste for periodicals. In the *Intelligencer* he had told simple stories in order to put readers to sleep; in the *Observator* he grabbed their ear to lecture them on the crimes of Oates and the Whig press.

L'Estrange intuited what the "reader-response" literary critics tell us of the effect of serial publication. One can tantalize readers with very dull stories, by breaking into them constantly and promising that they are "to be continued."[39] Investigative reporting was learning to sell news by offering a strip tease. In time, the investigation itself became news, seeming fresh long after the event lay cold in the grave. L'Estrange's dialogue form was obviously designed to involve readers, and it is amazing how long the periodical lasted and how many people bound their collected copies as a history. As history it appeared half-baked, but when he started in 1681 L'Estrange didn't feel that he could wait until his historical investigations were completed. He was forced to compromise with periodicity again. But as he said in his first issue, "Tis the Press that has made 'um Mad, and the Press must set 'um Right again."[40] When he closed the door behind his own paper, he hoped to turn off the light for all independent journalism.

Other Tories overcame their distaste for journalism, producing the *Weekly Discovery* (5 February 1681), the *Loyal Protestant and True Domestick Intelligence* (9 March 1681), and *Loyal London Mercury* (14 June 1682).[41] The most remarkable of them all was *Heraclitus Ridens* (1 February 1681), possibly the work of Edward Rawlins. It seemed to enjoy the cut and thrust of journalism in a way that one does not expect of true conservatives, mocking the Whig press by a parody populated by Mr. Popular, Mrs. Apparition, Mr. Turbulent, Cain, Judas, Pilate, and of course "Manassus Ben Harris" and his fellow Whig Anabaptist publishers. There were parody advertisements to match: "A most ingenious Monkey, who can both Write, Read, and Speak as good sense as his Master, nurs'd in the Kitchin of the late Common-Wealth, and when they broak up House-keeping, entertained by Nol Protector [Cromwell], may be seen do all his old Tricks over again, for Pence apiece every Wednesday, at his new Masters Ben. Harris in Cornhill."[42] It was, of course, an ad for Harris's penny paper.

Heraclitus Ridens is widely credited with having invented comic commentary on the serious news. But it was only responding to the Whig's own *Popish Courant* (later simply the *Courant*) which had been running for two years. There is no question that *Heraclitus* was a superior production, however, and it justified a 1713 reprint—in the wake of the *Spectator*'s similar success. At the time, the Whigs tried to answer, with *Democritus Ridens, or Comus and Momus* making light of the attempts to unmask a "Protestant Plot." Entertainment is never far from the periodical impulse.

The *Weekly Packet of Advice from Rome*, which had been the first opposition paper into the field, was also the last to close—in 13 July 1683—leaving only L'Estrange to grind away. After losing his paper, the most prominent of the Whig journalists, Benjamin Harris, opened Harris's Coffeehouse. But finding England too hot for him, he left for Boston, where he opened the London Coffee house—America's first. He also started the first colonial newspaper, Boston's own *Publick Occurrences Both Forreign and Domestick* (25 September 1690). True to his luck, it was suppressed after just one issue. Even such outposts as Massachusetts knew the effect that periodical news could have on a well-managed community.[43]

In England, the Whig cause was fatally compromised by the uncovering of their own Rye House Plot, which convinced many that the Tories had been right all along. When Parliament finally met again in 1685 the Licensing Act was reenacted, and chastened citizens were reduced to almost the same news economy as before 1678. Things were not quite the same; English newssheets were printed in Holland and smuggled into the country, and the coffeehouses and a penny post remained.[44] Newsletters proved hard to get rid of; L'Estrange estimated the circulation of John Dyer's newsletter at above five hundred in 1688.[45]

More surprisingly, the new king, James II, who is seldom given much credit for insight, recognized that even an authoritarian government now needed to cultivate public opinion. So he encouraged two Catholic newswriters to operate behind Muddiman's back.[46] James also sponsored a published periodical, *Publick Occurrences Truely Stated*, which began on 21 February 1688, at the beginning of a difficult year. The public was shocked to find that the government's new paper was produced by Henry Care, none other than the editor of the *Weekly Pacquet of Advice from Rome*.

Some remembered that Care had been a royalist before his Whig period. Anthony Wood called him "a little despicable wretch," who "after all his scribbles against the papists and the men of the church of England, was, after King James II came to the crown, drawn over so far by the Roman catholic party, for bread and money sake and nothing else, to write on their behalf." One would think that the country would have been getting accustomed to these "turncoats."[47] But while journalistic professionalism did not suit seventeenth-century notions of honor, James, at least, recognized that journalism was about talent rather than sincerity.

Care's editorial introduction offered an astonishing tribute to public opinion, as he anticipated the question of why the government needed anything beyond the *Gazette*: "He must wink hard, that does not see to what disadvantages the Government is daily Exposed by false Reports; Every thing liable to Misconstruction, [is] Trumpetted through the Kingdom, . . . whilst what tends to its Honour, and giving a right notion of our Superiours proceedings, is industriously stifled."[48] In short, he was complaining that a public without a free press had found means of "stifling" an authoritarian government's efforts to express its position! Despite what looks like total success in suppressing independent journalism, the unofficial institutions of public opinion seemed to the government to have the field to themselves. One would hesitate to contradict this assessment, given how smoothly the invasion and consti-tutional revolution proceeded late in that year. Regular, periodic discussion had proven more important than formal, legal freedom in creating, if not an informed public, at least a confident one.

In an effort to even the scale, *Publick Occurrences* offered domestic news to complement the *Gazette*'s foreign reports. It usually began with a short editorial comment written in a tone of sweet reasonableness, reminiscent of Muddiman's old newsbook. But as 1688 wore on, there was less news and more pleading in both papers. When excitement and consternation began to build around the birth of James's heir, the *Gazette* filled up with letters of congratulation, ignoring the ominous news from Holland.

Finally, on 27 September the government acknowledged the imminent invasion and the *Gazette* began printing loyal letters of "Horror and Amazement," as well as expressions of thanks for the king's hurried restoration of municipal charters. The paper began to appear three times a week in November, to prevent "False News and Reports," and the government again ordered the closing of all coffeehouses in London that made news available. But it was too late.[49]

In the event, newspapers proved an important instrument in the peaceful reso-lution of the crisis of 1688. Just as periodicals had helped sustain opposition, so they calmed a situation in which public opinion felt that events were moving in the right direction. Historian Peter Fraser suggests that things went so smoothly because of the development of public opinion. The revolution, he says, "was essentially a series of defections from the Crown in each of which an assessment of popular opin-ion, and a calculation of other persons' moves, were deciding factors. Without the extraordinary development of unlicensed newsmongering that preceded it, the Revo-lution could hardly have taken such a smooth course."[50] We should recall that he is speaking of a population that remembered only three years of printed domestic political news, some years in the past. However surreptitious the news was, its periodical tempo had created and maintained a new society, much calmer than the England of 1640.

Other historians agree. It would be a mistake, in Lois Schwoerer's view, to suppose that the revolution was entirely the work of a small elite, which in any event found itself divided. Such a change needed the acceptance of a wider public. William's propaganda, in the form of tracts, prints, and medals, helped. But beyond that, the tone of the licensed and unlicensed papers of the winter of 1688–89 helped to make the revolution bloodless. Of course, revolution is one thing and government is another, so we will not be surprised that William took immediate steps to stop the presses before they could turn on him.[51]

The *Gazette* itself proved indispensable to the revolution, when rumors could still be bizarre. Abraham de la Pryme, a Yorkshire clergyman, had heard "many a strange story" and thought it "wonderful how such rumors as then was could be in-vented." One had it that the Papists had raised horses underground on human flesh and were about to loose them on the Protestant population.[52] Samuel Newton, alderman of Cambridge, had learned only to trust published accounts, and noted on 7 November that "Newes came in the publick Letters to this Towne, That the Dutch were landed on Munday last at Dartmouth in Devonshire."[53] It was a far cry from the opening of the century, when Sir John Oglander had recorded that the false alarm of a Spanish invasion of Portsmouth in 1627 had sent "most of England" into a panic; the government itself had sent an armed force under the duke of Buckingham to investigate—so rudimentary was the government's own intelligence.[54]

At a time when rumors would have created difficulties, even a single trusted paper could contribute to stability. The *Gazette*'s carefully fostered authority made it a good vehicle for announcements and for registering the orderly transfer of power. The issue of 10 December 1688 carried "the Declaration of the Lords Spiritual and Temporal, in and about the Cities of London and Westminster, assembled at Guildhall," announcing that James had "withdrawn Himself." It went on to announce their intention to "attend his Highness the Prince of Orange" with a further declaration. On the twentieth, William printed his first order, on the suppression of disorders, with a list of those who were authorized to issue such government orders. The next issue reverted entirely to foreign news, which is what the English had come to expect under a secure regime.

Later issues carried the proclamations necessary to effect the revolution. Finally, on 11 February 1689, the *Gazette* gave its wording of the transfer of power, over which historians still contend. The public read that the Convention first agreed on "an Instrument of Writing for Declaring the Prince and Princess of Orange, King and Queen of England," who were then asked to add "their Consent thereto." This might be considered the determinative account of the conditional nature of the monarchy, if it governed the subsequent public debate on the constitution.

All those who had been troubled by the drift of Stuart administration now read the official *Gazette* with new eyes. Back in 1685 John Evelyn—Tory that he was—expressed disgust at the fact that the official paper had ignored Louis XIV's violent suppression of Protestants in France: "Whence this silence, I list not to conjecture, but it appeared very extraordinary in a Protestant countrie." Things were different by 2 December 1688, when Evelyn remarked wonderingly that "Every thing (til now conceiled) flies abroad in publique print, & is Cryed about the streetes."[55] Press freedom had not quite arrived, as it turned out, but given the real revolution in the nation's affairs, it was only a matter of time until it would. And in no small measure England's revolutionary development was due to the habit of periodicity.

EIGHT

Turning Culture into
News: Science

R eal press freedom—the freedom to follow political issues—did not arrive in England with the Revolution of 1688. The implications of the revolution for a news industry were not realized until 1695. But in the meantime, in the less sensitive area of intellectual culture, periodical publication began to change the tempo of the arts, science, and scholarship. The demands of a publishing schedule began a long process by which England would exchange culture for news about culture. Novelty would move up the scale of values involved in artistic expression and philosophy.

First, we may note that it is understandable that the revolution should not immediately lead to press freedom. The new regime owed much to the pressure of periodical media, and therefore knew it could not trust such a potentially powerful force. Even a very limited press had helped push the country toward revolution in 1679 and again a decade later. Parliament, which had protected the media in 1680 when Parliament itself needed support, was no longer interested in sharing the power it had gained.

As one would expect, however, a flurry of periodicals appeared in the confused winter of 1688–89. By January there were ten independent papers in London. And, naturally the sudden change of regime produced more renegade journalists. George Croom, whom James II had allowed to print the *Test-Paper* in order to attack the anti-Catholic Test Act, was, within months, serving the new regime by publishing the *Roman Post-Boy*, obscenely satirizing Papists. An historian's unsurprising comment on this businessman is that his "motive appears to have been commercial profit."[1] By June all but two of the new papers had been suppressed. Those that were left were precisely those that carried the least news.

It was not that William's government was displeased with the news that was appearing, for the press was initially supportive. The *London Intelligence* (19 January 1689) printed a story of the prince meeting the oldest lawyer in England and congratulating him on that fact, to which the latter replied, "I have outlived [a] great many Lawyers and Judges; and indeed I was afraid, had not your Highness come just when you did, That I should have outlived the Law it selfe." The *London Mercury, or, Moderate Intelligencer* (18 December 1688) enjoyed announcing the freeing of Titus Oates, and the news that L'Estrange had been required to enter recognizances "for his future forth-coming when called for." The English version of the *Harlem Currant* (19 February 1689) carried news of James's pitiful party as it arrived in France. It was just that the government did not want partisanship or participation encouraged. It is in the nature of the news to take sides, and an authoritarian regime was not interested in a press that might change sides.

William was as authoritarian as James had been and foresaw a very risky future for Europe; he did not see any advantage in having England's role debated in coffeehouses. The Bill of Rights, the cornerstone of the new constitutional settlement, guaranteed freedom of debate within Parliament but said nothing of freedom of the press. And the newly liberated Parliament saw to it that licensing was reimposed on the press.[2] Unofficial newsletters revived furtively, but they still cost four or five times what one would pay for a personal subscription to the *London Gazette*.

Still, there was some provision for England's news habit. Parliament resumed the daily publication of *Votes of the House of Commons* in October 1689, during parliamentary sessions. And the government revenged itself on L'Estrange's defunct *Observator* by sponsoring *Mercurius Reformatus: Or, the New Observator* (15 May 1689). Like its namesake, it contained no news, but only panegyric reflections on the general situation. It should be given some credit for introducing a new journalistic diction, smoother and more literary than any seen before. In time this language would grace the serial essays of Steele, Addison, and others. For the moment it was used to reflect on the hegemonic ambitions of France. The government also licensed two monthlies of foreign intelligence, which were both translations of Dutch publications. Knowing the Dutch press, William may have trusted the discretion of the originals. Or he may have understood the difference between the effects of a monthly and a weekly schedule of publication.

Monthly publication involves something less like news and more like history or reflection. Until this time a monthly schedule had scarcely been tried in England. The first English monthly appeared for three months in 1645, under variants of the title *The Monthly Account*. It could hold itself to a mere eight quarto pages, it said, because it was "not filled with flatteries, forgeries, and contradictions: but the face of matters of this Month is drawn in a true and compact form."[3] It never settled on a format before going out of business. No further monthlies appeared until January 1682, during the Exclusion Controversy, when the *Monthly Recorder, of All True Occurrences Both Foreign and Domestick* claimed that the public was disgusted by the mistaken reports in the weeklies and the "sham letters" that filled a partisan press. But its own jumble of miscellaneous news and reflection did not gain a following either.

The first to show any measure of success was *Modern History, or, The Monethly Account*, which lasted from October 1687 until allowed or forced to close in October 1689. It was Dutch in origin and had been on watch during the revolution itself—reporting William's farewell to the Dutch Estates, his request that they care for his wife if he should die, and his seasickness in the invasion voyage. The point of its monthly format was to offer longer, more connected narratives rather than the choppy reports of the *Gazette*. In line with its pretensions, it promised to separate "the News from the Reflexions."[4]

In July 1690 a journal appeared that emphasized the difference between news and reflection, while trying to maintain a weekly schedule. It was called *The Politicks of Europe, Or, a Rational Journal*, and the "Rational" in its title was meant to distinguish its deliberations from raw news. Indeed it contained nothing that could be called news, but consisted of one long essay, tying recent events into remote history and global politics. In its own words, it was "to draw the best use we can, from the several Occurring Events, which may not only serve for a Manuduction to the Art of Reflecting, which certainly is the most excellent of all others, but also to Emancipate us from the Surprize and Wonder, which is so common to persons, who never accustom themselves to foresee the consequences of things."[5] It resembles what we would now call the syndicated column. Whether it failed to win a following or was closed by a nervous government, it was soon gone.

The fact that the government licensed two monthlies at a time when it did not permit weeklies suggests that it thought monthly publications could not inflame opinion. In the absence of weekly competitors, the licensed monthlies were commercially successful. The *Present State of Europe, or, the Historical and Political Monthly Mercury* (July 1690) was printed in Edinburgh and Dublin as well as London and ran on into the next century. *Memoirs of the Present State of Europe, or the Monthly Account* (January 1692) appeared for two years. They both organized their reports by geographical area (always leading with Italy) and were allowed to have short sections on English domestic news. The "reflections" on the English situation often got into personalities, and they carried a surprising amount on England's military preparations.

On the whole, the English public in 1690 was back to the situation of the Restoration, in which it was up to readers to assemble the news as best they could. They could draw from the *Gazette* and the *Votes*, from newsletters and pamphlets. There was monthly news translated from the Dutch, as well as the foreign corantos found in coffeehouses and taverns. And there were still the Bills of Mortality and the *Philosophical Transactions*, commercial periodicals and advertisers, and for comic relief, *Momus Ridens, Or Comical Remarks on the Publick Reports* (1690), which briefly offered doggerel reflections on the wars with France. The ballad news tradition was not dead even yet, as another smutty reincarnation of "Poor Robin" indicates.[6] To these was added, in 1684, the irregularly titled *True Accounts of the Behaviour and Confessions of the Condemned Criminals in Newgate*, which appeared roughly eight times a year. In short, readers were not being offered the world on their plate each morning; they had to search to find the key to events.

In a situation where weekly domestic news was not allowed and foreign news was satisfied with a monthly schedule, a market developed for periodicals on culture, most of them monthlies. It was natural that science would be the first of the areas of culture to be given a periodical treatment. The monthly *Philosophical Transactions* had already proven an admirable vehicle for the new science, reporting and stimulating its steady progress. It was obvious that a monthly appearance was more appropriate than the ponderous volumes of old. Indeed the ponderous volumes that continued to appear had to be reduced to abstracts if they were to enter the stream of scientific information.

But when Henry Oldenburg died in 1677 the *Philosophical Transactions* lapsed. Various Fellows of the Royal Society tried to fill the void. In January 1678 Joseph Moxon, F.R.S., began the serial publication of the chapters of his *Mechanick Exercises*, the first book so marketed. It was the centerpiece of the society's Baconian project of opening "the Secrets of all Trades . . . because much Experimental Philosophy is Coutcht amongst them; but also that the Trades themselves might, by a Philosopher, be improved."[7] John Houghton, F.R.S., began *A Collection of Letters for the Improvement of Husbandry and Trade*, also monthly, in September 1681, which ran for two years. It then reappeared in 1692 as a weekly in a newssheet format and flourished for many years. It was so successful as a commercial weekly with articles on technical subjects that it doubled its size to a four-page folio to accommodate the flood of ads submitted.

Robert Hooke's monthly *Philosophical Collections* (1679) was much closer to the earlier *Transactions*, and on a slightly higher plane, containing Latin and logarithms. Its forty pages of reviews and book ads made it worth the price of one shilling, but to a very limited public. Only seven issues appeared, and the Royal Society had to consider what to do next.

There is tantalizing evidence that at this point the society considered an entirely different approach to scientific publication. In the records of the society and in Hooke's diary for January and February 1680, there are several references to a project they were calling a "Philosophical Gazette." It is described as a half-sheet publication to be priced at twopence. That is, it was to be in the same format as the *London Gazette* and every other newspaper produced since the *Gazette* appeared. So it would have been something quite different from the *Philosophical Transactions*. In the end, the society's officers could not agree on it. Their meetings on the subject ended without decision, except to ask Hooke to make a trial of an issue. Hooke's diary reports two meetings at the Crown Coffeehouse, involving such luminaries as Sir Christopher Wren and William Petty, but the meetings were inconclusive and even angry.[8] It would be interesting to know whether the apparent intention to address a wider audience in a newssheet format was the reason for the contention Hooke recorded. Did the new scientific elite already sense that science could easily be debased by journalistic treatment?

On 16 January 1682 an anonymous *Weekly Memorials For the Ingenious* began to appear, filling the void in scientific publication. It was especially important in translating Latin work for a public which had trouble keeping up in that language. For a year, the journal maintained a weekly, eight-page schedule with one or two book abstracts and another two or three translated from the French *Journal des Sçavans*. The interests of the *Weekly Memorials* were scientific and geographical, but it also liked to publish timely material, such as reports from the recent earthquake in Paris. The editor displayed a little lighter touch than editors of other scholarly journals, as when he warns that "Mr. Heindreich, Library-Keeper to the Marquess of Branden-burgh, threatens the world with a terrible Dictionary, which will contain no less than a Hundred thousand authors."9 The success of the publication was demonstrated by the appearance of a counterfeit of the same name, which survived from March to September 1682.

When the *Weekly Memorials* ceased publication in January 1683 it was because the *Philosophical Transactions* itself had revived. It was not changed; it still made no effort to be popular, except in the sense that the new science scrupulously avoided a specialized diction and intellectual pretension. Reports were direct and precise. They were not cut to the length of a gentleman's patience, but varied from fifty words to the nine thousand words once allowed to John Wallis. Issues varied from eight to thirty-two pages, based on the significance of the work included rather than its enter-tainment value. So it never became a popular journal. As the *Transactions* explained itself, it was for "preserving many experiments, which, not enough for a book, would else be lost."10 Thus it continued to be more a repository than a periodical, in that issues did not supercede each other.

In January 1687 the *Transactions* was joined by the first journal directed at students of history and philosophy. The *Universal Historical Bibliotheque: or, An Account of most of the Considerable Books Printed in all Languages* made it pos-sible to keep current with books in Latin, Dutch, French, and Italian by means of very extensive abstracts and the translations of foreign reviews. The title itself sug-gested that keeping current with scholarship could be the work of a couple of hours per month. But the level of discussion excluded all but the university educated. And the journal lasted only three months.

Obviously, periodical scholarship did not hold out any promise of being com-mercially successful. These journals were not the form in which science or scholar-ship was to trickle down to the public. They were, in fact, the form in which it was ridiculed by the satirists of the day, like Samuel Butler, Aphra Behn, and Thomas Shadwell, whose *The Virtuoso* (1673) was very popular with London audiences.11 Polite society had no taste for pedantry, and the truly commercial media would en-courage this prejudice. In the 1730s, when the editor of the immensely popular *Gentleman's Magazine* was begged by several mathematicians to publish their papers, he objected that this would bore his readers, whom he pictured as "the polite and gay, the politician and the patriot."12 Science would become something different when it was written with those groups in mind.

The public could have followed much of the scientific debate in the translations, the extracts of articles and books, and the reviews offered by the *Transactions*. At about nine shillings a year it was within the means of many, and most of those who bought it were not "professional" scientists.[13] But it took something else to make science a part of popular culture.

In 1691 the publisher John Dunton hit upon one of the most successful ideas in English journalism, up to that point. It was a periodical devoted entirely to readers' questions in all fields—science, religion, manners, courtship, history, anything at all. Called *The Athenian Mercury* (17 March 1691), it initiated the "club motif" in English journalism, which would shape the way the public thought of itself.

Readers were to send their questions by the penny post to Mr. Smith's Coffee-house in Stocks Market, where they would be considered by a group of experts. Though anonymous, this club was chatty in its responses, inviting curiosity about its members. In a later publication, *The Young Student's Library*, Dunton even presented a highly imaginary picture of the "Athenians" in a frontespiece, showing twelve gentlemen at a table being served by a coffee man, with a crowd of men and women handing in notes containing their questions.

In fact, the work was originally done by Dunton and two of his brothers-in-law. Samuel Wesley—clergyman father of the famous evangelists—handled history, theology, and literature, while Richard Sault wrote on mathematics and science. All three helped on social and personal questions. Readers were given the impression that it was a larger group, and told that it had university connections, meaning Wesley. Inevitably, there were satires written on the celebrated "Athenians," but some of the ablest men of the day, including Sir William Temple and the marquis of Halifax, complimented them on their efforts. Nahum Tate and Jonathan Swift wrote odes in their praise.[14] Dunton was pleased beyond measure at this, but always identified his audience as the "populace" rather than "the politer sort."[15]

The reference to Athenians harked back to Acts 17:21, which describes the Athenians of St. Paul's day as "spending their time in nothing except telling or hearing something new." The apostle had taken advantage of this to preach the Gospel (which means "good news"), and Dunton acknowledged that he had more than a little of the preacher in him. There was a moralistic, educational, and theological purpose behind many of his publication projects, so that he could style himself not just a printer, but a "Promoter of Learning and Vertue."[16]

But the *Athenian Mercury* let the English public speak for itself. In its long life it must have done more than any other periodical to define the English reading public, as Dunton pretended to hold up a mirror to the public. The interests of his correspondents proved wonderfully diverse. Readers who were used to being addressed from above, now heard each others' voices. The letters were selected, edited, even rewritten in the interests of encouraging a higher standard of expression. But the public took on a more substantial form in its own imagination.

Important to this process of self-realization was the anonymity of Dunton's correspondents. Identifying them would have inhibited the imagination of readers and stood in the way of the perfect communication of sentiments. The first issue announced that anonymity would "remove those Difficulties and Dissatisfactions, that shame or fear of appearing ridiculous by asking Questions, may cause several Persons to labour under." The possibility of shame is, of course, part of the price of real human community and of real personal identity.

Just as periodicals created a politically conscious public sphere, so they might create a private sphere by way of balance. In this new "community" one could display "personal" concerns to the whole world, without risk. Correspondents might be known better to thousands of strangers than to their own spouse. Indeed, some of them said they had no one else to turn to, and that no other soul in the world knew what they were now revealing—to the wide world.[17] The editors assumed an avuncular role, to the extent of getting involved in family quarrels. They even threatened to print the names of notable miscreants, in hopes that the threat alone might shape some families up.[18]

To create such a community, its commercial sponsors had to maintain their anonymity as well. Elkanah Settle's play, *The New Athenian Comedy* (1693), describes the public's extreme curiosity about their identity—and milkmaid Dorothy Tickleteat's efforts to deliver them a pot of cream by way of thanks. (She was grateful for their advice on how to comb her hair, which had won her a husband.) Anonymity preserved their fascination, even while it allowed them immediate access to their readers' minds. And it allowed playfulness, which extended to answering versified questions with versified answers.[19]

The *Mercury* created an alternative to traditional culture as well as traditional society. For the disoriented population of a rapidly growing city, the Athenians knew the newest answers in medicine, law, religion, and etiquette. Readers could ask the religious questions and make the confessions that should have gone to their parsons. For a penny readers could hire philosophical research done by "several Cambridge and Oxford Scholars."[20] But it is an open question whether the public learned more from the questions submitted or from the answers given. Dunton thought he was giving priceless instruction. At the same time, he was giving a voice to classes that had never been heard from.

By the second week of their twice-weekly operation the editors were asking that letters stop until further notice. The closely printed half-sheet wouldn't hold the answers. Dunton assured readers that all questions would be answered in due course (excepting riddles, obscene and scandalous questions, and matters of current politics).[21] And both commercially and educationally, Dunton was concerned lest all this advice vanish as each issue was superceded by the next. So he was soon offering to collect the individual issues in book form, creating a repository as well as a periodical. In warning readers that they would not answer the same question twice, he was suggesting that they keep their back issues for reference purposes—saving the answers to questions that hadn't hit them yet. To this end, his bound volumes were indexed, like the *Transactions*. Dunton assumed that his humble audience would defer to wiser heads; we shall see that the public was learning to call the journalistic tune.

The first things that customers wanted to ask about were religion and science. This was not simply their idea of what was expected of them; even after the editors showed that questions about manners and morals would get respectful attention, science continued to fascinate correspondents. The very first five questions were on religion, and specifically on the nature of souls or spirits. Questions on whether it was lawful for a man to beat his wife (no, or hardly ever) and on the origin of the spots on the moon (which made fun of an Islamic legend on the matter) rounded out the first issue. And from that beginning, questions of the nature of material and spiritual substance were frequent, as the public seemed to realize that it was living through a time of philosophical revolution.

After little more than a month, readers ventured into more intimate territory, and philosophy found itself in strange surroundings. The issue of 5 May 1691 fielded fifteen questions on marriage, and Dunton took the occasion to make this epoch-making announcement: "We have received this week a very Ingenuous Letter from a Lady in the Country, who desires to know whether her Sex might not send in Questions as well as men, to which we answer, Yes, they may, our design being to answer all manner of Questions sent to us by either Sex, that may be either useful to the publick or to particular Persons." It was the most dramatic invitation yet for women to be part of the reading public. A week later, the issue of 22 May was entirely made up of questions from women, with the announcement that the first Tuesday of each month would be set aside for their concerns.[22]

There is, in this, a hint that philosophy and women would have to be segregated from each other, with the excuse of a chivalrous respect for their special sensibilities. In fact, women's questions—when identified as such—covered the whole range of interests including the philosophical. And women proved useful to Dunton and his successors when it came to justifying their reforming purpose. They often appealed to their "female readers" as an excuse for raising the moral tone of popular literature.[23] The ribaldry that might appear in almost any of the earlier periodicals was unthinkable when "ladies" had been especially invited. Kathryn Shevelow, in a recent study of this issue, acknowledges that the earliest editors (Dunton, Motteux, Defoe) were fairly generous in their appreciation of women's abilities. But she found that later editors like Steele and Addison began to refine the feminine ideal into something more confining and eventually "Victorian."[24]

No sample of the questions addressed could do justice to the diversity of this publication. It shows a wide-awake audience, interested in many subjects neglected by earlier periodicals.

Whether the Fourteenth Ode of the first Book of Horace be rightly interpreted of the Roman Commonwealth?

Why are Common Women seldom or never with Child?

Whether the Doctrine of Passive Obedience and Non-Resistance be Absurd?

Who are the most happy in this world, wise men or fools?

Why Rats, Toads, Ravens, Screech-Owls, etc. are ominous: and how come they to foreknow fatal events

Why Copper yields a better price than Brass, Brass being made of Copper with much Labour?

What is Majesty?

Whether satyrs or sermons have been more successful towards reforming Men's Manners?

Whether a man ought to neglect his children by a first wife, to please a second, when nothing else will do it?

Whether of the two is the more serviceable weapon, the Gun or the Bow?

The *Mercury* demonstrated to the English public that science was one of its greatest interests—that it rivaled religion. When periodicals started, in mid-century, they were more attuned to miracles than to anything that sounds like science. Newsbooks were alert to reports of ghosts, visions, or monstrous births—in the manner of some papers today. But by the 1690s, science provided a fifth of the questions to the *Athenian Mercury*.[25] Science proved adapted to a periodical schedule earlier and more successfully than literature did. Science revisited the same reality every day, rather than transfiguring that world in the manner of the artist. It dealt in facts, as the same appear in the news. And the intellectual mood was shifting in favor of a quotidian reality that now seemed bearable and even interesting.

When it eventually entered the world of news, science was often made sensational and conflictual, to give it a greater interest. For example, Michael MacDonald and Terence Murphy have shown that England's reputation as a world leader in suicide was a media creation, despite a show of statistical grounding. Newspaper attention to suicide—during slack news periods—convinced readers that England led all other countries put together! Suicide was glamorized by association with the aristocracy and humanized by false detail, including made-up suicide notes. Some of this took the short step into novelistic fiction.[26]

The science of the *Mercury* was sober and knowledgeable by the standards of the day.[27] The editors got the nature of the tides wrong, when Newton's answer was already available (31 March 1691). But they often referred to the fact that recent authorities were split, and would describe both views without presuming to determine the issue. Of course, we should not be surprised to find that the science in the paper—good as it was for its day—has been superseded; the same will be said of ours in another two hundred years.

Why is the Water in the Baths more hot than in either Springs or Rivers? By reason of their passage through saline and sulphurous Minerals, whose Nature they Imbibe, and with whose Spirits they easily mix by reason of their Tenuity. (9 June 1691)

Whence the wind has its Force, and the Reason of its Changes? From several Causes, the first may possibly be the motion of the Elementary Bodies, as the Sun, Moon, and Stars. . . . If it be objected, That those bodies moving one way, viz. toward the West, we should have always Easterly Winds; we answer, 'tis a mistake, for some move obliquely, and some retrograde. (18 April 1691)

Where extinguished Fire goes? The more gross excrementitious parts of it fall down
to the Earth, and the more subtle and pure mount up to its Element; the reason why
we cannot see it so soon as ever its nourishment and combustible matter is taken
from it, is very satisfactorily answered, . . . that a Diaphonous or transparent Body,
except it be so condens'd (as fire is when 'tis nourish'd with matter) is not visible.
(14 April 1691)

This was the sense that bright men made of what they themselves had read, without
the qualifications that would appear in full-scale scientific reports. Just as today, the
tone of the reports suggests that the few things unknown about nature only represented a challenge, and not a gaping abyss. For, as we have a hard time remembering, until a science is finished (which is hardly conceivable) the "meaning" of
interim reports is clear only to working scientists. Journalistic reports from the
scientific frontiers will forget qualifications and ignore the radically provisional nature of the enterprise.

The further point to be made about the popular science of the *Athenian Mercury* is that it was not the science that was being produced at that time. The reports
of the *Philosophical Transactions* were admirably conceived and carefully expressed, but Dunton's customers were not asking about them. What readers want to
know defines the news—of science as of every other subject. Their questions and
interests might not be the matters that science was able to discuss. Readers did not
expect to see them discussed; they only wanted to be told what facts had been entered onto the rolls of philosophy. Whatever Dunton's educational motives, his commercial motive required that the steering of the enterprise be left to the customers.

A later scientist, the visiting American Benjamin Silliman, described the state
of popular science in London after a century of such treatment: "Popular lectures
are delivered here and only the most splendid and fascinating parts of the science
are treated of; for, where you have no compulsive power over your audience, you
must please them, and people always prefer entertainment *without* labour, to
Instruction *with*."[28] Periodical news has no compulsive power, of course, which is
why it has a hard time being educational. Just a year after the *Athenian Mercury*
began, the *Gentleman's Journal* was including a science section in which the editor
might interrupt to observe, "But of all the Philosophers, those, in my opinion, seem
the pleasantest, who maintain . . ." as if the reader's approval was the real issue.[29]
Nothing could be beyond the judgment of those who might buy a copy next month.

The *Athenian Mercury* was discontinued in June 1697, Dunton said, only for lack
of further worlds to conquer.[30] The printed volumes insured that he was not forgotten. And satires on the journal continued as a tribute to its popularity. The *London
Mercury* (later *Lacedemonian Mercury*) lampooned the Athenians for stooping to
their witless correspondents and for offering Whiggish and self-righteous opinions.
Like many before him, Tom Brown was offended to think of anything resembling
literature abasing itself before an uncultured audience.[31] He must have relished the
"Athenian" debate carried on in Settle's play, of whether the flea or the louse is the
nobler animal (decided in favor of the one that inhabits men rather than dogs).[32]

But Charles Gildon's *History of the Athenian Society* (1692) shows a very different appreciation of this effort. Gildon seriously compared the "Athenian Society" to the Royal Society. At that time he may have believed Dunton's boast that it was composed of eight experts, plus four translators. He viewed them as operating at a level only slightly below that of the most distinguished philosophers, accomplishing a form of popularization of which the latter were not capable. To Gildon's mind, the *Athenian Mercury* was the beginning of a general enlightenment, working against an elite monopoly on learning. He had harsh words for the clergy, who were content to leave the public in ignorance. And he was critical of a humanist tradition that disdained the effort to translate its Latin wisdom for a wider public. On the other flank, he observed, the Athenians had to fight popular superstition, which was especially (but not exclusively) prevalent among women. In Gildon's view, the Athenian model was nothing short of revolutionary—"the Scholar without the Pedant, the Philosopher without the stiff and obscure Expressions."[33]

Five years of publication and 580 issues suggest that the English had the makings of Athenians. But falling sales indicate that the effort exhausted the public as well as the small staff.[34] There can be little doubt that periodicity kept up interest in this sort of inquiry longer than any other approach could have done. One might well suspect, however, that the real meaning of this episode has to do with the self-identification of the reading public rather than its philosophical enlightenment.

Science never again came so near to dominating the public's interest after the excitement of political journalism resumed in 1695. The other thing that worked against it was that science was not sufficiently genteel for polite society. When the *Tatler* appeared in 1709, Richard Steele was more devoted to elevating taste than to following investigation. Science found a very small place in his paper, and references were uniformly dismissive. Scientists were represented by "Nicholas Gimcrack," who was so intent upon "Trifles" that he exposed "philosophy to the Ridicule of the Witty, and Contempt of the Ignorant."[35] A journalist like Steele could not afford to ignore the opinion of the witty and the ignorant, once the public had become the arbiter of all questions. While Dunton's "populace" might be drawn to science precisely because it was not part of the older culture, his "politer sort" were uneasy with it for the same reason. What this division would mean with regard to literature remained to be seen.

NINE

Turning Culture into
News: Literature

By the time that the *Tatler* was dismissing science, it would have been widely understood that the public was moving on to other interests. For the interval had seen the development of literary periodicals. More surprising, it would not be long before England saw the development of an imaginative literature that turned news discourse into an art form.

In July 1691, four months after the appearance of the *Athenian Mercury*, a general review appeared in London. *The Works of the Learned, or An Historical Account and Impartial Judgment of Books newly printed, both Foreign and Domestic* was edited monthly by a Huguenot immigrant, Jean de la Crose, who had experience in this line on the continent. In fact, it was de la Crose whose translations had been marketed in the unsuccessful *Universal Historical Bibliotheque* (1687), noted earlier. So it was his own experience that made him lament that his adopted England was behind Europe in the matter of reviews: "The great Encouragement they have received in Holland, France, Germany, etc. . . . seems to reproach us for having so long neglected it."[1] Science might be well served in England, but the other areas of scholarship—history, literary criticism, theology, travel, for example— were not.

In the long run such journals would achieve a measure of power over English culture by their choice of what to review and what to ignore—an invisible censorship. They could shape intellectual life even more than the authors of the works reviewed, by directing the cultural traffic. Since de la Crose promised to "chuse only such [works] . . . as may most deserve the perusal of the Studious Reader," it followed that what it ignored could safely be ignored by the public as well. He bluntly said as much, promising "to make good Books more known, read and esteemed, by putting down an infinite number of mean ones, amongst which they are confounded."[2]

As demonstrated by newspaper advertisements, authors were already dependent on periodicals in their hopes of penetrating the market.[3] Thomas Hyde, librarian of Oxford University and an author in his own right, told Thomas Bowrey who had compiled a Malay dictionary, that

> you should get it put into the Gazet, or into the Post-boy, or among the Works of the Learned. . . . As for inserting my book with Mr. Benet, I shall forbear it at present, because mine will be in the Acta eruditorum of Leipsic. . . . And besides, you ought to have some loose tables to past[e] up at the Parliament dores and at Westminster and the deanery of St. Pauls, and at the Royal Exchange. And if its in the gazetts or newspapers, it may do well and help to promote the sale.

There were no guarantees, of course, either with advertisements or reviews. Hyde's own Malay New Testament enjoyed an eight-page abstract in the respected *Acta Eruditorum* and still failed.[4]

De la Crose sensed the antagonism of his author-dependents almost at once. They ask "by what right I take upon me to give out an impartial judgment over their Books, and erect my selfe into an Universal Critick. I'll answer, by the same right as they have publish'd 'em." Indeed, his readers had the same right: "May not every Reader say, it is good or bad?" As editor, de la Crose even invited his customers to criticize himself.[5] Of course, he would have little to fear on that score. As a journalist it was his job to sense his customers' moods, and not, like an author, to create them.

As it happened, de la Crose misjudged the public's mood. If his goal was to win an audience that would sustain his journal, he had taken too serious an approach to literary culture. For one thing, he had made it a matter of principle to exclude fictions, "which are fitter to corrupt men's morals, and to shake the grounds of Natural Religion, than to promote Learning and Piety." But he also disdained devotional works or sermons, since they can be read nearly as fast as an abstract of them. So his reviews were reserved for philosophy and scholarship, which attracted too small an audience. The one innovative note he sounded was to promise to concentrate on facts and arguments rather than on mere style—rather on "Things than Words"—showing the influence of science's new project in culture more generally.[6]

The failure of *Works of the Learned* did not keep it from being a model for later reviews. Its formula must have seemed naturally right, in assuring readers of being in step with a general intellectual advance. For a shilling a month, its thirty-two to seventy-two pages guaranteed that they would be informed on a European scale. This involved a dozen reviews per month, half of them of Latin or French works, along with one or two original submissions. In January 1692 a "News of Learning" section began to appear as a regular department, amounting to several pages of obituaries and announcements of forthcoming works. It may have created a community, but not a public.

Those who would have been most anxious to see the newest *Works of the Learned* were the authors of books which might be reviewed. This was very different from the *Athenian Mercury*; its readers were probably breathless with pride at seeing their questions printed. Real authors, on the other hand, would have lived in terror of the hoped-for review in England's one literary periodical. The shame of an unenthusiastic review would only be surpassed by the dismay of those who were not reviewed at all. Nothing would more clearly show how periodical publication had turned the cultural life of England over, with the public on top and authors on bottom.

Soon a literary journal appeared that avoided de la Crose's overestimation of public taste, and appealed to Dunton's "politer sort." In January 1692 Peter Anthony Motteux began his remarkable *Gentleman's Journal; Or, The Monthly Magazine*, which, as the title indicates, did not limit its appeal to pedants. Another Huguenot immigrant, Motteux acknowledged that he was following the lead of the French *Mercure Galant* (begun in 1672).[7] England did not prove as ripe as France for a popular magazine, and Motteux would only keep it going, single-handedly, for a couple of years. But the formula would find a really spectacular success in the later *Gentleman's Magazine*.

England had never seen a magazine before. It promised nothing less than a capsule of all the "News, History, Philosophy, Poetry, Musick, Translations, Etc." that made up England's intellectual culture. Dedicated to William, earl of Devonshire, it pretended to be "By Way of Letter to a Gentleman in the Country" who wanted to keep up with things in London. And from the very first, the editor made sure that women felt included as well. They need not fear being "exposed to the Blush," for Motteux promised that it would be as much the lady's journal as the gentleman's.

Entertainment was the watchword, although Motteux would have been disappointed if his efforts to refine the taste of his readers had gone unnoticed. The first issue contained a poem by Tate, the actual score of a song by Purcell, a discussion of the musical scene in London and Italy, announcements of the new plays with some reflections on the same, the "character" of a stockbroker, an imitation of a Horatian ode, some science, and veiled literary criticism in an allegory of "the Kingdom of Poetry." There was also a humorous "novel" of a widow's grief, Horace on rural/ urban differences, discussion of the upcoming military campaign, and some critical glances at the deposed James II and "our false Politicians." To be sure, this first issue was twice the normal length of thirty-some pages, but there would always be a similar variety.

Along the way, England's first magazine kept inviting its readers to be the judge of this and that: "pray tell me whether the following Description of it be true." Science was not above the competence of this jury. Describing a French treatise on astronomy, Motteux remarked that "you may judge of it by what relates to the Spots or Maculae in the Sun, and to Comets." Everything was reduced to the same chatty level: "But of all the Philosophers, those, in my opinion, seem the pleasantest, who maintain . . ."[8]

So that readers could cast their votes on things, the second issue gave the address of the Black-Boy Coffeehouse in Ave Mary Lane for their correspondence, including submissions of news and fiction. A public that felt lucky to be included in high culture at all now found itself deferred to by an editor who was constantly apologizing and anticipating reaction. That second issue describes the reactions of a half dozen imagined readers.

The result of such deference would be that readers became conscious of themselves as a group, the *beau mond*. The goal of the publisher, naturally, was to make the journal so much a part of their identity that readers would need it to feel dressed. Motteux sketched roles that readers could try out, playing upon the Horatian theme of town versus country and pressing the debate between "ancients" and "moderns." The magazine tilted in favor of the moderns, flattering readers with the suggestion (à la Descartes) that moderns are more rigorous reasoners. Of course, readers could also expect a few (ancient) Latin flourishes to give the journal tone. They were translated, lest anyone feel left behind.

The fictions of the *Gentleman's Journal* were a major innovation within periodical publication. The *Athenian Mercury* is sometimes cited as a source of short fictions, in the sketches that presented its cases of conscience. But those were realistic, whereas the gallantry of the *Gentleman's Journal* was archly genteel. Altogether, some thirty short stories of amorous intrigue, of sixteen hundred to two thousand words, were published in the journal.[9] While often ribald, they were not obscene in the manner of the ballad fare. They might have no improving character, but they amount to the first appearance of "decent" entertainment in periodical form.

The tone throughout the magazine is gallant but also moralistic, and it is facile and brief in its treatment of all themes. It was for amusement, not for education, and was exceptional in ignoring religion altogether. It included expressions of respect for science, but the editor's allusions to it were as superficial as everything else. Science was not a serious matter for a man who thought it was relevant to recall that "the Pythagoreans, Platonists, and Stoics likewise had a pleasant Fancy, who believed that the Earth was a great Animal which . . ." (April 1692, 19). For polite society everything was a matter of taste. The editor might gently cast doubts on astrological interpretations (of earthquakes), but he included them for the sake of reader interest (August 1692, 19).

Motteux was soon complaining delightedly of the journal's mountainous correspondence and the submissions for which it simply had too little room. He only complained that too many of the submissions were weighted toward "melancholy love and grave panegyric" for a magazine meant to be cheery (July 1692, 1). A large part of the correspondence was in response to his riddle section, which made each issue like a party. Eight readers, at least, solved the one that read "A pudding hath that which every thing hath; pray what hath a Pudding?" One did it in verse: "All things undistinguish'd be / Without a *Name*, nay, so would we" (September 1692, 16). Solutions by female correspondents were often acknowledged.

When the journal disappeared after more than two years Motteux complained that his readers had not helped him enough and had become mere spectators.[10] He could hardly blame readers for that. Entertainment media are precisely for the purpose of making personal exertion unnecessary. Motteux had described his job as "to wait on the Guests, . . . placing the Dishes in order, and perhaps gracing them here and there with a Flower" (September 1692, 1). He may not have realized that he could be trying too hard. With periodicals to fall back on, society was forgetting how to amuse itself.

The periodicals that immediately succeeded the *Gentleman's Journal* were also of a literary nature, but in a more serious vein. It took some time to locate the middle ground between high culture and something more "polite" and commercial. First, John Dunton bought out de la Crose's *Works of the Learned*, restyled it *The Compleat Library: Or, News for the Ingenious* (May 1692), and kept it going for two years. In his usual, overconfident manner he announced that "nothing shall pass in Europe worthy of the Consideration of the Learned World, that shall not be met with in this Journal."[11] But readers saw it dwindle from sixty-some pages with over a dozen reviews of foreign-language works to thirty-some pages with five or six reviews of English works. They were still primarily of philology, philosophy, ethics, and history.

Dunton did understand, however, that the job of a periodical is to sell the next issue. So those reviews became more personal, in line with Dunton's intention to "innocently Divert our Readers." Whether or not he was inspired by the relative success of the *Gentleman's Journal*, he likewise thought that an interest in literary culture need not eliminate things "savouring of Railery and Satyr which pass not the bounds of Decency . . . to Wed Pleasure to Profit" (May 1692, 57f). Nor did the search for profit allow him to forget the female audience; his first issue reviewed a *History of Women Philosophers* by Aegidius Menagius.

Jean de la Crose, meanwhile, attempted a literary periodical devoted entirely to original submissions, in the *Memoirs for the Ingenious . . . in Miscellaneous Letters* (January 1693). Unfortunately, his invitation to send submissions to the Latin Coffeehouse in Ave-Maria Lane went largely unheeded. So this "Philosophical Entertainment" consisted almost entirely of his own articles, reviewing three or four major questions each month—in cosmology, theology, natural history, especially.

De la Crose was becoming exasperated at the difficulties of keeping a scholarly journal going and observed that they had only flourished where they were given state support. In France, for example, such publications might be maintained by a staff of four persons (January 1693, sig. B). He failed, in other words, to understand the essential point of commercial publication, which is that one cannot speak down to one's audience. Subsidies make one forget that it is demand that sustains a periodical.

De la Crose dropped *Memoirs for the Ingenious* after a year, to start *Miscellaneous Letters, giving an account of the Works of the Learned* (17 October 1694), which was another review journal. He hoped to make it a weekly, to see whether the usual period of political news would work for intellectual affairs. After two months, however, it fell back to a monthly schedule, which was maintained for a year and a half. Perhaps no one less determined than de la Crose could have maintained such an effort with so little encouragement.

By this time, licensing had ended and newspapers were reestablishing themselves. A later editor remembered the excitement of the scene: "About 1695 the press
was again set to work, and such a furious itch of novelty has ever since been the
epidemical distemper, that it has proved fatal to many families, the meanest of shop-
keepers and handicrafts spending whole days in coffee-houses to hear news and talk
politics."[12] There seemed to be less need for literary journals. *Miscellaneous Letters*
began reviewing more political and historical books than earlier reviews had done.
The *Athenian Mercury* itself disappeared in June 1697. And while another *History
of the Works of the Learned* survived from 1699 to 1712 on the old principles—half
on foreign works and half on religion—that was apparently all the activity of this
sort that the market would bear.

For a time, scientific and literary journals had met a social need. In the absence
of political papers, they kept up the news habit. Several such publications appeared
concurrently, mostly on a monthly basis. And in the process, they gave the public a
sense that it was the proper judge in cultural affairs, as it was now the judge of constitutional issues. But in the long run only the *Philosophical Transactions* survived—
with the somewhat different task of creating knowledge rather than reviewing it.

The larger influence of periodical publication on literary culture was not to be seen
in literary journals. It was in the development of novelistic realism, which has more
to do with journalistic, scientific, historical, and legal fact than with the traditional
forms of the literary imagination.

The novel was a revolutionary development within literary art, but its ready reception was the result of generations of training in news realism. The pace of the novel
was the pace of the news, which had come to seem the pace of life itself. The ordinary lives of novelistic characters were anchored in a social and physical world that
had been made literary by periodical publications. And novels often returned the compliment, by masquerading as journalism.[13] Daniel Defoe is the most notable example
of a newsman who could step over into fiction—or novelistic fact. Perhaps we should
not be too surprised to see how much this political journalist was drawn to figures
from the criminal world—some real (Avery, Cartouche, Sheppard, Wild) and others
more imaginary (Captain Singleton, Moll Flanders, Colonel Jacque, and Roxana).

Periodicals helped spread the novel-reading habit quite directly when they included short fiction—in the essay serials, for example—and when they serialized
novels. Periodicity was perfect for this subliterary activity, having the magical property of making dull stuff exciting. For periodicity means that readers' imaginations
keep busy in the intervals. The *Athenian Mercury* professed to see some danger when
lower-class readers took realistic fiction for sober truth. But its readers' submissions
offered models for the letter-series of later novels, which is why scholars speak of a
"news-novel discourse."[14]

There was always a danger that the distinction between news and fiction would
collapse altogether. Editors were so reckless as to accuse each other of inventing news

to sell papers, raising questions about their own reports.[15] Just as the novelist's art might disappear into the advertisement and the editorial essay, so journalists had a job to keep from fictionalization. We worry more about the news in this regard, from a concern to keep mere fictions out of the serious business that we think the news is. That is a measure of how far art has fallen in our esteem. In the eighteenth century, educated persons would worry more about the state of literature. Even journalists like de la Crose did not dignify the early novels as literature and would not review them, and this prejudice was to last for generations.

The issue of the contamination of literature by news was part of a cultural struggle that even had a name at the time—the "battle of the books," between "the Ancients and the Moderns." The *Gentleman's Journal* was important for encouraging the contest between the Ancients and the Moderns in 1692, and the *Athenian Mercury* frequently commented on it. In a recent study of the controversy, Joseph Levine admits that "the quarrel did not advance much" in their pages. But no argument does advance in the small space that periodicals have. What they offered, as periodicals often do, was their sense of which direction their readers were leaning.[16] Evenhandedness is a favorite editorial stance, and *Miscellaneous Letters*, for one, tried to hold to a balance. It reviewed William Wotton's *Reflections Upon Ancient and Modern Learning* in the issue of 24 October 1694, to see "what Parts of Learning are still unfinished, what in a manner perfect, and consequently what deserves the greatest Application, because Imperfect." But the forward spin of periodicity would make the Ancients' position—that major areas of thought would never improve on the Greeks—impossible. Literature would have to progress along with everything else to be a proper subject for the news.

In *The Dunciad* (1728) Alexander Pope offered the traditionalist's comment on the contribution of journalism to literary life, in his allusion to two editors, Whig and Tory: "To Dulness, Ridpath is as dear as Mist."[17] In general, Pope was lamenting the dominance of "sense" over "wit." Sense experience was what characterized news discourse. To a traditionalist, sense and fact failed in literature's essential task of increasing self-knowledge. In the *Dunciad*'s final scene, Dulness "uncreates" the world, as one by one the arts flicker out.[18] Or, in our terms, as the arts are replaced by news about the arts.

As both author and editor, Richard Steele was caught in the middle of this conflict, but we shall see him drop news from the *Tatler* in order to promote that journal's more literary qualities. Literary criticism—which often amounts to news from the literary frontiers—held no attractions for him. He foresaw how criticism would deaden art by making one too attentive to mechanics and self-conscious about one's reactions. As he put it, "A Critick . . . never looks upon any Thing but with a Design of passing Sentence upon it; by which Means, he is never a Companion, but always a Censor. . . . A thorough Critick is a Sort of Puritan in the polite World."[19] So in trying to further the education of society in manners and taste, Steele actually tried to wean it from the journalistic world that he fit so poorly. Believing that literature formed the truest context for life, he turned his periodical against the tendencies of the medium, and sought to absorb life into art.

A generation later, the critic Archibald Campbell surveyed a cultural landscape of devastation. In *Lexiphanes* (1767) he tried to account for the decline in English literary ability and taste and was reminded of the influence of the news. In particular, he thought, the political excitement of Robert Walpole's long administration bore a large responsibility: "So violent were the disputes and contentions raised about him, and on his account, that the whole attention of the publick was diverted from every other object, and turned into one channel, into that of politicks and party wrangling and altercation, producing only temporary pieces [of writing, i.e., journalism], which as soon as their turn was served, were thrown aside." To the historian, this seems absurd. The issue in Walpole's long administration—concentration of power through corruption—was hardly on a level with the issues in 1680 or 1710, when periodicals were much less in evidence. A furious politics did not produce a furious press; it was just the reverse. Periodicity alone can keep things on the boil. Campbell's comment simply shows that after a century of journalism, news was taken for granted as a window on a reality beyond itself. Pope's and Steele's sense of its artificiality was fading, as news discourse became the cultural reality.

Actually, Campbell did have some sense of how periodicity created a culture substitute. Booksellers no longer waited for authors to bring them polished copy, he complains, but hire hacks to keep their presses busy. They now give us "monthly, weekly, nay, daily lumber and trash which they are continually dispersing, in immense loads among the people, under the titles of journals, magazines, miscellanies, Records, etc. . . . Most readers, seduced by . . . the perpetual puffing of Newspapers, and a silly notion that the last writers on any subject must be the best . . . lose all relish of the old approved writers." Readers have so spoiled their appetites with this "garbage" that they are nauseated by "the nicest dainties." Periodical reviews have gotten in the way of literature. For readers now "will not so much as cast their eyes on a new production . . . till they have consulted their monthly Oracles, a Magazine, a Museum, or a Review, and have seen what judgment is past upon it by a Master Labourer" from Grub Street. With the latter, there is "no erazement, no rejecting, no waiting for the lucky moment, but away it must come, generally as wet from the brain as from the press."[20] Reviews dispose of books when they come out, like the news disposes of public events.

News of literature, in the guise of reviews, changed the tenor of English cultural life. It encouraged literary celebrity and self-consciousness. Neither necessarily promotes an appreciation of literary art. The effects of the news approach on our own mentality can be seen in one historian's lament at those early reviews: "Commonly they do not treat of the works we now revere or propose judicial opinions of the books which they presented. . . . They have better value as forerunners of the later reviews than as sufficient organs of critical principles."[21] This should be no surprise; it is the essence of book news to concentrate on fads. And there are critical fads as well as fads of taste. Whether by summary or criticism, periodicity was getting in the way of literature.

The same profit motive that produced periodicals prompted the odd practice of the serial publication of books of all kinds. In 1710 the *Tatler* advertised the sale of fascicles or "numbers" of books, consisting of perhaps three printed sheets (twenty-four quarto or forty-eight octavo pages). Dunton had observed that very common people would be glad to put down a penny for a sheet's worth of a travel account, who could not have justified a shilling for the whole book.[22] The formula was a success, and serial publication was soon a booming business. Profits proved to be larger when books were dismembered, and so poems, geographies, novels, anatomies, histories, bible commentaries, memoirs, dictionaries, trial records, penmanship manuals, theologies, plays, biographies, sermons, art, architecture, and medicine were all produced on a periodical schedule. They were hawked in the streets or delivered to subscribers.

This enterprise was encouraged by a political accident, when the Stamp Act of 1712 made it cheaper to print newspapers of several sheets than of single halfsheets. Since we will look at this development in more detail later, it will suffice to say that a generation of weekly newspapers found space on their hands and often filled it up by serializing books. This created a habit. After the act was corrected in 1725, there was not the same advantage in bulking up a newspaper, so serial publication became a separate business. By 1750 at least 450 books had been produced in this manner, and the fashion continued into the nineteenth century. One issue of the *Gentleman's Magazine* listed twenty books currently being published serially.[23] Careful customers could have put this knowledge back together, no doubt. But how many readers never discovered how things turned out? Getting one's culture in bits became as normal as getting one's politics that way.

Previous chapters have alluded to an opposition between news and books, between a periodical discourse and something with a better claim to conclusiveness. But there is another side to the story. Periodical publication was closely associated with book publishing in a day when both might be the business of the same printer. And in many respects news helped books more than it hurt them, at first.

For one thing, reading periodical news must have been a stimulus to literacy. And it was the main way that a public was created for something as similar as the novel.[24] Book ads were the most common advertisements appearing in periodicals, well into the eighteenth century. The literary journals we have just described certainly spread the fame of certain books, even while confining others to oblivion.

And it is also true that periodicals and books crossed into each others' territory very readily. Some essay periodicals—the *Tatler, Spectator, Guardian, Rambler*, and *Idler*—were of such a timeless quality that they became known mostly in their subsequent book form. Serial publication of book chapters may bring out all the oddity involved in periodicity, but it made "book" purchases feasible for many. We should note too that the publishers of books often depended on the income from periodicals to get them on their feet, especially in the provinces. Part-books enabled even well-established publishers to get through slack times. And a news market was a vital help to the provincial book trade, as news agents for London newspapers became booksellers, and vice versa.[25]

On the other side of the scale we have to think what weight to give to the way a news mentality would change the practice of reading. News consumption could lead readers to literature but erode the powers of sustained thinking that books represent. In the words of *Memoirs for the Ingenious; or, The Universal Mercury*, cultural periodicals offered a harvest of all "the Fruits of the Studies of the most Learned in all Faculties" for "a very small Expense, either of Money, Time, or Pains."[26] Periodicals promised that customers would not miss anything. For being cultured had become a matter of being informed about culture. A matter of one's spare change and spare time. One is reminded of Samuel Johnson's sour judgment on (political) news, that it "affords sufficient information to elate vanity, and stiffen obstinacy, but too little to enlarge the mind."[27] There were traditionalists of his day who, like Archibald Campbell, were happy to extend that judgment to the news of culture as well.

Turning News
into Politics

W hole books have been written on news and politics in eighteenth-century England. They describe the government's attempts to license or tax the press, or to subsidize some papers and intimidate others by libel actions. They mention the press's influence in shifting power between political parties or against a particular "ministry." And of course they are especially alert to any possible contribution the press may have made to the American or French revolutions.[1] This study views the issue of news and politics quite differently. Our interest will be the way that news directed attention toward politics and away from society's other institutions. We will be seeing how the news revolution helped in modernity's project of politicizing life.

Normally, when we speak of a political bias in the news, we mean that papers lean toward one party or ideology as against a rival, or that they are critical or supportive of an existing administration. But there is a deeper, more pervasive political bias in news, which is to insinuate that political attention is the mark of a thing's importance. By now, this has become an assumption. But the scope of politics is not a natural constant; it has grown or hypertrophied in recent centuries, absorbing functions once performed by institutions whose growth was more natural.

The habit of identifying a political dimension in all events has been aided by the tendency of periodical news to call for the reader's response. If one knows a tool (government) that can be used to deal with a situation, it becomes a mere problem to be solved. There is an obligation to use the means available. Partisanship is not required, but engagement is. But it is perfectly natural for partisanship to enter the picture, if it proves necessary to generate a response.

Early in the seventeenth century, before periodical news, national politics had dealt with dynastic claims and the religious settlement, diplomacy and trade policy, and taxes. The essential duties of national government were to maintain the defenses against outside aggression and ideological chaos, enforce justice, secure its currency, and raise the revenues necessary to these purposes. That seems absurdly limited to the modern mind, which hopes for political solutions to a wide range of social, economic, and moral problems. It is by directing our attention to politics that the news has helped to marginalize other agencies, and delegitimize them.

When press licensing ended in 1695 the news from the world of culture largely disappeared in favor of the news of diplomacy and politics. It was an exciting time politically, given the establishment of Parliament as a permanent feature of government. At first, the things that the press covered were the issues of the previous century, and certainly not local affairs. The public's pleasure at being included in the traditional political debates made it unnecessary to broaden the range of subjects. But there proved to be a dynamic within periodical reporting that would absorb new subjects into media—and political—attention. Reporting on the world's suffering—and what is news if not that?—seemed to call for the relief of that suffering, at a time when the state had overcome its rivals in English society.

In 1700, the main form of serial performance in England was still the sermon. Sunday might bring the parson's slant on temporal concerns as well as spiritual ones—or temporal ones in the light of spiritual ones. Newspapers began to compete with this arrangement, by offering social and political commentary before Sunday. But mental habits proved hard to change. Indeed, so slow was the process of redirecting attention to politics that it might throw doubt on the thesis that periodicity was driving the change.

There were several factors working against this politicization. In the first place, it took time for people whose deference was so ingrained to think of themselves as having a right to their opinions, much less a right to influence affairs. Also, the news had to overcome its own traditional (foreign) focus and format. In addition, some have argued that the capitalist ownership of papers (which was common by 1720) worked against innovation; regular profits were more important than rising profits in an uncertain industry. Fear of losing advertisers and readers suggested caution in political reporting. Nor should we underestimate fears of government action in what was still a sensitive enterprise.[2] Finally, politicians do not seem to have realized, or valued, the possibilities for self-advertisement afforded by a political focus in the news.

All this indicates the magnitude of the mental change involved in politicizing life. The slow beginnings of the process were noted by historian Jeremy Black.

> In contrast to modern British governments, their eighteenth-century progenitors neither had massive legislative programmes nor assumed that the purpose of power was legislation. . . . [The] Whig ministry conceived in 1718–19 what was by contemporary standards a radical programme, including substantial constitutional and ecclesiastical changes. Walpole was interested in significant fiscal reforms, Pitt in major changes in foreign trade. However, . . . most legislation was private and the parliamentary session, having begun just before or after Christmas, rarely lasted long after Easter.

Obviously, the short session of Parliament was a problem for periodicals, which could not simply suspend publication in the intervals. One response, therefore, was to make the character of the ministry a continuing issue, including its treatment of the press.

> The paucity and general repetitiveness of the programme led them [journalists] to attack nearly all new schemes, whatever their value. They had to be made to appear to characterise all the supposed vices and sinister intentions of the ministry and to be of fundamental significance. . . . The relative absence of new public political developments was possibly one reason for the serious attacks made on ministerial legal action against the press. Issues that could be made to appear crucial could be discussed long after the session was over.

In the absence of policy debate, periodicals had to comment on administration, by way of continuing a political discussion through the summer. News could "concentrate on general attacks on the supposed stance and methods of administration. This inevitably led first to attacks on alleged corrupt practices and attitudes, attacks that were easy to make and generally accessible in their message, an often felicitous mixture of wit and moral outrage." Foreign news (often given a policy perspective) was also a useful filler, whether or not the public preferred it.

Historians have usually treated the international news of the early papers as filler, provided by nervous editors until it was safe to report about the domestic scene. But we should remember that during a century in which foreign reportage was the only news allowed, readers had gotten used to thinking that this was what news meant. Even the unlicensed newsletters of this period, which enjoyed freedoms printed news lacked, still gave foreign intelligence first, and in greater quantities than political news.[3] And Black notices its advantages, from the standpoint of periodicity.

> Foreign news had the major advantage of being a sphere in which information and speculation altered daily, at least as long as the posts arrived. Its real and apparent importance was magnified both by this constant provision of events and by the relative ease with which information concerning them could be provided. This constant availability helped to make British foreign policy a major issue in the press. . . . As an area for partisan struggle it had much appeal.[4]

It was foreign news that filled the first papers to revive after the lapse of the Licensing Act.

Of course, the essential development behind a politicization of consciousness was the lapse or, as it turned out, the end of press licensing. One may puzzle over why politicians allowed news that would create a politicized public. Assuming that Parliament would naturally resist the end of licensing, historians have tended to accept the view of Laurence Hanson, who thought politicians had concluded that licensing "had failed completely of its purpose."[5] That was an argument used in Parliament at the time, which may have originated with John Locke. But insofar as the purpose of the law was to prohibit unlicensed periodicals, it cannot be said to have failed. Carolyn Nelson and Matthew Seccombe's bibliography of seventeenth-century periodicals cannot trace any unlicensed ones in the period 1689–95. Of course, there was more to the Licensing Act than restrictions on periodicals. But the government had shown itself well able to keep printed news from appearing. If legislators imagined that letting licensing lapse would make no difference, they would soon be wiser.

The issue of press freedom was brought to a head by political struggle. In 1692 one licenser was fired for being too Whig, and the following year another for being too Tory. In 1694 several licensers were in trouble. But in 1695, when a largely Tory administration found itself being edged out of power, it recognized the necessity of a press to present its position—something that Whigs had realized since the Exclusion controversy. And thus it was that Parliament was allowed to end on May 3 without a renewal of the act. An independent newspaper appeared on May 7. When the next Parliament met in November, it was presented with a new licensing bill. But this Parliament included many new members who apparently did not anticipate trouble from the press, and that bill and others were lost.[6]

Perhaps politicians took the view that historians have, that libel law gave the government the power it needed to control the press. If so, they were proved wrong. Libel prosecutions could be brutal, but they were clumsy and judges were becoming scrupulous in holding government prosecutors to the rules. So, according to Hanson, ministries in the first decade of the eighteenth century were truly "alarmed at the spate of libels with which they were confronted." And they "had neither the energy nor the time to spare to deal with erring pamphleteers." Even Defoe complained of the state's "criminal moderation" in restraining critics. If a journalist could take that line, think what Parliament must have thought.[7]

And yet Parliament voted down six new bills for renewing limits on the press in the next seven years. Hanson thought that the failure was due to distrust between the houses of Parliament and to the animosity of parties. England's new political parties had not yet agreed to alternate in power peaceably, and felt that no single licenser could be trusted with the job. Or it may simply have been short-sightedness that kept politicians from protecting their domain from an unlicensed press. They had not yet seen what it could do, or even what it would look like. The news they could remember had been foreign intelligence, and it had been fairly objective. So they may have connived at freeing the press, from a feeling that discussion not only could not be stifled, but need not be.

By 1712 attitudes had changed, as all parties had learned to use periodicals for their purposes. Hanson reminds us that while politicians had dropped plans for press licensing, there was no trouble at all in getting both houses to pass the Stamp Act in 1712, which only restricted readership a little. That act did nothing to govern what the press said, but only who read it.[8] For by then, politicians had discerned the need for a press to report their activities.

It takes an effort of our imagination to realize that no one could have thought of newspapers as having political possibilities in the 1690s. Libel actions were for pamphlets, which worried politicians much more than newssheets.[9] Politics was a matter of argument, and it was understood to take at least a pamphlet to develop an argument. Matthew Tindal's *Discourse for the Liberty of the Press* (1698) had nothing to say of newspapers in developing his theme. His topic was the freedom of debate and argument, not freedom of fact or assertion.[10] Newspapers were not part of his subject because they were not a forum for debate. His generation had not foreseen the importance of daily news in enlarging the field of political action or maintaining an atmosphere of suspicion and unrelenting criticism.

The new ministry in 1695 expected that the Royal prerogative could be used to suppress mere newspapers, even in the absence of Parliamentary legislation. For newspapers were not yet as sensitive an issue as pamphlets. And indeed, the courts began to threaten the new papers. They succeeded in frightening Benjamin Harris away, who had come back from New England to have another try at journalism. But the intrepid *Flying Post* of 7 May 1695, along with the *Post Boy* (16 May) and *Post Man* (22 October), held their ground and would appear thrice-weekly for many years.

The London resident of the government of Brandenburg reported that the new members of Parliament refused new laws on the subject because they did not trust the *Gazette* and wanted to preserve these new papers.[11] We need not suppose that they wanted to see partisan views. They may not even have thought that the papers would carry any domestic news. The resident's report suggests that they wanted more foreign intelligence than they were getting in the *Gazette*. And that is what the early papers provided—out of continental sources.

Contempories did not have our hindsight on what should count as news in a free press. Previously, when English newspapers had operated freely, there had been national crises that clamored for attention—the Civil War in 1642, and Exclusion politics in 1679. These upheavals were themselves the cause of press freedom. In 1695 the great national issue was foreign rather than domestic. England was committed to war against the greatest power Europe had yet seen, which had shown an appetite for conquest and religious persecution. So both the habit of foreign news and the real concerns of Englishmen for their liberties directed attention abroad. *The Protestant Mercury*, despite its subtitle of *Occurrences, Foreign and Domestick*, did not bother with domestic news. For years after it was safe to venture into national and local news, the papers concentrated on the international scene. In the *Tatler* issues in which Steele and Addison lampoon the news craze of Queen Anne's reign, it is still international news that has the coffeehouse statesmen all agog.

But even while they were emphasizing diplomatic affairs and uncertain of the propriety of domestic reporting, the newspapers were encouraging the public's political imagination. While they were slow to trespass into the politics of England, they felt perfectly free to comment on the politics of Ireland and Scotland. Covering the Scottish Parliament, the *Flying Post* of 16 June 1702 reported that "the Duke of Hamilton, accompanied by many Lords, Barons and Gentlemen, came to the House, where immediately after prayers, he made a short Speech, and then entred a Dissent against any thing that should be done or acted there, because he and those that join'd with him conceived themselves not warranted by the 7th Act of the 6th session of King William's Parliament to meet, sit or act." This was not simply a report of government institutions in motion, but showed the initiative of individuals. And it was not only great magnates who were involved. The *Post Boy* of 19 October 1695 reported the petition of the Protestant porters of Dublin against discrimination by Catholic businessmen, and one man's private bill to recover the debt the government owed him. Weekly reminders of political initiatives elsewhere would make English readers reflect on their own situation.

To that end, the papers occasionally found the nerve to print letters or editorials which took a political line. The *Post Man* of 25 September 1697 opened with the editor's response to a letter said to have come from a Jacobite supporter of the deposed James. The "Jacobite," of course, was standing in for all Tories. The editor insisted that ordinarily "I have taken such a care in the Writing of this Paper, to avoid giving offence to any Body in the World." It would take years to overcome this habit—or pretense—of impartiality. But during the reign of Queen Anne (1702–14), when party conflict hindered the government's power to act against journalists, editorial partisanship became more open.

Party lines were drawn in the journalistic terrain during the first years of Anne's reign. A determinedly Whig paper—another *Observator* (1 April 1702)—was answered by an ultra-Tory one, the *Rehearsal* (5 August 1704). These were twice-weeklies and were filled with political allusion or comment rather than news. John Tutchin's *Observator* looked like a newspaper, as had L'Estrange's earlier one, but was a running anti-Tory diatribe with only occasional references to current events. Its importance for the growing politicization of the public was that it related everything to party.

The papers of the late 1690s had assumed a national ideology, implying that the nation had finally recovered its long-lost unity. Tutchin knew that his partisan divisiveness would be disapproved and tried to disabuse his readers of the notion that England's internal peril was past: "It was not the Design of this Paper to recriminate; but to forward a Union among such as differ in some Points, and yet are all entirely in the Interest of their Country. But to oppose such Men as I have been speaking of, is our highest Duty, because they are Enemies to our *Civil Liberty*, and are by Inclination no Friends to the Present *Settlement*."[12] To the Tories who criticized him for introducing partisanship into news, he cited the example of L'Estrange.[13] Tutchin appears to have adopted this divisive approach for ideological reasons rather than for profits. Like L'Estrange, he was naturally contentious, with a reputation for fistfights. But it would not be long before others found that highlighting political divisions was good business, giving one a corner within the market.

The *Observator* was also a politicizing agent in that it commented on the issues before Parliament while that body could still be influenced. Tutchin was quite frank in telling Parliament when it was making mistakes and in labeling bills good and bad. And within three months, he decided that for political purposes L'Estrange's dialogue approach was better than the essay form. Essays offer "Positions and Assertions, which tho' true in themselves, were less Evident, because the Scruples and Reasons on the other side, were not by this Method so plainly Remove'd or Answer'd."[14] In short, dialogue helped the less reflective sort, who needed the editor to provide the semblence of discussion.

Tories could not let such a paper go unanswered and commissioned Charles Leslie to begin the *Rehearsal*. Also in dialogue form, it was far more jocular and mimicked the *Observator* in a way that drew attention to Tutchin's angry tone. Readers now had twice-weekly reminders of the respective sides and could choose identities within the positions presented.

In 1704 England was hardly faced with issues of the magnitude of those of 1642 or 1680, but periodical news always strives to make readers feel that they live in revolutionary times. In fact, England was moving from politics-as-unacknowledged-warfare to politics-as-fairly-civil-debate. But editors did more manipulating of symbols than discussing of issues. They argued over who had inherited Elizabeth's legacy, for example—the Tories, who emphasized its uncompromising ecclesiastical settlement, or the Whigs who emphasized Parliament's supposed resistance? Still, the *Rehearsal* differed from the older Royalist press—*Mercurius Aulicus* and *Heraclitus Ridens*—in having legislation to discuss, and in time that would bring discussion down to earth. But for the moment, politics was taken up with matters of religion, which did not invite compromise.

Tories were not sure they wanted religion to be a matter for politics. They thought it might be better left at the level of symbol than of news and negotiation. Leslie admitted feeling uneasy about producing news, and asserted that he was driven to do so despite his better instincts. News was becoming a national obsession, he complained. Longer treatises would have been more appropriate to the importance of the issues, but "the greatest Part of the People do not Read Books." Even the illiterate, however, "will Gather together about one that can Read, and Listen to an Observator or Review (as I have seen them in the Streets) where all the Principles of Rebellion are Instilled into them, and they are Taught . . . to Banter Religion." What he could try to do by adopting periodicity was to spread the necessary arguments over several issues for those "who read them at a Coffee-House" and do not ordinarily read in a way that could "be call'd Studying."[15] In other words, periodicals were not the ideal medium, but he would make the best of it.

As new enclaves were discovered within the news market, new papers were founded that would depend on political gossip to fill their space. The appearance of the first evening newspaper in England (*Dawks's News-Letter* in 1696), the first daily paper (the *Daily Courant* in 1702), and the first colonial and provincial papers (clustering around the year 1700 in Edinburgh, Dublin, Norwich, Bristol, and Boston) were not initially in response to the growth of politics. Indeed, they began with very distant news and only later edged into domestic politics. The *Daily Courant* (11 March 1702) explicitly declared that in an increasingly politicized society, there should be a market for impartiality. So, like an old-fashioned coranto, it promised that the editor would not "take upon him to give any comments or Conjectures of his own, but will relate only Matter of Fact; supposing other People to have Sense enough to make reflections for themselves." He would spare readers "the Impertinences of ordinary

News-Papers," meaning their political advocacy. To the editor, Samuel Buckley, advocacy seemed to have become the standard practice among his fellow journalists.

The most chaste intentions could be subverted, however. There were no limits on what the *Daily Courant* would print if one could pay, and politicians soon began to take out space to advertise themselves. On 31 December 1702 readers learned that

> Whereas Mr William Fazakerly stands for Chamberlain of London; this is to let his Friends and all Gentlemen know, that he stands [for election] solely by himself, and will not joyn his Interest with any other person.

> Whereas it is Industriously given out That Sir Robert Bewdingfield declines standing for Chamberlain of London; This is to let his Friends and the World know, That the Report is False, Groundless and Malicious.

> It appears by the many Bills dispersed abroad, that there are sundry Citizens put in for the Chamberlain's place now vacant, but it is generally believed the Citizens of London will now bestow the preference of their Favour on Mr. Dockwra, who had obliged them with so Memorable a Service, by setting up the Penny Post, as no City in the World has the like Conveniency.

Dockwra was back with more ads as the election drew closer, once buying half a column to vindicate his management of the Penny Post against "malicious reports." And thus paid political advertisements entered the periodical press. Papers did not find it easy to stay clear of politics.

For those who embraced politics rather than avoiding it, the most direct line was through the editorial essay. That was the significance of Daniel Defoe's long-running *Review*, originally called the *Weekly Review of the Affairs of France* (17 February 1704). Unlike Tutchin, he managed to stay with an essay format. Readers might have supposed the journal to be Tory, since its announced purpose was to temper the reports of the duke of Marlborough's military successes. But Defoe was coy about his partisanship and even paid his respects to the ideal of impartiality; when the unglossed facts are presented ("Fact, as it really is") he had no doubt that "men are easily capable to Judge, what and why Things are done, and will begin to see before them in the world."

Deep down, Defoe's journalism was of the commercial rather than the political variety. Unlike Tutchin again, he was only hiring out his pen. His friend, the great political innovator, Robert Harley, was the first conservative politician who saw news production as an opportunity, rather than a necessity. Berkenhead, L'Estrange, and Leslie had left no doubt where their papers stood, but Harley was more subtle. He was somewhat below the highest social rank and made himself indispensible to the ministry by generating its popular support. In Defoe, he recognized a writer of genius and they reached an agreement—involving money—that would insure that the *Review* insinuated Tory principles.

The paper resembled *Mercurius Aulicus* in its liveliness and readability, but it was not the product of desperation. Its humor was in a more generous vein. Defoe made light of the errors of rival papers in a department called "Mercure Scandale:

or, Advice from the Scandalous Club." It reported the activities of a club in Paris whose purpose it was to punish scandalous activities, and as Defoe tells it, they were kept busy dealing with journalists alone. For the future development of periodicals, this little feature's importance was in its image of a club as representative of the public. Defoe may had come by the idea while serving his journalistic apprenticeship with Dunton's *Athenian Mercury*.[16]

Harley worked with Defoe but he didn't own him. With Marlborough's continuing military success, the administration gravitated back toward the Whigs, and so did the essays in the *Review*. And when the Tories were swept into power in 1710, the *Review* turned up in their camp. When dynastic change again brought the Whigs to power in 1714, Defoe was recruited to use his Tory credentials to infiltrate several Tory papers in order to temper them. Governments had become too smart to close papers when they could divert them.[17]

The public would not have understood; we have seen how Marchamont Nedham, Henry Care, Nathaniel Thompson, and Charles Croome were despised as turncoats. But markets have a way of finding those who will supply them. The publisher John Morphew produced Whig and Tory journals *concurrently*.[18] Defoe had simply recognized that there were profits to be made in political journalism. And beyond that, as Laurence Hanson explains him:

> The key to the interpretation of Defoe's character seems to lie rather in this—that he knew he was a great writer who could write to more effect on most topics than any of his contemporaries; and that he saw no reason why the world should be deprived of the fine writing which he could give it. He could and did write on both sides in many controversies. He wrote both for and against the Septennial Act. He espoused both parties in the Bangorian controversy. His justification, if there were need of it, would be that his pamphlets represent the best work on both sides.[19]

To a journalist, the point was not so much which side prevailed as that politics be kept moving, and absorb more and more of the public's attention.

When Harley turned his mind to the political management of news, naturally he also thought of the official *Gazette*. Now that it was no longer the only paper available, its reputation had declined. Harley fell in with the fashion to the point of allowing Defoe's *Review* to point out mistakes of fact (and of grammar) in that paper. But Harley did think it was worth the government's while to run a paper of quality, not to argue with the public so much as to maintain its respect. So in 1707, in order to generate more reader interest, he hired an erstwhile playwright, Richard Steele, to try to reestablish the *Gazette*'s reputation. This appointment would lead to introductions to Joseph Addison, an undersecretary to one of the Secretaries of State, and also to Jonathan Swift. Periodical publication was attracting the best talent around.

Steele had ideas on how to raise the "credit" of the *Gazette* over its rivals, but was hamstrung by superiors who were satisfied to keep it "very innocent and very insipid." So in his spare time he began a different sort of periodical, which first ap-

peared on 12 April 1709.[20] The *Tatler* is a landmark in the history of English literature, as well as journalism. Its contribution to the politicization of English life was
in further refining the periodical essay, later so useful in pushing politics forward.

In the first several months of production, Steele included a section of news in
the *Tatler*, and he later claimed that it had helped the periodical gain a following.
As official Gazetteer, Steele had access to better and fresher news than any of his
competitors. A thrice-weekly schedule, as opposed to the twice-weekly *Gazette*, allowed the *Tatler* to scoop the latter twice each week. For various reasons, however,
Steele gradually dropped the news.[21] It had never fit well with the facetious tone of
everything else in the paper. In its place, Steele moved to a single essay per issue,
which might be on any subject.

Essays had been used only fitfully by journalists. The *English Lucian*, which ran
briefly in 1698, had given the observations of a time traveler who had dropped in on
contemporary London. It was an early instance of the relativizing "anthropological"
perspective, a facetious enthnography that became a favorite form of social criticism
among the philosophes of the French Enlightenment. Then Tutchin's *Observator* had
tried essays, before deciding that they were less effective than dialogues. Defoe's
Review essays revealed themselves as the chapters of a book when they were, eventually, published together. But after Steele's delightful essays began to captivate
London, other journals were eager to emulate them, often for political purposes.
Essays could give a dignity to political comment that was lacking in the partisan
dialogue or the editorial aside.

Just as the *Tatler* appeared, England fell into a spasm of political activity. In
1710 the growing opposition to the French Wars and general unhappiness with the
Whig grandees produced a Tory electoral landside. The Tory camp was especially
encouraged by a tide of public support for a Tory firebrand, the Reverend Henry
Sacheverell, during his show trial. All this convinced the Tories that they had a wide
popular following and that they would be able to use the press as effectively as the
irreverent Whigs. So they did two things of some consequence for political journalism. First, the party produced a new paper that specialized in political essays. Second, it argued Lord Bolingbroke out of his plans to restore press censorship and
passed the Stamp Act instead. The importance of the latter is in unintentionally
spawning larger, weekly papers that found space for political essays.[22]

The new paper, the *Examiner. Or, Remarks upon Papers and Occurrences* (3
August 1710), was to answer Defoe's *Review*—now that it was expressing its independence—the aging *Observator*, and Steele's faintly Whiggish *Tatler*. Jonathan
Swift, who had fallen out with Steele over political matters, was one of the group
that produced it. Both parties realized the need to rally their forces in a more open
political arena. So the new party papers were not so much for changing the minds
of their enemies—or even the undecided—as for keeping supporters informed and
defining the rapidly developing issues for them.[23]

The new journals seemed more interested in dividing than in uniting the
audience. The first number of the *Examiner* declared that

I meet with a great Variety of Papers, neither so Correct, so Moral, nor so Loyal as they ought to be: I see the Town every Day impos'd upon by false Wit, false Learning, false Politicks, and false Divinity: These sort of Writings, tho' they are in contempt among the Few that judge well, yet have their Influence upon the Generality of Readers; and many of them are adapted by the Cunning Men who contrive them, to the Capacities of the Weak, who are to be misled by them. Some of these Papers I intend to Examine, and set People right in their Opinions.

Insulting "the generality of readers" was a time-honored way of advertising one's paper. It was understood that those clever enough to have picked up the paper were among "the few that judge well." Fortunately, that is always a large majority.

The Whigs, suddenly out of power, felt even more acutely the need to produce an effective political organ, and countered with the *Whig Examiner* (14 September 1710), which soon became the *Medley* (5 October 1710). It started on as high a level as the *Examiner*, drawing on Addison and others to answer the Tories. Indeed its wit could be as elegant as Swift's:

I have resolved never to say anything to the *Examiner*, unless a word or two by chance in passing: He gave his Reasons, in his last Paper, why he wou'd have nothing to do with the *Review* and *Observator*, because of *their authoritative Manner, and insipid Mirth*. I do not pretend to have the same Reasons for not arguing with him. . . . I know the Criticks find numberless Faults with him, but they are an envious Generation; and I defy any of them to shew me an author that has one Perfection in a higher degree than he has, I mean the Talent of Painting or Drawing a Character: A pregnant Proof of this may be seen in his Piece of November the 9th, where he has given us a Picture to the Life of a very great Friend of his, that first set him to work, and in all likelihood pays him his Wages. He had been speaking of a *Political Lyar*, and then proceeds to this lively Description.[24]

In the long run, the Tories had the best of the match, in the view of contemporaries like John Gay.[25] The Whigs fell back on the old *Flying Post*; its issue of 21 June 1712 attacked the Tory paper, which had recently given "the Publick a new Specimen of his Learning, Wisdom and Honesty, for which, among others, I congratulate those who employ him."

Meanwhile, the Tory leader Bolingbroke was still thinking in terms of silencing rival journalists. But his party, perhaps under Harley's influence, settled on a simple economic limitation through the Stamp Act of 1712. This did not involve the elimination of daily publication. The government only wanted to discourage some of the underfunded and scrambling papers that kept nipping at its heels. By raising the price of papers a halfpenny they hoped to eliminate a certain class of papers and readers.

Unfortunately, they were not sufficiently careful in drafting the bill. Assuming that news always came on halfsheets—as it had done for the past fifty years—Parliament taxed halfsheets one halfpenny per copy. A folded whole sheet was taxed a penny. But anything over a sheet (i.e., a pamphlet) had to pay only two shillings *per edition*. Actually, the wording was ambiguous; publishers insisted that "in *one* printed copy" (for pamphlets) must have meant something different to Parliament than "for *every* printed copy," as elsewhere in the act. Understood in that way, it was actually cheaper to produce a newsbook of one and a half sheets—twelve very small or six larger pages—because it effectively escaped the tax. Accordingly, the papers founded after the Stamp Act were weeklies of this greater length—usually costing only three halfpence. Unable to provide much more news of the usual (foreign) kind, they began to develop the political essay to fill the space.[26] We should note that the loophole was closed in 1725.

So the weeklies of the period 1712–25 were more naturally political than the standard thrice-weeklies. Since the latter had already printed the foreign intelligence, there was nothing left but to comment on the domestic scene. And apparently the recent political activity had given readers a taste for this sort of thing. The *Weekly Packet* of 9 July 1715 complained of the pressure it felt from its readers: "Those Gentlemen who are importunate with the Author of this Paper, to insert an Account of the Proceedings in Parliament, are desir'd to observe, that whosoever does it, acts contrary to a standing Order." But others were doing it, and readers now expected it. Indeed the same paper had commented on bills making their way through Parliament just two weeks before.

Even after the resolution of the political crisis in 1714, with the accession of the Hanoverian dynasty and the dismissal of the Tories, the papers found that politics had become a habit. The *Weekly Journal, or British Guardian* of 7 January 1716 rubbed salt in Tory wounds with a "Character of a True English Subject" and a very transparent "Diary of a Preston [Jacobite] Rebel." It printed many loyal addresses, which rehearsed parts of England's political creed almost weekly. Editorial paragraphs, inserted in the flow of the news, only became more frequent as the years passed. *The Shift Shifted: or, Weekly Remarks and Political Reflections Upon the most Material News Foreign and Domestick* (18 February 1716) lived up to its name by tacking "Remarks" onto every story. Readers no longer needed to exert themselves to come up with their own reflections, and soon these remarks became lengthy editorial essays. The *Weekly Journal: Or, Saturday's Post* of 8 June 1717 still began with foreign news, but followed that with a full-scale editorial on the position of the established church. The *Freeholders Journal* (begun 31 January 1722), a *Tatler* imitation, filled up six pages with nothing but political reflection. Nothing like this had appeared in the seventeenth century.

It is not clear whether the public's interest was leading newspapers away from foreign intelligence and toward political involvement. Addison's funniest writing for the *Tatler* describes the enthusiasm of his neighbor, a politically obsessed upholsterer, for *foreign* news.[27] As news of the international situation was thinning out in 1709, Addison made merry over the discomfiture of the journalists.

> The Approach of a Peace strikes a Pannick thro' . . . the ingenious Fraternity of which I have the Honour to be an unworthy Member; I mean the News Writers of Great Britain. . . . The Case of these Gentlemen is, I think, more hard than that of the Soldiers, considering that they have taken more Towns, and fought more

Battles. They have been upon Parties and Skirmishes, when our Armies have lain still; and given the General Assault to many a Place, when the Besiegers were quiet in their Trenches. They have made us Masters of several strong Towns many Weeks before our Generals could do it. . . . Where Prince Eugene has slain his Thousands, Boyer [of the *Post-Boy*] has slain his Ten Thousands. This Gentleman can indeed be never enough commended for his Courage and Intrepidity during this whole War: He has laid about him with an inexpressible Fury. . . . It is impossible for this ingenious Sort of Men to subsist after a Peace: Every one remembers the Shifts they were driven to in the Reign of King Charles the Second, when they could not furnish out a single Paper of News, without lighting up a Comet in Germany, or a Fire in Moscow. . . . I remember Mr. Dyer [the newswriter], who is justly look'd upon by all the Fox-hunters of the Nation as the greatest Statesman our Country has produc'd, was particularly famous for dealing in Whales.[28]

There is nothing in this to suggest that readers were eager to turn from the excitement of foreign affairs to news from their own drab neighborhoods. A view of their papers shows that events along the Turkish-Austrian border were still a major interest.

But in 1720 an explosion occurred that would turn the English press irrevocably toward national affairs. That was the year of the first great stock market crash in England—the South Sea Bubble—which devastated ancient families and generally upset a nation that had experienced a generation of notable successes. And it was the year that the *London Journal* began to publish "Cato's Letters."

These anonymous editorials caused a sensation and kept the country in thrall for months. Clearly, their attraction was in their intemperate tone. On 24 December 1720, for example, readers were told that "all our Loses, Pillages and Oppressions, since the Conquest, do not ballance the present great Calamity: From a Profusion of all Things, we are reduced to a Want of every Thing, . . . and even the Rich complain that they can hardly find Money to buy Bread." The loss of historical scale that periodical publication encourages is clearly on display. The South Sea scandal gave plausibility to old complaints against an increasingly closed oligarchy, and the disaster was presented as the scheme of a government that had planned its whole course.[29] The country is in the grasp of "a corrupt and wicked Ministry," "Bloodsuckers and Traytors," "Publick Robbers," who were grinding down "honest Men," "worthy Citizens," "innocent Britons," who must rouse themselves.

The main author, John Trenchard, a prominent freethinker of the day, was edging toward caricature in these essays, picturing diabolical forces in apocalyptic struggle with the innocent. He protested his own virtue: "No man living laments the Calamities brought upon his Country more than I do."[30] And he glibly assumes that readers will understand how to seize on the fact that "the Benefit and Safety of the People constitutes the supreme Law." This was revolutionary rhetoric; it only lacked the circumstances of 1789 to make it dangerous.

Dire as the situation was, there was still hope that Parliament would act, and "Cato" appealed to the legislators to consider whether treason charges were appropriate to those "who, being entrusted with the Wealth, Security, and Happiness of Kingdoms, do yet knowingly pervert that Trust, to the undoing of that People." After all, "Parliaments, in almost every Reign since the Conquest, claimed and exercised this Right" over those "who have abused the Favour of the Royal Master, and endeavour'd to make him little and contemptible to his People."[31] If Parliament failed to act, "it is certain, that the whole People, who are the Publick, are the best Judges whether Things go ill or well with the Publick," and will take action.[32]

And who, exactly, constituted this irresistible public? Speaking of the French Revolution, historian Jeremy Popkin has observed that periodicals then served "as a symbol and a stand-in for 'the people' in whose name all political acts were now carried out, but which could not assemble and speak in any concrete manner." That is, newspapers could easily seem a more convincing expression of a people's will than its elected representatives.[33] This is especially true if they take the position that the people are always right and that they speak with a single voice.[34] Fortunately, circumstances in England did not allow this "public" to turn into a tyrant.

It is hard for historians to discover the same depths of evil in the ministry of that time that Cato did. But the *London Journal* became wildly popular in its day; someone computed its sale at fifteen thousand copies—far beyond its competitors. After trying to destroy its presses, the government decided to buy the paper in 1722. Its publisher warned that by "turning off the strength of expressions" the government might reduce "the sale to about 7 or 8,000."[35] Profits were the last concern of the government, whatever they had been to the pseudonymous journalists.

If Cato overreacted to political malfeasance in 1720, there was more substantial reason to oppose Sir Robert Walpole's administration. Walpole monopolized political power so successfully that the ruling class felt its place in the constitution to be threatened. To meet that threat, in 1726, another journalistic landmark was raised. The *Craftsman* set out to mobilize public opinion, because that was the only political force that Walpole did not control. At first, the paper soberly discussed the kind of political issue to which periodicals had become accustomed—official inquiries into official misconduct, the question of the public debt, foreign trade, and tariffs. But in its sixteenth number, on 27 January 1727, it hit its stride with a vivid political caricature entitled "The First Vision of Camilick."

> In the midst of these execrations enter'd a Man, dress'd in a plain habit, with a purse of gold in his hand. He threw himself forward into the room, in a bluff, ruffianly manner. A Smile, or rather a Sneer, sat on his Countenance. His Face was bronz'd over with a glare of Confidence. And arch malignity leer'd in his eye. Nothing was so extraordinary as the effect of this person's appearance. They no sooner saw him, but they all turn'd their Faces from the Canopy, and fell prostrate before him. He trod over their backs without any Ceremony, and march'd directly up to the Throne. He open'd his Purse of Gold, which he took out in Handfulls, and scatter'd amongst the Assembly. While the greater Part were engag'd in scrambling for these Pieces, he seiz'd, to my inexpressible Surprize, without the least Fear, upon the sacred *Parchment* itself. He rumpled it rudely up, and cramm'd it into his Pocket. Some of

the people began to murmer. He threw more Gold, and they were pacified. No sooner was the Parchment taken away, but in an instant I saw that august Assembly in Chains; nothing was heard through the whole Divan, but the Noise of Fetters and Clank of Irons.

The political cartoon had arrived. In the *Craftsman* literary caricatures won a hearing for well-informed comment by people who had been insiders, like Lord Bolingbroke himself. The much-admired paper created the expectation of an absolutely relentless journalistic opposition to overbearing authority. So it promoted the grievances of the day, and especially the refusal of Walpole to bend to a public clamour for war with Spain. It was no longer enough to complain of what the government was doing; now there were complaints of what the government refused to do.

Until Walpole was at long last forced from power, in 1742, the periodical press conditioned readers to an oppositional mentality. Historians observe that the press was more engaged in inflaming public opinion than in reporting events, building up anticipation for Parliamentary sessions before there was news to report.[36] After years of unrelenting criticism and scurrility, newspapers would continue to be in opposition simply by reflex, in the provinces as well as in London.[37] In retrospect, the opposition to Walpole seems overblown and petulant, but whether Walpole could have been removed without a wildly partisan press is a question. He controlled, to various degrees, five of the leading London papers as well as other lesser lights. After he was gone his accounts revealed payments of £50,000 to sweeten the press during his last decade in office.[38]

By then the press seemed to belong with politics. It might seem that we are only seeing, once again, the effort to use the press *against* government, just as Shaftesbury had. But when we say that papers were relentlessly antigovernment, we only mean they were antiministerial. At the same time, they were beginning to encourage government *involvement* in society in a general sense. As one journalist put it during the struggle against Walpole, "as Government concerns every man, so it seems but natural that every man should concern himself about Government."[39]

Jumping forward a generation and dipping (at random) into the *Gazetteer and New Daily Advertiser* for 1 January 1772, one sees the change that had sprouted through the crust of earlier custom. Though the English Parliament was in recess, the paper reported the proceedings of the Irish Parliament—for customers who needed politics with their morning coffee. And in anticipation of the next parliamentary session, a report of a French tax raised the question, "Does not this hint merit the attention of the legislature?" The removal of restrictions on the publishing of Commons' debates in 1771 (and Lords' debates in 1775) opened a floodgate of helpful suggestions by readers who urged government into new areas.[40] On 3 January the paper suggested a government role in the private construction of Battersea Bridge, and on 4 January it hoped to see the government more involved with East India Company affairs.

Picking up the *Whitehall Evening Post* for 6 January 1781, one finds a call for

the government to help hurricane victims in the West Indies, along with a long editorial on "that arch-rebel Dr. Franklin" and his traitorous British friends. The
St. James's Chronicle; Or, British Evening Post for 1 January 1778 commented on
government commercial policy, and two days later on the likely effects of a projected
policy with regard to the number of military officers. Readers' letters urged other
jobs on the authorities, including the regularized numbering of houses.

Even provincial papers like *Felix Farley's Bristol Journal* urged a distant government to action. At random, on 6 January 1787 it suggested a bill to facilitate the
recovery of insured losses, and a week later listed the political business pending when
Parliament would next meet. A week after that it was advising the government not
to give up certain forts on the American frontier and "to see justice done to the various British creditors of the [now independent] Americans."

The promotion of government, as such, was a notable departure from earlier ages.
The traditional view had held that the subject's liberties required constant vigilance
against government encroachment. Sometime in the eighteenth century the subject's
liberty came to be associated with *using* government for a growing list of desirable
ends. It was very natural for periodical publications to promote this government
activism. Maintaining pressure on government gave newspapers a purpose and
rationale. In time, the media would discover their essential function in providing daily
reminders to voters and legislators to seek out problems to address. On the other hand,
the international situation was increasingly displaced from the front pages from the
exciting days of the mid-1720s forward.[41]

Living on our side of this great historical watershed, we may be surprised to hear
periodical news faulted for politicizing all areas of life. It is a measure of the success of the media in conditioning us, that we no longer think of politics as a last resort.
But politics can be viewed as an exercise of power when better means of resolution
have broken down. Discovering conflict, and listening only to the most clamorous
voices in debate, the march of periodicity increases the scope of power in our world.

To generations on the far side of the news revolution nothing about modern life
would seem so odd as our complicity in the constant changing of the rules through
relentless legislation. It seems natural primarily because of the forward momentum
of a news industry. Of course, none of this is a choice that newsmen have made,
but is part of the dynamics of the medium. The note was struck as early as 1720,
when the founding editor of the *Independent Whig* sighed that "whoever goes
about to reform the World undertakes an Office obnoxious to Malice and beset with
Difficulties."[42]

ELEVEN

Turning Religion
Upside Down

If periodical news found a natural affinity for politics, it discovered the opposite with religion. Religion is about the abiding realities—about the eternal, if you like—while periodicity encourages a concentration on the transitory and the mundane. Religion tries to deepen the mystery of our existence, while news of religion transforms it into fact. The distorting effect of news on religion had nothing to do with an antireligious bias among early journalists. Indeed, it can even be detected in the earliest efforts to create religious periodicals.

Religion had once provided the frame within which the events of life found their place. After the news revolution, religion became simply a *part* of the world of news. Daily news replaced religion as the master text of a modernizing society, even for illiterate persons. Theology, meanwhile, became literal-minded, in imitation of the discourse of scientific and historical fact, turning its back on a symbolic language that was its natural idiom.

The Restoration period has long been seen as England's first self-consciously secular period, following the failure of religious enthusiasts to initiate a religious millennium.[1] Coffeehouse culture seems almost an alternative to the church. As historian Michael Hunter puts it, "The principal milieu of atheism" which so concerned contemporaries was "the culture of 'wit,' an educated but not learned environment in which intellectual agility was at a premium, which was seen as thriving in the fashionable atmosphere of the court and the coffeehouses of late-seventeenth-century London. . . . What they lacked in intellectual sophistication they made up for in arrogance and iconoclasm."[2] After a century of intense religious interest religion was being marginalized, in part by a "scientific revolution" in which facts were supposed to overcome mystery, but also because of a news consciousness.

Jeremy Black observes that "the amount of space devoted to religious and ecclesiastical topics in the press was less than might be expected. . . . Religious developments produced less newsworthy material and events than the world of politics."³ This should not be surprising; religious events are not like others. Periodical news is not a convincing medium for reporting providences or epiphanies. Or as historian Josef Altholz has put it, "In the Protestant traditions that predominated in Britain, there was little sense of timeliness or periodicity. The 'good news' had been once delivered to the saints and was timeless; a concern for current information smacked of worldliness."⁴ A mid-century editor expressed as much in his comment that "through the goodnesse of God wee still can say we have not much Newes at home."⁵ Another described the contrast between a prefunctory devotional life and the daily news: "Should a Hawker come by his Door crying, *A New Mail from Holland*, he would leap up from his *Prayers*, run to the next *Coffee-House*, and leave God and his Family, to enquire what *News*."⁶ Time was more pressing than eternity in the emerging modern consciousness.

Journalists would not have acknowledged an animosity toward religion per se, but only toward religious excesses. There were editorial attacks on the "priestcraft" practiced by the official clergy and on an unseemly "enthusiasm"— spiritual "possession"—among the sects. The controversies that could be reported kept antipapist, anti-Dissenting, anti-Methodist sentiment high.⁷

Religious news came naturally to be about the politics of toleration and religious establishment. While news has a hard time expressing respect, which is what religion is all about, it is good at expressing pity. And from the beginning the most prominent theme of "religious news" was the rights of those who were in opposition to the established church.⁸ Religious "Dissenters" would become prominent in the history of journalism since, as a minority, it was in their interest to ally with the forces of change. Not only did they pioneer in the founding of a "religious press," but Unitarians would be prominent in liberal journalism more generally. They found it as natural a medium for their progressive message as preaching.⁹

There were a couple of interesting exceptions, however—periodicals that really saw religion entwined with everything in life and giving a point to it all. Of course, by the conventional rhetoric of the day God often made the front page. But on a strict definition, perhaps the only periodical that truly deserved the description "religious" was the very first one, called *New Christian Uses, Upon the Weekly True Passages and Proceedings* (7 October 1643). In the midst of England's troubles, a nameless editor made diurnal readers reflect on how the week's news appeared to the eye of faith and what the proper response of believers should be. "Let us not be meerly Athenians in asking for Newes, but let us all stay a little and consider what the Lord hath done." So the editor led his readers in prayer. After each news item culled from the diurnals the editor added both "The Providence" he thought it showed and also a petition ("Use of Approach") or a thanksgiving ("Use of Acknowledgment") in which readers could join.

This is not news as we know it, but an actual exercise of religion. Its strangeness, to our thinking, is a measure of how far news and religion diverge. With only one issue surviving, it appears that even readers at that time thought it peculiar. But it does provide a benchmark for tracing the divergence of religion and news, the former discerning a realm behind the world of news and seeking a knowledge of the divine will embodied in events.

And yet, the structuralist critic Roland Barthes has shown how, in an odd way, a religious sense is preserved even within the modern news consciousness. He is not thinking of the world of political, diplomatic, or economic news, but of the humble sphere of the "fillers" (*fait-divers*). This miscellaneous stuff does not belong to any context that would give it "importance" or meaning; it is not about a politician's cancer or the burns on a starlet's face. Fillers have no context and must have an interest all by themselves. They do this by showing something incongruous, coincidental, or strange in their causation—qualities that seem to call for explanation but defy explanation at the same time.[10]

Almost necessarily, fillers must be something outside the normal. They trade on the same incongruity as humor does. Barthes's own examples include a murderer identified by his bicycle clips, a train derailed when a moose tripped the switch, the same diamond brooch stolen for the third time, fishermen who net a cow, a woman who died the day she bought an annuity. There are coincidences that seem downright spooky and crimes that are particularly horrific. The public seems to like the mystery or incongruity better than they would like some officious attempt at explanation. Readers like the "peculiarity," as Barthes puts it. Of course, coincidence is beyond explanation, and yet we cannot help sensing that nature is signifying when it repeats itself, or when there are ironies, symmetries, or reversals in events. Like religious miracles—which may also be of this character—they seem to be "signs." As Barthes put it, "Paradox . . . belongs to a deliberately constructed world: a god prowls behind the *fait-divers*."[11]

Fillers, then, can keep alive what the phenomenological school calls a "religious sense." It will not rise to the level of a religious *understanding*, because the "meaning remains suspended," as Barthes says. But we still have signification: "Meaning is both posited and frustrated." Apparently we feel more comfortable with it there. So while modern readers might reject overt religious explanations, they have only retreated to a pretheological, prereflective form of religious consciousness. It seems that our "mastery" of causality has left mystery and coincidence intact, on the fringes of the world of news.

But the heart of the news does not lie in these fillers. The significance of most reports is perfectly apparent in their political or social context. And even the papers devoted to religious news show how quickly a devotional sense was lost in a periodical schedule.

The next two attempts at religious periodicals were from the Catholic and Quaker camps and did not survive their first issues (in 1648 and 1662). Their purpose was to encourage coreligionists through difficult times, so they served a religious *purpose*.[12] But the next group of papers, whose titles bore the term "Protestant," were Protestant only in the negative sense of the word. Appearing during the Exclusion Crisis, the name on these papers was only a party identification, meaning anti-Catholic.[13]

There were others that used sarcastic titles—*Catholic Intelligence* and *Weekly Packet of Advice from Rome*—to indicate the same religious nativism. English nationalism appeared in religious dress, but it was not a religion that made spiritual demands on its adherents. There continued to be papers with such titles into the eighteenth century, so long as Catholic or pro-Stuart "Jacobitism" was still a fear.[14] Like political papers, they served to strengthen the divisions within society.

But other papers had a more positive purpose. After the Revolution of 1688 there was widespread concern with the moral reform of English society. Many who looked back on the Restoration as a disgraceful period of laxity and irreligion joined Societies for the Reformation of Manners.[15] Religiously oriented editors like John Dunton thought of using periodicals in this effort to drive profanity, drunkenness, obscenity, gambling out of public sight, at least. The *Athenian Mercury* gave this reform impulse a public hearing, trying to do it in a humorous, and not simply a censorious, spirit.[16]

The seriousness with which the *Athenian Mercury* dealt with moral and theological questions was commented on at the time as a gratifying change from the frivolous and condescending tone affected by the Restoration wits. When Jonathan Swift offered his "Ode to the Athenian Society," it was primarily to express his sense of the cultural threat the *Mercury* was trying to face:

> *The wits, I mean the atheists of the age,*
> *Who fain would rule the pulpit, as they do the stage,*
> *Wondrous refiners of philosophy,*
> *Of morals and divinity,*
> *By the new modish system of reducing all to sense,*
> *Against all logic, and concluding laws.*
> *Do own th' effects of Providence,*
> *And yet deny the cause.*

This secularism was what the Athenians opposed, with their more reasoned and pious use of philosophy. Swift could be carried away by the contemplation of their more chaste Philosophy:

> *How soon have you restored her charms,*
> *And rid her of her lumber and her books,*
> *Drest her again genteel and neat,*
> *And rather tight than great!*
> *How fond we are to court her to our arms!*
> *How much of heaven is in her naked looks!*[17]

But the *Athenian Mercury* was more philosophical than scriptural. Religious moderates like Dunton still thought that Christianity could depend on support from *within* the new intellectual and philosophical culture.[18] That would soon change. "Evangelical" elements began to view English society as a pagan mission field. There was, after all, a new relation of religion to society when the *Mercury* had to address questions that correspondents should have taken to their ministers.

In 1697, when the *Athenian Mercury* expired, something similarly constructive appeared that was more specifically religious. Despite its title, the *Occasional Paper* seems to have been roughly periodical, apparently monthly, and ran for a year. In each issue the editor, a moderate Anglican, considered controversial question, at a length of thirty-some pages. These tended to be intellectual challenges, such as skepticism, Deism, anticlericalism, but might also be moral or spiritual issues such as suicide and playgoing. In any event, the issues were not recycled sermons. Sometimes they were lengthy reviews of books of current interest such as John Toland's *Christianity Not Mysterious*.

The author was clear on why a periodical format had become necessary in theology or religion. English culture was in motion and in the current climate of press freedom, he said, readers might see attacks on religion but miss the answers to these attacks. The church was not at a loss for arguments, but its pamphlets might go unnoticed. A periodical would assure readers that they were keeping up and would be shorter, cheaper, and more to the point than full-scale refutations. Defoe would repeat the same points in a pamphlet of 1699. Refutations of the current dismissals of religion and morality did not always come to the attention of the public, which was too apt to accept the last thing it read.[19] So in his *Review* he often put in a word for decency and piety.[20]

Nothing could offer better evidence of the new situation of English culture than this picture of religion on the run. Among the concerns of the *Occasional Paper* was the effect of Restoration drama, which lowered audience resistance by a constant display of "Lasciviousness and Prophaneness" to the point that it became banal and unremarkable. The editor expressed the wish that "some Lover of Vertue wou'd examine all [plays], or at least those of them which are most usually read and acted, and shew the natural tendency they have to Vice."[21] This was precisely what Richard Steele, former playwright, would attempt ten years later in the *Tatler*, in continuing these moralistic efforts.

While the idea that religion needed to compete in the public sphere was common enough, the proper formula for a religious periodical was proving elusive. Two appeared in 1700, *Mercurius Theologicus; or, the Monthly Instructor* and still another of Benjamin Harris's productions, the *Weekly Entertainment*. The former, which ran for twelve issues, consisted of chapters of a book on natural theology and may more properly be considered a serialized book. The latter, in newspaper format, saw religion's problem differently. Harris was making an earnest effort to counteract the many "light and frothy Pamphlets, as may Vitiate and Poyson the Minds of the Readers." So his paper was made up of items from the news, stories from ancient and modern history, and other relations—almost fables—of an edifying nature. Readers were assured that "if at any time we be a little Jocose, it shall be always within the Bounds of Sobriety," so that even women and children could become part of the audience.[22] Not enough of them bought it to keep it going beyond its first month.

Of course, weekly sermons provided the religiously inclined with periodical edification, but church attendance was widely thought to be falling off. So John

Dunton schemed to reach the public in a new way. In January 1701 he began the *Post-Angel*, a monthly of eighty-odd pages, which survived for two years. It may be considered England's second "magazine," ten years after the *Gentleman's Journal*. It also came the closest of any periodical after *New Christian Uses* to maintaining an alternative culture to the one disclosed in the political news, awakening the sense of a world beyond the world of periodical news.

Dunton had probably never heard of *New Christian Uses* and must have gotten the idea for a news of Providence from the Reverend Increase Mather on one of his trips to New England.[23] Mather had announced, in 1684, a scheme to collect and publish recent evidences of Providence in human affairs. In effect, he asked correspondents to help him to continue a Deuteronomic history of God's activity in the world. Historian David Paul Nord has shown how, by the publication of occasional pamphlets or news "relations," the press in New England sustained this interest in a providential history through the seventeenth century.

The historical sense of the Judeo-Christian religious tradition exists in tension with its more mystical and timeless elements. But the Protestant movement within that tradition tended to discount the liturgical and sacramental elements in order to concentrate on a providential history. Thus it opened a window on the news. Of course, it expected to fit news reports into established patterns of interpretation. In Nord's words "the recent comet was a remarkable event but not a mysterious one," because theology explained it. In time, however, the theological framework would fade and only the events would remain in a news consciousness.

In fact, New England's news orientation—begun by its clergy—would hasten its secularization. Fascination with providences gave readers an "orientation to events." More than half of the eight hundred titles printed in seventeenth-century New England were news related, despite the lack of a newspaper. At first they may have broadened readers' faith, but in the next century news gathering become an end in itself. As Nord puts it, "After the seventeenth century the meaning and purpose of much of the news was lost; only the news itself remained."[24]

Dunton's *Post-Angel* followed Mather's lead in collecting and publishing "Providences" both of judgment and mercy. These led off each edition, followed by obituaries of eminent persons (sometimes drawn from unpublished funeral sermons), questions and answers (often taken from the files of the *Athenian Mercury*), ordinary "publick" news, and book notices and recommendations. Each news item carried its spiritual application, and Dunton was just as tempted to "improve" the public news with spiritual observations as he was the Providences. The difference was generally that news involved important people, while Providences happened to ordinary people and had been missed by the other papers.

When a poetry section was added, the magazine truly became—as advertised—a "Universal Entertainment." But Dunton repeated Harris's promise that "if at any time I be a little Jocose, it shall always be within the Bounds of Sobriety."[25] Whether or not it was as entertaining as the *Gentleman's Journal*, it had as long a run.

Other editors had less sense of the requirements of religious discourse, and brought religion into the orbit of the political, as was natural to periodicity. Charles Leslie's *The Rehearsal* (1704), which we have treated as a political journal, showed an obvious feeling for the importance of the religious issue. But there is an erosion of the religious sense in Leslie's definition of the issue—as the place of the established church in the nation's life—and in his concentration on the purely political tactics involved. This became the normal approach of news to religion and exhibited the characteristic desperation of those who suppose that promoting God's power or honor depends on political agents.

Some editors thought the main threat to the nation's spiritual health was intellectual rather than political. The monthly *Censura Temporum* (1708–10) took a dialogue form in monitoring "The Good and Ill Tendencies of Books, Sermons, Pamphlets, Etc." Unlike the *Occasional Paper*, which thought that intemperate defenses of orthodoxy were counterproductive, it deployed sarcasm in the defense of religion. Dunton also took this general line in the *Christian's Gazette* (1709). "What's the News is the Grand Salute, and common Preface to all our Talk," he observed, and so he tried to turn theology into "news"—to get it talked about. He argued some theological "novelty" or paradox in each issue ("Novelty II. That the Saints in Heaven will be eternally making New Discoveries," or "Novelty V. Proving Brutes have immaterial Souls"). By then the *Post-Angel* was so far in the past that Dunton felt free to recycle large chunks of it in this later production, to no avail.[26]

Defending "religion" could be said to be a part of the purpose of the *Tatler* when it began in 1709. Steele did it, of course, with more subtlety than we have seen to this point. He had written a serious religious tract, *The Christian Hero*, in 1701 and his periodical can be seen as a new tactic toward the same end. Piety and charity could be promoted by humor as well as by didacticism. And the periodical format would make it harder for people to ignore.

The *Tatler* essays have been called "lay sermons on taste," but they often move into morals more seriously than that phrase would suggest.[27] While the journal never mentioned Christ, the others we have surveyed almost never did so either. The public's discussion of the religious issue in these decades concentrated on the intellectual, social, and moral virtues more than on spiritual ones. And this gave scope for Steele's wit, which could be far more entertaining at the expense of the freethinking opposition than the others we have met.[28]

The Tory John Gay paid Steele a high compliment in this connection, while speaking of the *Tatler* after its demise.

> There is this noble difference between him [Steele] and all the rest of our Polite and Gallant Authors: The latter have endeavour'd to please the Age by falling in with them, and incouraging them in their fashionable Vices, and false notions of things. It would have been a jest, sometime since [ago], for a Man to have asserted, that any thing Witty could be said in praise of a Marry'd State, or that Devotion and Virtue were any way necessary to the Character of a fine Gentleman.

Understanding the ways of authors, Gay knew how brave Steele had been to take on English society single-handedly. And he knew how remarkable was his success.

Instead of complying with the false Sentiments or Vicious tasts of the Age, either in Morality, Criticism, or Good Breeding, he has boldly assur'd them, that they were altogether in the wrong. . . . 'Tis incredible to conceive the effect his Writings have had on the Town; How many Thousand follies they have either quite banish'd, or given a very great check to; how much Countenance they have added to Vertue and Religion; how many People they have render'd happy, by shewing them it was their own fault if they were not so.[29]

Since, as Gay observed, "his reputation was at a greater height than, I believe, ever any living Author's was before him," there was evidently a market for morality—if not for religion—in the "informed public." And soon Steele and Addison's daily *Spectator* (1 March 1711) would again ply that market.

One last attempt was made at a more specifically religious periodical when an anonymous Anglican produced the *Hermit* (4 August 1711). In essays rather than sermons or chapters, it explored religious themes on a weekly schedule. But the author soon declared himself exhausted, and during the next thirty years of political strife there was not another "religious" periodical that required a second issue that was not merely a party paper or an anti-Catholic lampoon.[30]

The first really long-running religious party organ, which commenced in 1732, finally showed what it took to make religion commercially successful. An Anglican cleric, William Webster, launched the *Weekly Miscellany; Giving an Account of the Religion, Morality, and Learning of the Present Time* to make up for the deficiencies of the ordinary press in covering these areas. His formula for success included an essay on an issue involving theology, morals, or the established church, some general news including crime, and book notices, poetry, and ads. We shall see that the highly successful *Gentleman's Magazine* had begun in the previous year along similar lines (in fact, the *Weekly Miscellany* ran ads for it). Webster was showing the public that religion could be part of such entertainment. Not that he thought that earthquakes required reflections on Providence; the religion of his paper was largely a matter of hostility to Dissenters and Methodists.[31]

With George Whitefield's spectacular intercontinental revivals, starting in 1738, religious affairs truly became part of the news of the world. It did not strain anyone's spiritual sense to see the hand of Providence in events of that kind and scale. Crowds of tens of thousands were news, whatever the occasion. Jonathan Edwards, in New England, had first suggested periodicals that could coordinate the awakenings in America, Wales, Scotland, and England, and carry similar reports from Holland and Germany.[32] And the young Whitefield was extraordinarily attuned to public relations methods and at age twenty-two was already keeping track of the press he was getting.

Whitefield did not shrink from the sensationalism ingrained in the news. He immediately recognized the value of negative publicity, for instance. In his serially published *Journal* he relished the fact that "somebody or other thought me considerable enough to write a letter in the *Weekly Miscellany* against me, and with several untruths, about my preaching at St. Margaret's, Westminster." Five days later he was able to note that the writer had died.[33] As stated above, Webster's *Weekly Miscellany* did not itself deal in such Providences.

In 1740 (or possibly 1741) the evangelical party supplemented Whitefield's serial *Journal* with a periodical, *The Christian's Amusement*. It soon became the *Weekly History: or, An Account of the most Remarkable Particulars relating to the present Progress of the Gospel* and ran for several years. Similar papers were founded in Scotland and New England. A periodical appearance was perfectly natural, given the hope of a continuing revival, for these papers had the task of encouraging those who were carrying the good news into the dark corners of the land.

The *Weekly History* was an unusually clumsy production, splitting sermons between several numbers and simply breaking them off at the bottom of the page. But in printing letters from Whitefield and other preachers and from observers and converts, the journal must have done much to maintain the enthusiasm that a scattered campaign needed.[34] Indeed, the bonding it provided for the evangelical movement was such that the provincial and colonial fringe began to influence events at the center. Harry Stout has pointed out that Whitefield intended this, sending news to London of the success of the Gospel abroad, in order to make London itself feel left out. This, of course, would heighten anticipation of his returns.[35]

Other religious parties likewise formed around their periodicals, in the same way that political papers defined events and positions for the faithful in the first decade of the century. As the eighteenth century wore on, all the various nonconformist bodies founded such organs to preserve denominational identity into a new generation.[36]

More general periodicals did not find the eighteenth-century religious revival suitable for their news. Editors had little use for spirit-filled religion or deviant groups unless they made spectacles of themselves. The extravagances of the Methodists were a constant source of amusement.[37] And clergymen of the established church were a butt of the news, as they were of the novels of the day.[38] But there is no sign that editors suspected that evangelical religion would become a cultural force in the coming century. That would be a matter of process, which often eludes the news.

The essential reason behind a mutual antagonism between news and religion is that periodical news was even then bidding to replace religion as the "master text" of English culture. When Hans Frei wrote that until 1700 England's myth was Scripture, he meant that religion provided the names, identities, and narratives in which people lived their lives. It offered illiterates and philosophers a shape for their moral and social situation. Historians, scientists, and lawyers wrestled with the Bible in writing their treatises, not because they were forced to but because they wanted to be heard. The heterodox Thomas Hobbes used 657 biblical citations in *Leviathan*, despite his talk of creating a political science. As Christopher Hill has put it, "When scholars laboriously demonstrate that Levellers or Milton or Winstanley were primarily motivated by religion, they have proved no more than that these thinkers lived in the seventeenth century." People automatically expressed themselves in scriptural phrases and "read back into the Bible themselves and their problems."[39]

Using the Bible as master text did not imply a devout belief, necessarily. Nor did it guarantee righteousness. What is offered were shared meanings, which are the basis for community. It is that coherence which seems lacking today. No one, probably, would want to bring it all back in quite its old form, but one can wonder what might have developed out of it without the overpowering competition from a news industry and synthesized excitement.

Seventeenth-century theologians like Increase Mather who turned toward news fact to bolster religion cannot have recognized the dynamics involved in that move. They saw the respect accorded to the facts of science and tried to use them in a "natural theology." They used the facts of history to guarantee the trust-worthiness of the biblical records, and the facts of journalists to demonstrate Providence.[40] In doing so, they robbed religion of its more natural language. They adopted the assumption that language should correspond to something not of the subjective realm, when it was always metaphor that offered freedom to the spirit.

When communications theorists speak half-facetiously of news as ritual, it suggests periodic returns to some spiritual foundation. But if one returns and finds that things are changed, it's not ritual. Periodical news cannot admit that things have not changed. For example, crime represents one of society's boundary areas, but news of crime may not seem to indicate the transgression of real limits. Rather it may indicate trends in crime—new forms that may change the boundaries. Thus the periodical treatment of crime may not call criminals to account so much as it calls society and its values into doubt, as if news was consumed primarily by theorists.

Granted, one cannot dwell always in the eternal verities. But a society obsessed with relativities is one that will experience difficulty reaching certain satisfactions. It will have unusual difficulties in socializing and educating its children. If parents live in the news, they may imagine all the dangers coming from the other direction—that their own, conventional or traditional standards can only be a burden to their children and not a resource. It is a fear that periodicals can be expected to encourage, for the industry creates dependence by eroding confidence in settled opinion and habit. Periodical news destroys a bondage to tradition, but at the price of bondage to the next edition.

It is frequently observed that the things that replace religion end up becoming like religions. Analogies between news and religion are legion. Hegel described the news as modern man's substitute for morning prayers.[41] Indeed, Addison suggested that "all well regulated Families" should "set apart an Hour in every Morning for Tea and Bread and Butter" and the latest *Spectator*.[42] It is no stretch to see the news as a form of daily communion, in which readers collectively bow their heads over the miseries of the world and spiritually participate in them. Clearly, they mistake the elements for the Real Presence, and do not see them as mere symbol. It is what Carey and his school mean by news as ritual—the "maintenance of an ordered, meaningful cultural world." Whether periodicity allows it to be sufficiently ordered or ultimately meaningful is what is in question.

There is revelation as well as ritual in news discourse. Headlines give a dramatic account of the contending forces in the upper story of our universe, with a prophetic spin on all accounts.[43] The editorial essay constitutes a sermon, and denominational differences are seen in the groups that are shunned editorially and pictured in diabolical forms. Finally, news offers an absolute point of reference, which is some image of the public. For there can be no authority above those who form the media's market. If there is no getting away from religion in this sense, we must be concerned with one that cannot confess its true nature or take responsibility for its prophetic leading.

Periodical media now offer what bonding our societies now enjoy, given the state of our more traditional cultures. How those cultures would have developed in the absence of competition with a daily news product is a moot point. But we must wonder whether periodical news as culture text can really fulfill the necessary "mythic" function, when it takes change to be the only constant. Given the widespread adoption of a periodical tempo, recognized religions now rank as one "interest" of the news among others—with its own separate "section." This is not a new development; it has been fifty years since Robert Park observed that "news is a purely secular phenomenon."[44] It was implied from the beginning.

TWELVE

The Club Image and
Vicarious Community

The defining moment in the life of the English reading public came at around the turn of the eighteenth century, shortly after the press found itself free. That was when local affairs became part of the world of news, when the image of the club became symbolic of the informed public, and when caricature began to replace civil discourse. Together, these changes would tend to reduce periodical publication from a medium to a mechanism. That is, they reduced the effort needed to participate in public opinion, by marketing news and discussion as a product. No longer did readers need to search out a wider world when they could find it on their own doorstep. No longer did they need to engage with a diverse coffeehouse crowd when they could find a more like-minded group in the "club" to which they subscribed. And there was no longer any challenge to engage with alien views after seeing them portrayed in freakish shape. Readers could begin to live in a more subjective world, encouraged by a news industry whose expertise was in the knowledge of its customers rather than some outer reality.

Remarkably enough, all these developments can be traced back in large part to one person, who rarely appears in histories of journalism, the humorist Edward "Ned" Ward. Ned Ward is often described as a "scribbler." He had found his talent to lie in the description of low life in London and specialized in character sketches. Seventeenth-century "character" writing was satirical, and Ward's do not escape that designation entirely. But they were unusual in suggesting a measure of sympathy and understanding for the lower orders who had been ignored before, except in advertisement copy. In November 1698 he had the inspiration to begin producing characters in periodical form, as the *London Spy*.

There was nothing in the character-writing genre that required a periodical format, and histories of journalism often ignore the *London Spy* since it included nothing that could be called news. But the journal was a commercial success and ran monthly for a year and a half, offering Pickwickian rambles through parts of London that had always escaped literary treatment. Of course, the ribald papers of John Crouch and the coarse humor of "Poor Robin" had already appeared in periodical form. But those productions were so obviously directed at a vulgar, semiliterate audience that they cannot be compared with Ward's sketches and did not influence the main stream of journalism. Ward's protagonist, the wide-eyed bumpkin getting his first look at London, embodied a homespun wit and intelligence that appealed to the coffeehouse customers of the serious press.

Most important, it forced them to look at their city. Readers learned the tricks of the various trades in London and got to visit the Monument, the Exchange, the Abbey Tombs, the "lions" in the Tower, "Bedlam" Hospital, and Gresham College, in the company of Ward and his friends. All this suggested a change of focus to other journalists, a greater concentration on ordinary local affairs than had ever appeared in the news. As his biographer puts it, "Ward discovered the city of London for the journalist."[1]

News could begin at home. We have already argued that the assumption that Englishmen only put up with a steady diet of foreign news because of risks in covering the local scene only reveals a modern prejudice. Early papers apparently took the view that reporting local news was unnecessary, that people would naturally prefer to find out the neighborhood gossip for themselves. By the time local news could reach print it would be several days old, and an editor would be risking his credibility in expressing himself on matters that his readers would know as well and as soon as he. In 1700 Englishmen still thought of foreign news as the real news of their time. Addison's most hilarious sketches—involving his troublesome friend the "Political Upholsterer"—show him and his cronies to be crazed with interest in the most remote intelligence, from Sweden and the Turkish frontier.[2] The newsletters that flourished even after the appearance of newspapers began with foreign news, and gave it more space than the parliamentary news that was their reason for being.[3] Provincial and colonial papers, likewise, gave foreign news pride of place. The *Norwich Post* contained mostly foreign news, then London news, before local news and ads. As late as mid-century, the *Pennsylvania Gazette* was half from Europe, then 18 percent British, and only 21 percent from Pennsylvania and the other British colonies.[4]

The development of a local focus in the news, therefore, takes some explaining. Part of the explanation lies in advertising, a ubiquitous component of all periodicals of the period. Foreign news found itself surrounded and sometimes crowded by ads and personals, which began to create a neighborhood. If one read only the reprinted volumes of essay-serials like the *Spectator* one would not be aware of the large presence of ads in the original. They might take up half the space, and editors were increasingly aware that they provided all of their profits.[5]

Given the importance of advertising to the news industry, one can understand Addison's fond tribute, in the *Tatler* essay of 14 September 1710:

It is my Custom, in a Dearth of News, to entertain my self with those Collections of Advertisements that appear at the End of all our publick Prints. These I consider as Accounts of News from the little World, in the same Manner that the foregoing Parts of the Paper are from the great. If in one we hear that a Sovereign Prince is fled from his Capital City, in the other we hear of a Tradesman who hath shut up his Shop, and run away. If in one we find the Victory of a General, in the other we see the Desertion of a private Soldier. I must confess, I have a certain Weakness in my Temper, that is often very much affected by these little Domestick Occurrences, and have frequently been caught with Tears in my Eyes over a melancholy Advertisement.

By the end of its existence the *Tatler* had as many as fourteen or eighteen ads per issue, for books, wigs, slaves, wheelchairs, birdcages, shoe polish, lotteries, auctions, cosmetics, rental properties, professional services, and medicines. And there were the poignant personals to which Addison alluded: "Gentleman, who on the 20th Instant had the Honour to conduct a Lady out of a Boat at White-Hall-Stairs, desires to know where he may wait on her to disclose a Matter of Concern."[6]

There was pathos in the margins of the news. There was fortune, in the winning lottery numbers and the rewards announced for information. The arts flourished in those margins; theaters, which were sensitive to daily trends, had to have notices in each day's *Daily Courant*.[7] And there was fun, as readers had to be careful not to be taken in. Parody ads appeared as early as the papers of the Exclusion period—in the *Popish Courant* and the answering *Heraclitus Ridens*. But the *Spectator* did not really have to divert readers with its fake bankruptcy notices for its critics, when it could run ads for telescopes, a cure for stuttering, manuscript sermons, a lady's riding habit, sedan chairs lined in scarlet, Holbein portraits (genuine?), the sale of a government office, and of the next right of appointment to a parish.[8]

Some already understood that there was an art to writing effective ads. Thieves like Jonathan Wild ran notices such as the following: "Lost, the Ist of October, a black shagreen Pocket-Book, edged with Silver, with some Notes of Hand. The said Book was lost in the Strand, near the Fountain Tavern, about 7 or 8 o'clock at Night. If any Person will bring the aforesaid Book to Mr Jonathan Wild, in the Old Bailey, he shall have a Guinea reward." David Nokes decodes this to mean "that Wild already had the pocket-book and was offering to return it for an appropriate fee. The mention of 'notes of hand' implies that he already knew the owner's name and since the Fountain Tavern was a notorious brothel, probably amounts to a threat of blackmail."[9]

As the audience for periodicals broadened, the concentration on a wider world began to lose out to an interest in the bit that impinged most directly on the reader. This took some time, but the *Athenian Mercury* and *London Spy* began the process. Steele was the next to see the commercial possibilities in periodicals as a way of reading about oneself. He included Ward's cast of characters, but also the more polite elements of society, which he could sketch so delightfully.[10] Like Ward, he saw that one did not have to *make* local life interesting; he *found* it to be interesting. One did not need obscenity or scatology to hold reader interest, but only needed to awaken the public to the humor and the pathos all around them.

As part of this local scene, the image of the club became a way of making readers welcome. The very first number of the the *London Spy* visited a coffeehouse, where people were choking on the tobacco smoke and drinking their "Mahometan-Gruel." A coffeehouse figured in the second issue as well, and Ward soon found that there was no better microcosm of the bustling metropolis. So while producing this periodical he began another, entitled the *Weekly Comedy, As it is Daily Acted at Most Coffee-houses in London*, which ran weekly for several months in 1699. In it he introduced a club of twelve characters, including Scribble, a newswriter. It offered a background for his "characters."

The growing use in the eighteenth century of the club as symbolic of the public suggests a change in the way that periodical news was consumed. The imaginary club of the periodicals began to compete with the actual community of the coffeehouse. Picturing a club was a way to generate the brand loyalty that periodicals depend on. And during the eighteenth century the function of the coffeehouse would begin to be taken over by periodicals, making actual visits less important. News was increasingly consumed in private, so that the news industry had to manufacture public opinion rather than plant the seeds. The *Tatler* admitted as much, in its jocular announcement of a new approach to news. The paper, Steele said (12 April 1709), was

> principally intended for the Use of Politick Persons, who are so publick-spirited as to neglect their own Affairs to look into Transactions of State. Now these Gentlemen, for the most Part, being Persons of strong Zeal and weak Intellects, it is both a Charitable and Necessary Work to offer something, whereby such worthy and well-affected Members of the Commonwealth may be instructed, after their Reading, *what to think*: Which shall be the End and Purpose of this my Paper.

The eighteenth century saw the birth of gentlemen's clubs, which acquired their own premises. The few earlier ones had met in taverns, having at most the exclusive use of a room on the premises. When they became exclusive in membership they preferred their own rooms. For those who would never see the inside of a club, domestic life acquired a new importance and rationale, associated with the growing emphasis on sentiment. The new valuation of privacy is nowhere better seen than in the report that by the 1790s talkers in London coffeehouses were being shushed by readers.[11]

There were earlier uses of a club motif in periodical literature, including the "Athenians" who were hinted at in 1691 but never introduced.[12] *Mercurius Eruditorum: or, News From the Learned World* (5 August 1691) purported to be the transactions of a club of three members who discussed their somewhat high-brow reading—including the periodical *Works of the Learned*. Defoe's *Review* referred to a distant club, in France, but failed to bring it to life.

The more successful representation of sociability was in the dialogue, as we have seen it used in *Heraclitus Ridens*, the two *Observators*, and the *Rehearsal*. Their dialogue was to *begin* conversation, which may be taken as the proper function of periodicals. A club, on the other hand, was the full representation of a conversation. One can settle into a club's ambiance without being an active participant, and "Mr. Spectator" admitted that this was his usual practice. In a dialogue someone who does not participate is noticed, and there is pressure to become engaged. Engagement was what was being lost from the world of news.

But what, exactly, is the connection between the club motif and periodicity? The point of a club—as opposed to some more spontaneous gathering—is its continuing, regular, and periodical character. Thus it is analogous to the relationship between newspapers and their readers. The image of a family would not have worked as a symbol for news; families suggest demands, responsibilities, routine, and stability. Clubs suggest variety, stimulation, and excitement.

Ned Ward became increasingly involved with clubs—real and imaginary. He may have been the perpetrator of the *Secret History of the Calves' Head Club* (1703), which convinced many Tories of the existence of regicide societies that made merry over England's disasters. And he is known to have published the *History of the London Clubs* in 1709, in which one learned of clubs of cattle-dealers, beggars, thieves, bankrupts, fops, syphlitics, quacks, liars, and crossdressers. This number grew with the popularity of subsequent editions, to thirty-two clubs, some of which may actually have had some basis in reality. Of course, the contemporary Societies for the Reformation of Manners were real enough, arising in opposition to those that amused Ward.[13]

Periodicals offered readers clubs of their own, for vicarious participation. The *Tatler* and *Spectator* were only the most famous of those that adopted a club motif. The setting encouraged these papers to became self-absorbed, so that some, like the *Spectator*, did without news altogether. Other such "clubs" found that they, too, could get along without reference to anything outside themselves. The *Female Tatler* (8 July 1709) introduced the club of both sexes. As late as 1730, the *Grub Street Journal* (8 January) began as the transactions of a society. Its mission was ridicule of the newspapers of the day, continuing the satire of the *Dunciad* on a periodical basis.[14] Eliza Haywood's *Female Spectator* of 1744, the first periodical *by* women, featured a club of three members, along with letters from readers who were thereby admitted to the society.[15]

Thus there might be more than the mere simulation of discussion in these club journals. Letters were part of editorial technique, and readers who aspired to membership might actually address each other. A problem arose with the suspicion that letters were chosen, edited, or even manufactured to create the journal's substance and style. Editors expressed such suspicions regarding rival periodicals, and thereby about themselves.[16] Still, it was not at first unrealistic to think of the public as bonded in such an intimate way, when we remember the relatively small size of London and of provincial "society" at that time. When Steele became disgusted by the bad behavior of London audiences he promised to embarrass offenders by printing their names (16 April 1709): "After this Declaration, if a Fine Lady thinks fit to Giggle at Church, or a Great Beau come in Drunk to a Play, either shall be sure to hear of it in my ensuing Paper: For merely as a well-bred Man, I cannot bear these Enormities." Shame could still work in a society on this scale, and such periodicals were like group newsletters.[17] But by their self-referencing character—citing previous issues and alluding to future ones—a periodical eventually became a world in itself.

Periodicals that took this introspective turn regularly included women in their definition of the public. Kathryn Shevelov observes that women were "metonymic of the nonelite public," that part of the public in which the political gave way to more personal concerns. Politics was already being served by the periodical press, but domestic life and "society" offered new niches in the market. While this led away from politics, it did not reduce the natural bent of periodicity toward reform, which we noticed in reference to the politicization of life. There were paths to reform other than the political, and all of them could be encouraged by periodical publishing. Reminding readers of the ladies present allowed editors to be unabashedly reformist, since women so commonly served as moral symbols.[18]

Those outside of London may have found the club world of the periodicals especially meaningful. The isolation of rural gentry households and even of small town society is hard to imagine today. Periodicals would serve as a lifeline for those who felt isolated by their class pretentions or their cultural tastes. Certainly they took advantage of the opportunity to correspond with editors and contribute verse.[19] And they were also invited to identify with any of the various personae adopted by periodical titles.

The possibilities for chosing an identity within the periodical market were myriad. Readers might find a patriotic identity in journals entitled the *Englishman* (1713), *Guardian* (1713), *Patriot* (1714), *Briton* (1723), *True Briton* (1723), *Free Briton* (1729), or *True Patriot* (1745). Or they might think of themselves as cultural kin to the *Examiner* (1710), *Plain Dealer* (1712), *Monitor* (1714), *Reader* (1714), *Censor* (1715), *Critick* (1718), *Freethinker* (1718), *Advocate* (1720), *Auditor* (1733), or *Student* (1750). Or they could identify with a class, as *Freeholder* (1715), *Patrician* (1719), *Plebian* (1719), *Craftsman* (1726), or with one of the several journals containing the term "gentleman" (1692, 1721, 1731, 1741). Women might join with journals that included "ladies" (1694, 1704, 1749) or "female" (1709, 1744) in the title. Or readers might have to find themselves in the more curious ranks of the *Night Walker* (1697), *Tatler* (1709), *Spectator* (1711), *Hermit* (1711), *Lay Monk* (1713), *Lover* (1714), *Wanderer* (1717), *Comedian* (1732), *Prompter* (1734), *Tickler* (1747), *Midwife* (1750), *Rambler* (1750), *Adventurer* (1752), *Connoisseur* (1754) or *Fumbler* (1762). They could even flatter themselves that they were being addressed in the various journals addressed to the Learned, the Curious, or the Ingenious.

If a "public" is defined as a group that shares a common source of news, then these journals were creating the possibilities for new social divisions. Traditional societies are those in which one knows one's news sources personally, and must respond in a personal manner.[20] The proliferation of impersonal media allowed readers to retreat from face-to-face contact and make less effort to respond to those whose views were different. From the first decades of the eighteenth century it was possible for men and women to identify themselves with magazines or papers with more permanence than their families or neighborhoods, bonded by agreement on attitudes. The media could divide society as well as unify it.

The division of society was also encouraged by the third of Ward's innovations, the introduction of caricature within periodical literature. Ward foreshadowed caricature in the character-writing of his two periodicals, and also in his bizarre descriptions of imaginary clubs. While he retained his good humor, not everyone did. The development of verbal caricature began shortly after his time and would lead to the visual cartoons that began to appear in periodicals in 1767, with their puzzling ferocity toward Lord Bute.[21]

Illustrative prints developed independently of news and were not produced periodically at first. Nor, for the most part, were they satirical. Before 1720 the emblematic tradition persisted in England, in which familiar symbolic elements were woven into suggestive patterns. That genre was not as emotionally involving as caricature would be. It was didactic, moralistic, and often devotional, and hardly suited to the news. The first association of prints and periodicity was simply in the fact that by 1724 printmakers like William Hogarth began to advertise their new productions in the newspapers.[22]

The scandal of the South Sea affair, in 1720, produced the first outburst of satirical prints, at the same time that it was producing the scurrility of Cato's Letters.[23] And it roughly coincided with the introduction of caricature into England, from Italy. At first, caricature was a hobby for amateurs; Hogarth, who dominated English printmaking, despised it.[24] But even his more refined draftsmanship exhibited some of the rage that was becoming characteristic of the journalists. As evidence of that rage, we have already seen the example of "The Vision of Camelick" from the *Craftsman* of 27 January 1727, in which Walpole was vividly portrayed as the corrupter of his people. M. Dorothy George observes that "the frequent 'dreams' and 'visions' dear to the *Craftsman* and other papers" became an inspiration to printmakers.[25] Herbert Atherton agrees that we may think of visual caricature—operating through distortion—as the *result* of an earlier verbal caricature: "The prints of the late 1720s and early 1730s approximate the ideas, and occasionally even the imagery, found in the *Craftsman*." After 1730 print production became "a continuous form of journalism," though not actually appearing within periodical literature.[26]

So caricature, with its tone of political and social rejection, began with the "characters" authored by Ward, Steele, and others. It necessarily focused on human figures rather than on the symbols of the emblematic tradition. And this encouraged political antagonism to concentrate on personalities rather than principles. It was commented on at once, by John Mottley, for example, in his play *The Craftsman: or, Weekly Journalist* (1728). A character addresses the editor of that paper, on the subject: "Oh how I admire your excellent Invectives! 'Tis no difficulty to abuse a Person that we know is an ill Man; but the Art is to make a Woolsey or a Menzikoff of one we are convinced is honest and deserving, when we are resolved to hate him. This is what we all love you for; go on dear Caleb, pull down these Idols *Merit* and *Honesty*, they are the greatest Enemies of our Party." Mottley had no doubt of the reason behind such intemperance: "In order to increase the Publick Good, we must endeavour to distress it a little more; and then who knows but you and I may come to be Men of Power."[27]

Students of visual satire have been puzzled by its virulence as it burst on the scene in the 1770s: in the words of Professor George, "It was a malicious World. Wit and ridicule were admired and feared to a degree that now seems strange."[28] Foreign visitors expressed surprise at the violence and vulgarity that they saw in the prints they found in coffeehouses.[29] One is at a loss to explain this virulence in political terms, since the issues of the day would hardly justify it. It is a commonplace that eighteenth-century politics was primarily personal, or factional, which would be greatly encouraged by caricature. When issues are lacking, one must keep up interest by exaggeration, which is inevitably personal.

Part of the attraction of caricature is its brevity. Periodical publication typically involves space constraints that reduce the amount of discussion possible. Atherton says of the prints, that "the conjunction of diverse images with their innumerable connotations is a short-cut to and often a perversion of logic."[30] That could be said of daily news more generally, and simply suggests that news and cartoons were made for each other.

According to George and Atherton, virtually all political prints in the mid-century were antigovernment. And that antiestablishment tone proved natural in reference to other fields as well; all the professions were satirized in the prints of the day, with the clergy leading in attention. Scientists, too, were always treated derisively. By contrast, soldiers and sailors were viewed sympathetically, often as victims. They were in fashion, of course, because of England's recent military successes.[31]

All this reflected what could be found in the contents of even the most respected journals. Steele invariably made light of the scientists of his day, presenting them as "enthusiasts" in their own way. Nicholas Gimcrack, the scientific virtuoso, was "little versed in the world" but was "able to discover the Sex of a Cockle" and "will tell you, with a great deal of Gravity, That a Flea is a Rhinocerous." The "Tatler" admitted that "I have been present at the Dissection of a Mite, and have seen the Skeleton of a Flea." Ordinarily he avoided this company for fear of boredom: "When I meet with a young Fellow that is an humble Admirer of the Sciences, but more dull than the rest of the Company, I conclude him to be a Fellow of the Royal Society."[32] Literary scholars seemed just as ridiculous. Steele had fun with Tom Folio, the "learned Idiot, (for that is the Light in which I consider every pedant)." And he allowed that "I have arriv'd by Laziness to what others pretend to by Philosophy, a perfect Neglect of the World."[33]

The world of fashion and taste was where Steele's profits came from, not the world of erudition. He was helping polite society to assert itself as the arbiter of fashion in science and scholarship as well as in politics and the arts. Steele could chuckle over fashionable society as well, but did so without being dismissive. For example, while trying his best to ignore the biggest political event of the *Tatler* years— Sacheverell's trial—he diverted himself at the expense of the ladies who were attending with such unaccountable interest. As he put it, the singer

> Nicolini himself is commanded by the Ladies, who at present employ their Time with great Assiduity in the Care of the Nation [attending the trial] to put off his [concert] Day till he shall receive their Commands and Notice, that they are at Leisure for Diversions. In the mean Time, it is not to be expressed how many cold Chickens the Fair Ones have eaten since this Day Sevennight for the Good of their Country [in box lunches at the trial].[34]

The glamour of his audience was reflected in Steele's wry observation that some of these fair ones were getting up early enough to discover that daylight began before nine in the morning.

By their very nature, periodical publications had a "democratizing" influence on culture. Selling the next issue meant changing the composition of the jury that sat in judgment on the issues of the day. Periodicals offered the "informed public" the confidence to assert its understanding of things over the views of "experts." Verbal, and later visual, caricature played its part in this by undermining the dignity of traditional elites and culture. Historians use the term Enlightenment to describe the attacks on an outmoded science, a decadent humanism, and philosophical and theological scholasticism, and the reopening of all questions on a new, popular basis. Caricature helped to clear the ground.

Creating this informed public meant identifying opposition groups. Intellectual and professional elites, politicians, Papists and religious enthusiasts did not exhaust the list of those who were used in this way. Criminal biography inspired a periodical all its own, which began to portray them more colorfully in the early eighteenth century. The seventeenth-century *True Account of the Behaviour and Confessions of the Condemned Criminals in Newgate* had been low-key and sympathetic. But as time went on, the reports became more exciting, furnishing the lively accounts of criminal life that made up the later collections of "The Newgate Calendar."

The early editions of the serial, which emanated from prison chaplains, puzzle historians by their dullness and are dismissed as sermons. The crimes for which the subjects were executed or (often) pardoned are sometimes trifling and hardly ever entertaining. The focus was on the penitence of the condemned. Ellenor Rogers is fairly typical of the early cases offered to the public (27 May 1686):

> Condemned for Felony; She was Born in Cheshire, is 26 Years of Age; she hath been married to a person very lately, who pretended he had some means whereby to maintain her, yet was only a Gentleman's Servant, and Service was her best imployment; she denys not the Robbing of her Mistress, but saith her Husband came to her in service for Mony, which was a temptation to commit the Fact to supply him and other bad Company, which she was acquainted with: She saith, it is the

first wrong she hath done to any person, and if she may obtain a Pardon, she resolves to live honestly and justly for the time to come.

Ellenor was hung. It was not a story designed to titillate readers.

When journalists took over criminal biography, things became more colorful. The later publications that were excerpted in the various *Newgate Calendars* included lengthy stories of celebrity pirates like Captain John Kidd, or professional thiefs like Jenny Diver, or of those who murdered their lovers. Such characters were demonized rather than converted.

Sensationalism is a constant temptation for publishers who must sell one edition after another. And it was not long before England seemed to be in the grip of a crime wave. As one historian notes, "In 1712 the violent activities of a gang of upper-class hooligans, the Mohocks, were almost entirely a 'media-event,' the result of a sudden panic in the Tory press."[35] As another has put it "To judge impressionistically from newspaper reports of robberies committed, highway robbery was at an epidemic level for much of the period. . . . On the other hand John Wesley testified that he had travelled hundreds of thousands of miles all over England by day and by night and was never stopped by a highwayman."[36] Guarding the moral boundaries of society was no longer done by clergymen, with a message of moral reformation, but by journalists who created audience revulsion by surrealism.

Another group—women—presented a puzzle for editors. While women's interests and contributions were often encouraged and praised, Kathryn Shevelow thinks that the new periodicals had the effect of circumscribing women's approved roles. The situation was paradoxical; periodicals were moving women into the cultural mainstream while confining them to a special social sphere. The approved image of womanhood—which Shevelow believes developed very largely through periodical literature—associated them with "love and romance, matrimony, children, and the household," and with "genteel codes of conduct." An older view—that women were similar to men but inferior—was giving way to an admission of equal strengths, which should be confined to separate spheres. Even women editors joined this campaign.[37]

In short, periodicals were torn between the need to be socially inclusive—appealing to as wide a market as possible—and socially divisive—strengthening readers' self-identification by contrast with groups who were beyond the pale. So long as the focus was on foreign news it had been easy to assume English inclusiveness. As the focus became domestic, periodicals had to look for aliens within the nation's borders. While the club motif encouraged a kind of inclusiveness, caricature and stereotyping strengthened identity through discrimination. Women, criminals, and religious enthusiasts were defined more sharply for news discourse.

So long as the coffeehouse maintained a "public square" it would provide a reality check on social divisions of a primarily literary nature. Coffeehouses represented all elements within English society, to a degree that astonished foreign visitors. But an awareness of the variety of English society may have been more difficult for, say, provincial readers to maintain, if they depended on periodicals for their view of the world.

The very existence of provincial society might be forgotten by those who lived in the media. At one time it had been possible to regard the countryside as the real England, and London as a curiosity. The balance shifted when the gentry began to look to London as their media focus. Periodical newsletters and papers, with their abbreviated sense of society, must have been a major cause of this reversal.

One of the most notable events in the decline of provincial cultures and the growing hegemony of London standards was the establishment of the two great magazines. Magazines, which tried to include a little of everything, overcame the feeling that one was missing out. One did not have to visit London or rub elbows with the coffeehouse bourgeoisie to feel connected. When the *Gentleman's Magazine* was founded in 1731, its editor Edward Cave said that he was doing so because it had become impossible for the average man to keep up. And he had particularly a provincial audience in mind.

Cave's apprenticeship had been spent largely in Norfolk, helping to produce the *Norwich Courant, or Weekly Packet*. A later clerkship in the Post Office taught him the logistics of distribution. He understood his audience and the details of subscriptions and agents, and it was these provincial subscribers who gave him his initial success.[38] Periodicals were their lifeline. Magazines offered a digest of everything being printed, to allow society to keep together. Within a year a syndicate of booksellers created the *London Magazine*—essentially the same magazine—to compete. Readership went beyond anything England had seen before; one estimate had the *Gentleman's Magazine* alone selling fifteen thousand copies in the 1740s.[39]

Prompted by such sensational success, at least sixty magazines were founded in London by 1780, with ten more in Scotland and eleven in Ireland.[40] To compete with the *Gentleman's Magazine* they would have to combine political essays and foreign news, verse and sometimes prose fiction, prices and fair schedules, book notices, bills of mortality, executions, promotions, and marriages, in fifty to sixty double-column pages. For sixpence a month, customers had everything they could have found in a London coffeehouse, including digests of nearly two hundred separate issues of the London papers. Not only the news that should have initiated discussion but the essays which embodied that discussion were brought together for those who just wanted to listen in.

There were, as we have seen, precursors of this higher-order, metamedium. English miscellanies began with Motteux's *Gentleman's Journal* in 1692. There was a gap in the succession until Dunton's *Post-Angel* appeared in 1701, which proved too religious in character to have a universal appeal. At the same time a short-lived monthly, *Memoirs for the Curious* (February 1701), appeared, which specialized in "what Occurs that's Rare, Secret, Extraordinary, Prodigious or Miraculous, through the World, whether in Nature, Art, Learning, Policy or Religion." It was not so interested in breasting the tide of information as in finding a few items that would keep readers diverted. And although the editors insisted that they were not competing with the *Post-Angel*, being "willing to Content Themselves with such Intelligence as can be had by means of Substantial Flesh and Blood," their "occurences" were as "extraordinary" as the *Post-Angel*'s Providences. A weekly, the *Diverting Post, for the Entertainment of Town and Country* (28 October 1704), hung on a little longer—about eight months. It had a narrower concentration—on songs and verse, the news of plays and musical performances, society doings and court news—much of it contributed by women.

The most substantial of the early magazines, the *Monthly Miscellany: or, Memoirs for the Curious* (January 1707) survived until September 1710, finding room for a little of everything—divinity, law, philosophy, mathematics, science, medicine, book news, biography, letters, history, travel, poetry, husbandry and trade, and "reflections" on the news—in thirty pages. Its first issue was launched with a description of a club engaged in discussing religion, in the manner of a "Platonick Supper."

To show how quickly periodical editors were coming to realize their relationship with readers, this first issue featured a list of questions on which the public was invited to submit its "opinion." It was a reversal of the procedure in the *Athenian Mercury* by which the editors rendered judgment on the public's questions. It was now the public that would offer its judgment on questions submitted to it.

> What is the meaning of the word *Raca* in St. Matthew, ch. 5, v.22?
>
> What difficulties appear in the late Act of Parliament concerning Bankrupts, and what is the opinion of the Publick in general in relation to that Act?
>
> What Diseases are incurable?
>
> Who was the best Moral Philosopher?
>
> Whether it were not better to condemn such as are convicted of simple Felony to perpetual Slavery in publick Work-houses, than to take away their lives?

Things were becoming easier for readers, who were being polled for their opinions rather than having to wonder what their own questions might be.

In short, miscellanies or magazines were conscious of a duty to identify their customers' interests, as well as supplying them with information and entertainment. For it was not self-evident what should go into a magazine. Periodicals devoted to foreign intelligence, political news, or scholarly debate had not faced this uncertainty. When the field was as wide as life itself there were decisions to be made. As magazines became more sure of themselves, they would decide for their readers and place a frame around the public mind.

The *British Apollo, or, Curious Amusements for the Ingenious* (13 February 1708) was the last miscellany that continued the older pattern. Twice-weekly for three years it combined two folio pages of answers to readers' questions with a page of verse and another of news and ads. A gap then appeared in this succession during the 1710s and 1720s, decades dominated by historical and political journals and essay-periodicals. So it is fair to say that there was scarcely any real precedent for Edward Cave's magazine when it appeared in January 1731. He had not even begun his apprenticeship when the last of the old miscellanies expired. But he discerned the essential feature of the "magazine" (storehouse), which is that—even more than other periodicals—they are meant to be entertaining. They were also informative, but mainly in that they informed readers of what others were reading.

Of course, all periodicals had a sense of their relationship with readers. When the *London Mercury* began its political career in 1721 it worried that "to render a Journal acceptable to everybody, is one of the most difficult things in nature." Jeremy Black cites similar references from such sober serials as the *Flying Post*, *Mist's Weekly Journal*, and the *London Evening News*. From Motteux's time onward, editors had been fond of complimenting the "taste" of their readers, as if that should guide even the bare provision of information. For, as the *Cirencester Flying Post* (1742) observed, papers were "obliged to conform to the prevalency of fashion . . . and change the scheme of their writings according to the taste of the public." The result was that by 1775, as one reader complained, "the people of this country will not at present read any article in a newspaper longer than a paragraph."[41]

Magazines set the standard for entertainment. the *Gentleman's Magazine* and its imitators did this without being clever or stylish. The ribaldry of Crouch was no longer necessary, or the genius of Steele and Addison, or the vituperation of Trenchard. In Cave's view, readers only needed to be satisfied that they were current with things in London. Indeed "a Work of this Nature, well executed, can hardly fail of pleasing almost all Sorts of Persons."[42] Market dominance meant eschewing the aristocratic pretensions of the old *Gentleman's Journal*, and staying more on a level with the *Athenian Mercury*—pitched at the populace.[43]

The immediate and sustained success of the *Gentleman's Magazine* allows us to take it as an inventory of the mentality produced by a free press. For readers who wanted to keep up, Cave began with some thirty pages of abstracts from the essays of a dozen leading London papers, with an occasional glance at the provincial press. Debates between rival papers could be followed without the suspense of awaiting responses. The style of the better papers, of course, was lost in the abstracting process. And space constraints meant that debates were shortened to the simple presentation of positions taken. Foreign and domestic news was only glanced at, but one could keep abreast of society weddings and promotions in the army, court, and church. Then readers slowed down a bit over several pages of verse and a fairly complete list of books published.

This format changed little over the years, so that we may conclude that readers were satisfied that they were informed. The way that interests were proportioned in the magazines defined the reader's world. It was pardonable to miss news that had not registered with editors, but to be part of fashionable society one needed to be current with the magazines that "everyone" would have read. The monthly schedule successfully adopted by the magazines may even have tempered the notion that each day's political news is all important. Monthly production allowed time for reflection, and edged readers toward an historical perspective. In fact, a claim to that effect was useful when the *London Magazine* argued for an exemption from the tax on newssheets (May 1733): "The true import and meaning of the word news is the return of intelligence, of any kind, by the posts foreign or domestick. But all transactions of a month's standing are, long within that time, recorded in the Secretary of State's Office, then, by the law of nations becomes memorials, and all future recitals of them fall under the proper and only denomination of history."

The job of the first magazines was simplification, entertainment, and reassurance. It was not political excitement or cultural leadership. As the historian of the *Gentleman's Magazine* complains, "The literary essays were too much at the mercy of the interests of the moment."[44] The literature included was reduced to the middle-brow verse of those who could not find publishers elsewhere (and who might even pay editors to include their work).[45] Coverage of science neglected developing fields like physiology, except when they might report on the anatomy of a hermaphrodite. Thus the same historian notes that, in general, "science still appears as the plaything of gentlemen."[46] Reporting religion meant reporting religious controversies, turning spiritual awareness into a matter of theological puzzles and ecclesiastical conflict. Business was summed up in the movement of a few commodity and stock prices. In short, in a world that was becoming too complex to keep track of, periodical publication allowed readers to maintain a certain intellectual confidence.

A nascent "public sphere" was already disbanding after a promising start, as an innovative news industry supplied enough discussion to satisfy its customers. For the discussion encouraged by the coffeehouse, the magazines substituted something more synthetic. Jeremy Black's general comment on the eighteenth-century press is especially appropriate to the magazines: "There was little suggestion of anything to be discussed. Most pieces displayed a certainty that reflected an attitude that the reader would share the suppositions and intentions of the author. . . . [It was] didactic . . . in keeping with the tone adopted for political reflections."[47] It may be that a true public sphere depends on a class of people who have little to do except concern themselves with the affairs of state. The English middle classes had shown that they were indeed interested, but they had private affairs to deal with. Some had to settle for a convenient short-cut.

The magazine was invented with the English provinces in mind, to simulate the coffeehouse society of the metropolis. But in a sense, all England became provincial and dependent after the news revolution. Readers found themselves at the terminus of an information system, rather than at the heart of national debate. John Evelyn, who was at the center of politics, science and religion when in London, was pitifully dependent on the *Gazette* and the *Flying Post* when back on his estate in Surrey. He confided to a friend in 1697 that on "Wednesday and Saturday nights . . . my wife and myself take our turnes to read the packets of all the newes sent constantly from London, which serves us for discourse till fresh newes comes." With that as their window on the world, it is no wonder that his mind was filled with "horrible roberys, high-way men, and murders committed such as never was known in this Nation since Christian reformed: Atheism, Dissensions, profanesse, Blasphemy among all sorts [classes]: portending some signal judgement, if not amended."[48]

Some of Evelyn's rural neighbors may have been satisfied to do without London news, but the inhabitants of the towns provided a market eager for news of the metropolis. The number of towns numbering over ten thousand inhabitants went from seven to forty-nine in the course of the eighteenth century. And for this growing population, "the newspaper was the quintessential accompaniment to urban [i.e., small town] living."[49] By 1723 there were twenty-four provincial papers, filled with London news. After 1737 there were never fewer than thirty, and three times that number had run for a time before stopping.[50] The circulation areas of twenty of these papers covered almost all of England by the 1730s.[51]

Provincial papers may have done more to tie readers to London than to strengthen their own local communities. They served as local notice boards, of course, but avoided trying to mediate local debates. Seeing the stale news that they lifted from the London originals made some townspeople willing to pay the postage to enjoy the London press. By the 1760s over a million newspapers per year were being sent out of London, with over 3 million a year in the 1780s.[52] When the early provincial papers were pressed to fill their space they had depended on readers' contributions. But as the posts became more reliable, budding writers complained that their papers were no longer local. A letter to the *Newcastle Courant* of 3 March 1733 objected that there was no "arena for the Use of such of your Correspondents as have Courage enough to enter the List of Authors."[53]

The English were being spoiled. A news industry promised a world more real, or at least more interesting, than that of the reader's experience. Local culture had a hard time competing with a world portrayed in print, which can lend things an unwarranted significance. London life could itself became provincial, when lived vicariously through magazines. Imagined clubs could help satisfy a need for community, which was all the more intense for its caricature of unpopular figures.

Magazines completed the process by which periodicals could substitute for participation. What had been a medium for interchange became a mechanism for transmitting opinion. Periodicals had promised to keep readers informed, which is, in any real sense, an impossible goal. As they developed, their role become the different one of keeping readers together. When the circulation of the *Gentleman's Magazine* was added to that of the *London Magazine* and their many imitators, they could go far toward defining the nation's consciousness.

THIRTEEN

Living in a Permanent Revolution

We need news for the same reason that we need eyes—
to see where we are going.
—*Rebecca West*

A people without reliable news is, sooner or later,
a people without the basis of freedom.
—*Harold J. Laski*

Quotes like these make us wary of criticizing our news media and watchful of any threat to press freedom. Though we may rail against the bias of editors or incompetence of reporters, we seem unshaken in our conviction that news is vital and part of the natural order. One might, indeed, claim that our society is literally based on a communion in the news. On the other hand, we also have a feeling that modern societies are in some respects dysfunctional. We should consider connecting these two notions.

One problem in our thinking is to assume that news means periodical news and a news industry. As we face a future in which news is likely to be more irregular and gathered to suit individual need, we can begin to gain a perspective on what the commodification of information has meant over the last four centuries. Has the significance or the truth of commercially produced news ranked as high as some other values? And how has the structure of periodical news, quite aside from its content, shaped our minds? For one can resist the ideas one encounters more easily than one can resist the form of the underlying discourse. In facing such questions, reviewing the origins of English journalism offers a fresh perspective. It may also help us to understand why the market for news seems to be declining, even as the industry matures.

Periodicity produced a revolution in consciousness every bit as important as the introduction of printing, though it has gone unnoticed in our histories and even in communications theory. The adoption of weekly and then daily schedules for marketing information began developments the implications of which are still being worked out. Periodicity allowed information to become a business, where it had once been a part of personal relations. News became a product, where it formerly had been an excuse for social interaction. And like all industries, its commitment was to profits, which depended on pleasing customers.

Pleasing customers meant promising change to those who will come back tomorrow. Change is the industry's product. This has not had the unsettling effect on political or economic institutions that it has had on cultural and social values. Indeed, it has been a major contributor to the politicization of modern societies; however it may blast the careers of individual politicians. Once it became safe to deal in politics, the English news industry encouraged political approaches to the entire range of social and cultural questions.

It may be impossible today to recover a sense of the impact that regular, factual, sensible, straightforward news made when it first appeared in printed and affordable form. Before then, news had either been the guarded property of elites, vulgarized in ballads, or dressed up rhetorically in longer "relations." The first newssheets and newsbooks, following one another like clockwork, wiped the haze off the world. To be sure, we have seen humanist scholars and Renaissance playwrights who deplored the rage for news, understanding how it would tip the balance between fact and truth—mere *factum* as against philosophic *verum*. But the enterprise fit in so well with the new factual approaches to law, history, and science that older forms of discourse had trouble competing.

At first, customers received unadorned reports from foreign corantos, something close to the bare bones of military intelligence. The concept of fact and the juxtaposition of multiple items—the essential features of news discourse—did not develop over a period of time but sprang into being with periodicity itself. When the enterprise fell into the hands of a syndicate, an editorial voice was introduced, to harmonize accounts and personalize the product.

With the collapse of government in 1641 came the excitement of reading the diurnal proceedings of a revolutionary Parliament. Soon there was at least one newsbook appearing every day of the week, including Sunday. At first this news was gathered by a single source—Parliament—but it was not long before editors began developing their own domestic sources. And they began editorializing, as periodicals saw the need to choose sides. A whole range of techniques were developed—variety, caricature, statistics, humor, pornography, "human interest," impartiality *or* partiality—to rally readers and create brand loyalty. Competition brought out the energy in newsmen. And an emerging professionalism taught them how to change sides—scandalizing contemporaries and historians alike.

As governments regained control—first the Protectorate and then the Restoration—it seemed wiser not simply to forbid periodical news publication, as had been done once before. News consciousness had become too deeply rooted, and rulers realized that it could be a resource. So they saw that the nation's new addiction was supplied, if only by licensed or official newspapers. The magic of anonymity seemed to add societal authority to an austere product, and censored papers helped frame discussion for an entire generation.

Contemporaries did not dismiss this managed press as readily as historians do; they paid for those papers and even bound the back issues. Meanwhile, the dynamics of periodicity began to work beneath the intentions of official editors. Advertisements personalized the product, associating news reports with a more domestic reality. The government encouraged the publication of Loyal Addresses, only to find that these gave readers a political voice and made the official *Gazette* in some sense their own.

Of course, it was precisely the deficiencies of the official newspapers that encouraged the rapid development of the coffeehouse as a periodical medium. And in retrospect, it seems that the most active period of the coffeehouse in creating an authentic "public sphere" faded with the maturing of the journalistic product. Despite a meager provision of papers, newsletters, and other periodicals, coffeehouse patrons were forced by discussion to transmute them and the available pamphlets and prints into public opinion. Things would be simpler later, when the industry began to supply reflection as well as information. But during the Exclusion Controversy it was the discussion more than the news that was threatening.

Coffeehouse debate threatened more than government, however. News consciousness was a major contributor to the democratic impulse within seventeenth-century society. Demotic judgment devalued traditional elites and standards in literature, science, scholarship, and theology, as well as politics. There was an "anti-intellectual" atmosphere in this displacement of authority, and in the naive invocation of Reason. While science and history clearly needed new directions, theology and philosophy created problems for themselves by adopting the factual discourse that was so natural to news and to the coffeehouse audience.

Critics like Northrup Frye have explained why the language of fact—of representational accuracy—was not appropriate to religion and why news and religion have become locked in a sharpening struggle for our culture's soul. Restoration theologians, recognizing the shift of consciousness, made the mistake of adopting a language of fact, producing what Samuel Johnson termed an "Old Bailey Theology," referring to the central London courts. This meant presenting a brief—on the testimony of the resurrection witnesses or the balance sheet of Providence or the wisdom of cosmic design—to a popular jury that settled matters by the evidence of "sense."[1] But as Frye remarks, a language of myth and metaphor "is the only language with the power to detach us from the world of facts and demonstrations and reasonings, which are excellent things as tools, but are merely idols as objects of trust and reverence."[2] Journalists, for their part, found religion to be newsworthy only when it was freakish or uncharitable, to the point that many were convinced that it is always so.

Philosophy also suffered from the growing dominance of news. The third earl of Shaftesbury, publishing in the earliest years of the eighteenth century, is a fair example of the type of philosopher favored by the spoiled readers of periodicals. He took for his motto

Nothing in the text but what shall be of easy, smooth, and polite reading, without seeming difficulty or hard study: so that the better and gentler rank of painters and artists, the ladies, beaux, courtly gentlemen, and more refined sort of country and town wits, and notable talkers may comprehend, or be persuaded that they comprehend, what is there written in the text.[3]

By contrast with this polite society, Shaftesbury thought that "speculative men" or scholars generally perverted "the original plain principles of humanity" and "common sense." Unlike Locke, he could not help believing in innate ideas, which came to mean whatever his general audience found self-evident. He simply felt that "men's first thoughts . . . are generally better than their second: their natural notions better than those refined by study or consultation with casuists." Thus, "to philosophize, in a just signification, is but to carry good-breeding a step higher."[4] Polite society was now used to being addressed in this manner.

Somewhat later, Samuel Johnson reflected on the situation in which scholarly speculation found itself, wondering at its causes:

An opinion has of late been, I know not how, propagated among us, that libraries are filled only with useless lumber; that men of parts stand in need of no assistance; and that to spend life in poring upon books, is only to imbibe prejudices, to obstruct and embarrass the powers of nature, to cultivate memory at the expence of judgement, and to bury reason under a chaos of indigested learning.[5]

It was a situation encouraged, if not caused, by the anti-intellectualism of the coffee-house, which was better suited to an airing of political issues than to exploring more arcane topics.

The Glorious Revolution of 1688 was, to some extent, aided by the habit of periodicity, even if only embodied in a managed press. Society held together through that change, unlike the experience of 1641. But while the new regime might be grateful for the help afforded, it was not eager to magnify that effect of granting a wider press freedom. Accordingly it closed the papers that were beginning to sprout, except for a couple of monthlies that offered reflection on recent events.

Customers found ways, however, to keep the periodical habit alive during the early 1690s. Frustrated in their desire to resume unlicensed news, publishers began to experiment. Monthly publication fared well in a number of scientific and literary journals. Luckily, the *Athenian Mercury* and its imitators did not deflect working scientists out of the way. By contrast, satisfying newsreaders would have a more profound effect upon literature.

By its nature, a periodical approach to literary issues would mean enlisting on the side of "the moderns" in the emerging culture war. Literary journals naturally assumed that readers wanted to hear of the latest publications. For a generation already schooled in a canon of "classics" this may have created a salutary balance. Subsequent generations, however, might simply ride the surf of current literature, as novelty moved up the scale of artistic values.

Nothing embodied this taste for novelty better than the "novel," which grew out of the news-fact discourse. Those who only learned to read because of the newspapers they found lying about were not schooled in traditional poetry, drama, or scholarship. For them, as J. Paul Hunter dryly remarks, the new literature, whether in news-sheets or novels, "took events and rumors of the street and returned them to the street in printed form."[6] Newsreading habits dictated a new departure in literature, in line with John Dunton's "Athenianism" rather than Swift and Pope's "Augustanism." Swift's *Tale of a Tub* and Pope's *Dunciad* labored to discredit the new culture by exhibiting it in the context of earlier standards. Their education had encouraged them to see things whole and to work to achieve balance. They reveled in the pleasure of words and the rhythm of reading. But novelists, like journalists, concentrated on experience and immediacy, on novelty and surprise. Novelistic fiction eventually produced its own works of distinction, but has apparently failed to discipline its public in the literary habit.

This may have to do with the fact that published news has itself became an art form. The more that literary critics now speak of the character of "texts," the more we can see "the news" as having this self-referential quality. Just as novelistic texts are not exhausted by reference to raw experience but gain meaning and force by self-reference, so periodicals set up echoes to increase their resonance. Contemporaries were not unaware of such intratextuality; the *Grub-Street Journal* existed for the sole purpose of parodying the press. In other words, it recognized the conventions developing within a supposedly transparent medium.[7] For early editors could not help trying to give their periodicals a particular personality, despite the idea that news is not art but simple reality.

Steele and others of the old school made a game of getting in their readers' way, defeating attempts to treat the news as transparent. A regular parody of journalism would keep alive the realization that "the news" had become the master text, as argued earlier. For we are all too apt to think of it as the world itself, like a myth that contains all the possible stories. But like the Bible before it, news became a master narrative for everyone from illiterates to philosophers, regardless of how people personally *felt* about it.

Social philosophers caution us to be conscious, if not suspicious, of whatever serves as our metanarrative. Periodical news doubtless seemed liberating in a culture that confined thought under archetypes and other tropes. But the news would shortly have to develop its own habits if it were to make its news world familiar. So while it freed minds from certain static conventions of truth, it created dynamic conventions that form the rules of modern thinking.

There are two dangers in this. One is for the news to insinuate its own conventions, for as Peter Dahlgren observes, news can "create meaning independent of the specific events to which the stories refer." For example, we do not think to be suspicious of the politicizing effect of the front page, and of periodical news per se. Such tendencies are impossible to resist when they are structural and hence invisible, when news is better seen as socialization than as information.[8]

The other danger is its ability to silence other viewpoints. Alvin Gouldner calls attention to the fact that the news' "silences generate a kind of 'underprivileged' social reality . . . unworthy of attention."⁹ Oddly enough, the news industry can be a force of censorship in modern societies. Censorship goes deeper than the effort to keep certain books—already published—from being purchased for public libraries or assigned in the classroom. Properly speaking, it is deciding what should be published at all, so that it follows that only publishers can censor. Periodicals need not tell us of the books suppressed, since they never appear. And by misapplying the accusation of censorship, journalists appear to side with forward thinking and against mere convention. Being on the side of the future has always been the pride of editors, as when one boldly pronounced in 1756 that "persecution is the fate of all reformers; and from this, the authors of the *Critical Review* would have been sorry to find themselves altogether exempted."¹⁰ But from the first, they have exercised censorship by freezing books out of their review process, as unworthy of attention. In the words of A. J. Liebling, "Freedom of the press is guaranteed only to those who own one."¹¹

With news serving as the basic text—shaping and censoring our views—the position of what we used to call "culture" is problematical. For it is questionable whether anything could promote both culture and politics. The word "culture" is related to agriculture, after all, and is associated with slow growth; politics is the application of power to problems (or just issues) that have not been resolved by other processes. James Carey, in explaining a cultural theory of communications media, observes that at one time "society existed not only *by* art, religion, ritual, language; society existed *in* these forms of life." Nowadays, culture may be the *subject* of politics, rather than its base.¹² In the place of cultural expectations of a relative stability—allowing individuals the time to find a balance—everything becomes a matter of decision. Process might be defined as that which is too slow to attract journalistic attention.

When something becomes a subject for political action, this might be taken as a sign of failure. That is, society has failed to settle the matter by discussion and agreement, and must settle it by force of numbers. The modern world has adopted a different view, which assumes that society is dignifying an issue by politicizing it. Newspapers developed this view quite early, as Jeremy Black noticed in surveying the journalism of the eighteenth century: "The general thrust of the articles [on social questions] was on the need for action by those holding similar views. . . . The people were defined as a problem and treated as an undifferentiated mass that clung to past habits through superstition, ignorance, irreligion, indolence and folly." Noticing so many problems, newspapers frequently "called for action, the banning of begging and the moving of the poor to workhouses, 'useful necessary and elegant' urban improvements, . . . the setting up of schools 'for instructing indigent blind persons' for useful employment . . . and the adoption of a new method of baking bread for the army." There was no end of improvements that editors could imagine—on crime and slavery, drunkenness and bull-baiting, gambling and dueling, public health measures and taxation schemes—fostering an expectation of something like permanent revolution.[13]

When the weeklies established in the wake of the Stamp Act had to fill their extra space, the easiest thing, apparently, was to turn to political comment. And the first dailies met their frantic schedule by hiring the first reporters to search out news—or to see everything under the guise of news.[14] All of this—the political insistence, the demands of dailiness, and the confrontational tone of the essay periodicals—struck some contemporaries as little short of insane. There were complaints that editors would ruin the country for the sake of selling their papers.[15]

Actually, England's discovery of permanent revolution may have helped to save it from the kind of revolutionary violence that France experienced, and a post-revolutionary hangover. In normal times, however, politics may work better if it is not driven by a periodical schedule, for the convenience of publishers. Peter Golding argues that it is the periodical nature of news that makes structure and process invisible. And if periodical sales require personalizing the news, bureaucracy is ignored despite its enormous importance. Process cannot really be covered by a medium concentrating on the interruptions in the flow of life.

In the absence of a broader understanding of power and process—which one might begin to find in books—the news view of the world is incoherent.[16] After studying the coverage of the radicalism of the 1960s, Todd Gitlin concluded that daily news is "the novel event, not the underlying, enduring condition; the person, not the group; the visible conflict, not the deep consensus; the fact that advances the story, not the one that explains or enlarges it." As a result, he complained, the media has become the main instrument for blunting any reform of economic or political structures.[17] But "reform" would be a mild word for what was happening to other areas of life and thought at the time.

Thus a news consciousness promotes something like a permanent revolution in culture—including political culture—by contrast with firmer control in the commercial and bureaucratic base. Basic political and economic institutions are assumed by the news industry—which is part of both—while it churns a nation's cultural and social values. As Mitchell Stephens has put it, the news leads to the extinction of cultures as other technologies have led to the extinction of species.[18]

One might demand at this point whether a polemical critique of such an essential element of modern life as daily news makes any sense. Would we want to risk turning the clock back in some misguided search for a Golden Age of wisdom and social harmony? Isn't it precisely our mass media that have created the present atmosphere of relative enlightenment? Are modern societies even possible without published news, whatever its shortcomings? Wouldn't closing it down, if that were possible, plunge the world back into a Dark Age of superstition, witch-burnings, Inquisition, anti-Semitism, tyranny, disease and filth?

In the first place, one could be against periodical news—the industrial product—without being against news. We only assume that it must march along at a pace set for commercial purposes. Really important news, which is still privately transmitted, is still irregular. And the notion that our newspapers are really keeping us "informed" about the 180-odd nations of the world is too childish to deserve comment. Second, we are only trying to suggest why the news business is already in free fall. Per capita newspaper consumption has fallen steadily for decades, in all western countries. And evening news broadcasts seem to be dwindling to a single story for the day. If the remaining customers are not puzzled by the world, it is because they are almost entirely ignorant of its unimaginable variety.

Third, one might reflect that the Dark Ages have little to teach moderns about human misery. Centuries from now students may learn that our twentieth century was incomparably the most murderous century in history, a time of unimaginable ideological and world wars, of governments that slaughtered their own populations, of Holocaust, of quite unprecedented levels of torture, homelessness, abandonment, and pollution. We are too fond of contrasting our priviledged niche in this century with the most negative possible view of earlier ones. Indeed, inhabitants of the future will only need to watch reruns of our news to be convinced that it was the worst of times. If there is a lament in all this, it is not for a time that was, but for a time that might have been—not distorted by a giddy politics, puerile culture, and irresponsible social relations.

Shortly before making the first presentation of some of this material, a reporter who had seen my title called to ask whether I could summarize it briefly—in a couple of sentences, perhaps. Nothing simpler, I said; it amounts to the idea that one cannot summarize anything as complex as an idea or an event in a couple of sentences, and that the reason we don't realize this is because of an enormous change in consciousness which we could call the News Revolution.

Were we to proceed with a journalistic review of the study, the generalizations would seem too pat to be quite true. But we would have to begin with the fact that publishers found steady profits in the periodical publication of nothing more than the most ordinary information. As a result, a new mentality spread among those who did not balance weekly and later daily news with anything more substantial. The result of this "market press" was the politicization of life, to the detriment of something we have called culture. And society was divided by the new media as much as it was bonded—unless it is possible to be bonded by conflict. Readers became oriented toward the future, to the neglect of the resources of the past.

We have not tried to assess the other social and political factors that contributed to a new consciousness—class formation, urbanization, state development, literacy, and schooling. These have attracted study before, unlike periodicity. Of course, the notion of a news consciousness would be enriched by considering the relation of these other, more familiar themes.

Naturally, a news editor would insist that we go on to give some hint of what is coming next. Has the News Revolution run its course, and if so, what will the communications system of the future look like? Historians can see no further than others, but we all expect a fragmentation of the increasingly passive audience of our "consciousness industry." There will likely be some shift from the supply-side economics of the old media toward a demand side, with information becoming more irregular and user-specific.[19]

But a communication system is not just about the transmission of information. A "medium" is that which lies in the middle and fosters exchange. We have seen evidence that seventeenth-century periodicals were media in this sense; readers found ways of making their thoughts known to editors. But as the industry matured it began to produce a news mechanism rather than news media. The flow began to go only one way. That will not be so possible in the future, as customers are able to exercise much greater choice.

But humanity is social. If the past is any guide, people will want to maintain communication and hear common stories. They may still want something delivered every day so that they can feel connected. It won't have to be the "World News." If we were wise, we would arrange to have a book thrown in our driveway every few days. More realistically, we could continue to subscribe to a daily package of ads and announcements, how-to advice and local human interest, sports and comics, which is most of what we are getting now. At any time, of course, there could be a flurry of "extras" when something was actually happening—a serious development that we wanted to follow daily. That wouldn't be every month, or necessarily every year. These issues could be derived from the same press releases that we see rewritten for us nowadays. But we would have given up the quite unrealistic goal of being "informed" about the whole world—the illusion of omniscience, which the industry is happy to encourage.

A growing number of people have already moved into this new world, though they may be too embarrassed to admit that they are shirking the duty to follow the day's lead story. They need to be encouraged to find other ways of exploring their world. If they got a feel for solid information or knowledge, say through books, the inadequacy of periodical reportage would become too painfully apparent. An ideal future would be one in which the present proportions were reversed, where people read anthropology, political philosophy, poetry, biology, biography, gardening, or the history of rock music—and a few news reports as appropriate. We might recover something of the situation in which Francis Bacon found himself, when he could reflect from his own experience that "reading maketh a full man, conference a ready man, and writing an exact man."[20]

We can probably look forward to a more diverse future, with the problems involved in that condition. Some will continue to look to the surviving media for the excitement of the day. But there is a younger generation that is convinced that no effort is needed in keeping informed if a few television headlines will do the job. Others have allowed their cynicism about the news industry to justify an open identification with marginal cultures rather than the putative common discourse. And some will respond to the failures of the news industry by efforts to inform themselves about odd parts of a real world, in preference to keeping current with a mythic one. Local communities may actually benefit from opting out of a pseudo-public. They might at first feel the same uneasiness that Albert Einstein admitted, who seemed to have the daily news in mind when he reflected that "I am almost ashamed to be living in such peace while all the rest struggle and suffer. But after all, it is still best to concern oneself with eternals, for from them alone flows that spirit that can restore peace and serenity to the world of humans."[21]

Notes

CHAPTER ONE

1. See Denis McQuail, *Mass Communication Theory: An Introduction*, 2d ed. (London: Sage, 1987), 204–7, for the most notable attempts at definition, all of which view news as a kind of knowledge or event—rather than phenomenologically, as a product.

2. Benedict Anderson, *Imagined Communities: Reflections on the Origin and Spread of Nationalism* (London: Verso, 1983), 39.

3. Gaye Tuchman, *Making News: A Study in the Construction of Reality* (New York: Free Press, 1978), 164.

4. See Richard D. Brown, *Knowledge is Power: The Diffusion of Information in Early America, 1700–1865* (New York: Oxford University Press, 1989), 25–28, for an early example.

5. Marshall McLuhan, *The Gutenberg Galaxy: The Making of Typographical Man* ([1962] New York: New American Library, 1969); Elizabeth L. Eisenstein, *The Printing Press as an Agent of Change* (Cambridge: Cambridge University Press, 1979).

6. McQuail, *Mass Communication Theory*, 9.

7. Jürgen Habermas, *The Theory of Communicative Action* (Boston: Beacon, 1984–87), 2:391, speaks of a "professional code of journalism" and its obligations and mission, as if he would accept news if such standards were more conscientiously applied. He describes the early years of the English periodical press as something of a high point of "communicative action," from which later development declined, but without suggesting that the economic dynamics of periodicity was itself responsible (*The Structural Transformation of the Public Sphere* (Cambridge, Mass.: MIT Press, 1989), 32–43. Nicholas Garnham, "The Media and the Public Sphere," in Craig Calhoun, ed., *Habermas and the Public Sphere* (Cambridge, Mass.: MIT Press, 1992), 361, also sees the issue in terms of who has access to the news media, rather than how periodicity shapes the product.

8. Alvin Gouldner, *The Dialectic of Ideology and Technology: The Origins, Grammar, and Future of Ideology* (New York: Seabury, 1976), 107–10, cf. 123f. See Edward S. Herman and Noam Chomsky, *Manufacturing Consent: The Political Economy of the Mass Media*

(New York: Pantheon, 1988), 2; and Todd Gitlin, *The Whole World is Watching: Mass Media in the Making and Unmaking of the New Left* (Berkeley: University of California, 1980), 251–53, for similar critiques.

9. See McQuail's discussion of media theories in *Mass Communication Theory*, 51–106.

10. Max Horkheimer and Theodor W. Adorno, *Dialectic of Enlightenment* ([1944] New York: Herder and Herder, 1972), 134.

11. Daniel Bell, *The Cultural Contradictions of Capitalism* (New York: Basic, 1976), 33–37.

12. See Jacques Ellul, *Humiliation of the Word* ([1981] Grand Rapids, Mich.: William B. Eerdmans, 1985), 196f, and *The Technological Society* ([1954] New York: Random House, 1964). In *Propaganda: The Formation of Men's Attitudes* ([1962] New York: Knopf, 1965), 145, he says that daily news creates an "incoherent, absurd and irrational" world, which seems "catastrophic" in concentrating on "trouble, danger and problems," and which suggests the need for political responses. He seems to imply that this is an aberration and does not suggest that journalism is therefore an illegitimate enterprise. See also Brendan Dooley, "From Literary Criticism to Systems Theory in Early Modern Journalism History," *Journal of the History of Ideas* 51 (1990): 461–86.

13. Michael Harris, "The Management of the London Newspaper Press During the Eighteenth Century," *Publishing History* 4 (1978): 96–112; idem, "Periodicals and the Book Trade," in Robin Myers and Michael Harris, eds., *Development of the English Book Trade, 1700–1899* (Oxford: Oxford Polytechnic Press, 1981), 69–76; Robert Munter, *The History of the Irish Newspaper, 1685–1760* (Cambridge: Cambridge University Press, 1967), 37.

14. Wolfgang Iser, *Prospecting: From Reader Response to Literary Anthropology* (Baltimore: Johns Hopkins University Press, 1989), 10–15.

15. Nor did his mentor, Harold Innes, even in his *Changing Concepts of Time* (Toronto: University of Toronto Press, 1952). Innes did worry that the mass media, which created the public, would eventually threaten the possibility of public life and rational discourse, by doing our thinking for us, monopolizing discussion, and suppressing freedom of expression. See James W. Carey, *Communication as Culture: Essays on Media and Society* (Cambridge, Mass.: Unwin Hyman, 1988), 145, 163–67.

16. Marshall McLuhan, *Understanding Media: The Extensions of Man* (New York: McGraw-Hill, 1964), 204–7.

17. Marshall McLuhan, *The Mechanical Bride* (Boston: Beacon, 1951), 3f.

18. Roland Barthes, "Structures of the *Fait-Divers*" in *Critical Essays* ([1962] Evanston: Northwestern, 1972), 185–95. See chapter 11 for further discussion of Barthes's analysis.

19. Peter Golding, "The Missing Dimensions—News Media and the Management of Social Change," 70–80, and Gaye Tuchman, "Myth and the Consciousness Industry: A New Look at the Effects of the Mass Media," 91, in Elihu Katz and Tamas Szecskoe, *Mass Media and Social Change* (London: Sage, 1981).

20. Gitlin, *The Whole World is Watching*, 271–82, describes such a news paradigm, which he calls "the dominant hegemonic principles."

21. Peter Dahlgren, "TV News and the Suppression of Reflexivity," in Katz and Szeckoe, *Mass Media and Social Change*, 103–9.

22. See Hayden White, *The Content of the Form: Narrative Discourse and Historical Representation* (Baltimore: Johns Hopkins University Press, 1987), 21–23, on narrative closure.

23. Bell, *Cultural Contradictions of Capitalism*, 48.

24. C. John Sommerville, *The Secularization of Early Modern England: From Religious Culture to Religious Faith* (New York: Oxford, 1992), 182–85.

25. Northrop Frye, *The Double Vision: Language and Meaning in Religion* (Toronto: University of Toronto, 1991), 14–18.

26. Susanne K. Langer, *Philosophy in a New Key* ([1942] New York: New American Library, 1948), 227.

27. Ibid., 228–32.

28. Ibid., 234–36.

29. Ibid., 235.

30. Hans W. Frei, *The Eclipse of Biblical Narrative* (New Haven: Yale, 1974), 51.

31. Roland Barthes, *Mythologies*, trans. Annette Lavers (London: Jonathan Cape, 1973). In finding examples of myth in modern times, Barthes uses *Paris-Match*, *France-Soir*, *L'Express*, *Elle*, *Le Figaro* (116, 130, 149f).

32. S. Elizabeth Bird and Robert W. Dardenne, "Myth, Chronicle, and Story: Exploring the Narrative Qualities of News," in James W. Carey, ed., *Media, Myths, and Narratives: Television and the Press* (Newbury Park, Calif.: Sage, 1988), 67–86; Stuart Hall, "The Narrative Structure of Reality," *Southern Review* (Adelaide) 17 (1984), 3–17: "We make an absolutely too simple and false distinction between narratives about the real and the narratives of fiction," that is, between news and adventure stories (6). James W. Carey, "A Cultural Approach to Communication," *Communication* 2 (1975): 1–22; Robert Rutherford Smith, "Mythic Elements in Television News," *Journal of Communication* 29, no. 2 (1979): 75–82; Graham Knight and Tony Dean, "Myth and the Structure of News," *Journal of Communication* 32, no. 2 (1982): 144–61; Tom Koch, *The News as Myth: Fact and Context in Journalism* (New York: Greenwood, 1990).

33. See note 13 above.

34. Harris, "Periodicals and the Book Trade," 69–76; idem, "The Structure, Ownership and Control of the Press, 1620–1780," in George Boyce, James Curran, Pauline Wingate, eds., *Newspaper History from the Seventeenth Century to the Present Day* (London: Constable, 1978), 92–94; Anthony Smith, *The Newspaper: An International History* (London: Thames and Hudson, 1979), 61; cf. Michael Schudson, *Discovering the News: A Social History of American Newspapers* (New York: Basic Books, 1978), 93–98.

35. *Daily Courant*, 11 March 1702.

36. G. A. Cranfield, *The Development of the Provincial Newspaper, 1700–1760* (Oxford: Clarendon, 1962), 86f, 105; Gilbert D. McEwen, *The Oracle of the Coffee House: John Dunton's Athenian Mercury* (San Marino, Calif.: Huntington Library, 1972), 164.

37. Jack Goody, ed., *Literacy in Traditional Societies* (Cambridge: Cambridge University Press, 1968), 67. This should be considered in connection with the concept of "secondary orality," suggested by Walter J. Ong in *Orality and Literacy: The Technologizing of the Word* (London: Methuen, 1982), 136.

38. *Freeholder*, 23 March 1716.

39. Anthony Smith, *The Newspaper*, 61.

40. G. A. Cranfield, *The Press and Society: From Caxton to Northcliffe* (London: Longman, 1978), 32.

41. Ralph Straus, *The Unspeakable Curll* (London: Chapman and Hall, 1928), 26–32, 85, 102.

42. Thomas C. Leonard, *The Power of the Press: The Birth of American Political Reporting* (New York: Oxford, 1986), 28.

43. Straus, *Unspeakable Curll*, 128f.

44. Anon., *The Case of the Coffee—Men of London and Westminster* (London: G. Smith, 1729), 5; Mitchell Stephens, *A History of News: From the Drum to the Satellite* (New York: Viking, 1988), 234; James Sutherland, *The Restoration Newspaper and its Development* (Cambridge: Cambridge University Press, 1986), 32.

45. Henry Fielding, *The History of Tom Jones; A Foundling* ([1749] New York: New American Library, 1963), 64.

46. Laurence Hanson, *Government and the Press, 1695–1763* (Oxford: Clarendon, 1936), 118f.

CHAPTER TWO

1. Stephens, *History of News*, 14; H. S. Bennett, *English Books and Readers, 1603–1640* (Cambridge: Cambridge University Press, 1970), 179–89.

2. Stephens, *History of News*, 29, 44; McQuail, *Mass Communication Theory*, 206.

3. Ithiel de Sola Pool, "The Mass Media and Their Interpersonal Social Functions in the Process of Modernization," in Lewis Anthony Dexter and David Manning White, eds., *People, Society and Mass Communications* (New York: Free Press, 1964), 433–35.

4. Daniel Lerner, *The Passing of Traditional Society* (Glencoe: Free Press, 1958), 178, 190, 234, 317, 321–25, 330f, 337.

5. Stephens, *History of News*, 23, 56f.

6. Ibid., 87f; M. A. Shaaber, *Some Forerunners of the Newspaper in England, 1476–1622* ([1929] New York: Octagon, 1966), 11f, 63–130, 203.

7. Ibid., 295–97, 241.

8. Lennart J. Davis, *Factual Fictions: The Origins of the English Novel* (New York: Columbia University Press, 1983), 46–72.

9. Quoted in J. G. Muddiman ("J. B. Williams"), *A History of English Journalism to the Foundation of the Gazette* (London: Longmans, Green, 1908), 5.

10. Stephens, *History of News*, 72.

11. Ibid., 76f; George T. Matthews, ed., *News and Rumor in Renaissance Europe (The Fugger Newsletters)* (New York: Capricorn, 1959), 17–21.

12. Fernand Braudel, *The Mediterranean and the Mediterranean World of Philip II* (New York: Harper and Row, 1972), 365.

13. Brown, *Knowledge is Power*, 277, 25–28, 39.

14. Ben Jonson, *The Staple of News*, ed. Anthony Parr (Manchester: Manchester University Press, 1988), 23; Shaaber, *Some Forerunners of the Newspaper*, 168.

15. Anthony Smith, *The Newspaper*, 9f.

16. D. C. Collins, *A Handlist of News Pamphlets, 1590–1610* (London: South-West Essex Technical College Press, 1943), lists 462 for that twenty-year period.

17. Ibid., xiii–xvii.

18. Shaaber, *Some Forerunners of the Newspaper*, 138–46.

19. Ibid., 181f; Stephens, *History of News*, 92f.

20. Shaaber, *Some Forerunners of the News*, 199f, 228.

21. Ibid., 301, 310f; Stephens, *History of News*, 149f; Eric W. Allen, "International Origins of the Newspapers: The Establishment of Periodicity in Print," *Journalism Quarterly* 7 (1930): 313–19; Joseph Frank, *The Beginnings of the English Newspaper* (Cambridge, Mass.: Harvard, 1966), 2.

22. Stephens, *History of News*, 59.

23. Robert E. Park, "News as a Form of Knowledge," *American Journal of Sociology* 45 (1940): 675–77.

24. McLuhan, *Understanding Media*, 204–7.

25. McQuail, *Mass Communication Theory*, 9f.

26. Ong, *Orality and Literacy*, 74f, 102, 136, 176–79.

27. Frank, *Beginnings of English Newspapers*, 7–9.

28. Folke Dahl, *Bibliography of English Corantos and Periodical Newsbooks, 1620–1642* (London: Bibliographical Society, 1952), 31–41; Cranfield, *Press and Society*, 6; Frank, *Beginnings of the English Newspaper*, 3, 8f.

29. Dahl, *Bibliography of English Corantos*, 51–54; Cranfield, *Press and Society*, 6; Fredrick Seaton Siebert, *Freedom of the Press in England, 1476–1776* (Urbana: University of Illinois Press, 1952), 151.

30. Leona Rostenberg, *Literary, Political, Scientific, Religious, and Legal Publishing, Printing, and Bookselling in England, 1551–1700* (New York: Burt Franklin, 1965), 1:76–83.

31. Stanley Morison, *The English Newspaper* (Cambridge: Cambridge University Press, 1932), 13.

32. Stephens, *History of News*, 159.

33. Dahl, *Bibliography of English Corantos*, 55–85.

34. Ibid., 86–113.

35. Matthias Shaaber, "The History of the First English Newspaper," *Studies in Philology* 29 (1932): 568.

36. Cranfield, *Press and Society*, 6.

37. Shaaber, "History of the First English Newspaper," 565f.

38. Morison, *English Newspaper*, 13.

39. *An Abstract of Some Speciall Forreigne Occurances* (London: printed for Nathaniel Butter and Nicholas Bourne, 20 December 1638), sig. A3.

40. Mark Eccles, "Thomas Gainsford, 'Captain Pamphlet,'" *Huntington Library Quarterly* 45 (1982): 259–70.

41. 19 March 1624, quoted in Shaaber, "History of the First English Newspaper," 582.

42. 20 November 1623, 24 February 1624, quoted in Ibid., 581.

43. 26 July 1622, quoted in Dahl, *Bibliography of English Corantos*, 73.

44. 16? July 1630, quoted in Ibid., 167.

45. Rostenberg, *Publishing, Printing, and Bookselling*, 1:87.

46. Siebert, *Freedom of the Press*, 157.

47. Contrast this attitude with that of the French government. M. Solomon, *Public Welfare, Science, and Propaganda in Seventeenth-Century France* (Princeton: Princeton University Press, 1972), 118–60.

48. Dahl, *Bibliography of English Corantos*, 22; Cranfield, *Press and Society*, 8; Michael Frearson, "The Distribution and Readership of London Corantos in the 1620s," in Robin Myers and Michael Harris, eds., *Serials and Their Readers, 1620–1914* (New Castle, Del.: Oak Knoll, 1993), 1–25.

49. Quoted in Richard Cust, "News and Politics in Early Seventeenth-Century England," *Past and Present* 112 (1986); 70.

50. Robert Burton, *The Anatomy of Melancholy* ([1621] New York: Random, 1977), 1:18f.

51. Ibid., 2:81.

52. Ibid., 2:199f.

53. Quoted in Cranfield, *Press and Society*, 8.

54. Quoted in Frearson, "Distribution and Readership of London Corantos," 7.

55. 13 December 1623, quoted in Shaaber, "History of the First English Newspaper," 576.

56. Jonson, *Staple of News*, "To the Readers"; I, v, 62; I, ii, 22–28, 34–36, 50–52, 65–66; I, v, 85, 48–54; "Intermean," 37–40; III, ii, 161. Some of the same points are made in Jonson's earlier *News from the New World Discovered in the Moon* (1620).

57. Richard Brathwait, *Whimzies; Or, a New Cast of Characters* (London: Ambrose Rithirdon, 1631), 12–22.

58. John Davies, *A Scovrge for Paper Persecutors . . . with a continu'd inquisition by A[braham] H[olland]* (London: for H. H., 1625), 24f.

59. Anthony Parr, in Jonson, *Staple of News*, 23.

60. 9 January 1640, quoted in Siebert, *Freedom of the Press*, 160.

61. 23 April 1640, quoted in Shaaber, "History of the First English Newspaper," 585.

62. Dahl, *Bibliography of English Corantos*, 221–23, 242, 251.

63. Rostenberg, *Publishing, Printing, and Bookselling*, 1:87–96; Sheila Lambert, "Coranto Printing in England: The First Newsbooks," *Journal of Newspaper and Periodical History* 8 (1992): 13.

CHAPTER THREE

1. Morison, *English Newspaper*, 29.

2. Carolyn Nelson and Matthew Seccombe, *British Newspapers and Periodicals, 1641–1700; A Short-Title Catalogue of Serials Printed in England, Scotland, Ireland, and British America* (New York: Modern Language Association of America, 1987).

3. Muddiman, *English Journalism*, vii–viii.

4. Frank, *Beginnings of the English Newspaper*, 23; Peter Fraser, *The Intelligence of the Secretaries of State and their Monopoly of Licensed News, 1660–1688* (Cambridge: Cambridge University Press, 1956), 20.

5. Carolyn Nelson and Matthew Seccombe, *Periodical Publications, 1641–1700: A Survey with Illustrations* (London: Bibliographical Society, 1986), 20f.

6. Frank, *Beginnings of the English Newspaper*, 24.

7. Ibid., 41, 68.

8. Ibid., 268f.

9. Ibid., 26, 33.

10. Ibid., 43, 146.

11. Morison, *English Newspaper*, 16.

12. Ibid., 97f.

13. Ibid., 22f, 27.

14. Ibid., 25f.

15. Ibid., 79.

16. Ibid., 42–44.

17. Ibid., 27.

18. Frank, *Beginnings of the English Newspaper*, 68–70; Michael McKeon, *The Origins of the English Novel, 1600–1740* (Baltimore: Johns Hopkins University Press, 1987), 49; see Nelson and Seccombe, *Periodical Publications*, 27, for the practice of selling bound series of newsbooks as historical chronicles.

19. Frank, *Beginnings of the English Newspaper*, 41, 46, 64, 90, 155.

20. P. W. Thomas, *Sir John Berkenhead, 1617–1679: A Royalist Career in Politics and Polemics* (Oxford: Clarendon, 1969), 56f.

21. Ibid., 60; *Mercurius Britanicus*, 19 September 1643.

22. Thomas, *Berkenhead*, 35.

23. Ibid., 38, 90.

24. Frank, *Beginnings of the English Newspaper*, 58.

25. Joseph Frank, *Cromwell's Press Agent: a Critical biography of Marchamont Nedham, 1620–1678* (Lanham, Md.: University Press of America, 1980), 13–21; Thomas, *Berkenhead*, 17.

26. Frank, *Nedham*, 16–24, 28.

27. Ibid., 26; Thomas, *Berkenhead*, 95.

28. Frank, *Nedham*, 27.

29. Ibid., 28.

30. Ibid., 29.

31. Ibid., 40–43.

32. Ibid., 45–47.

33. Ibid., 54, 61–63.

34. Ibid., 64, 107.

35. Cust, "News and Politics," 60–90.

36. Frank, *Nedham*, 42, 88, 105–7.

37. Ibid., 91, 102.

38. Ibid., 78–85.

39. E. A. Wrigley, "A Simple Model of London's Importance in Changing English Society and Economy, 1650–1750," *Past and Present* 37 (1967): 44.

40. Frank, *Beginnings of the English Newspaper*, 54–57, 113; E. S. Chalk, "Circulation of XVIII-Century Newspapers," *Notes and Queries* 169 (1935): 336, gives the case of an eighteenth-century newspaper which regularly went through fifteen hands.

41. Anon., *Character of a Coffee House* (London: Jonathan Edwin, 1673), 1.

42. *City Mercury*, 20 March 1694.

43. Donald Coleman, *The British Paper Industry, 1495–1860* (Oxford: Clarendon, 1958), 172f.

44. Muddiman, *English Journalism*, 2, 182f, 192, 196.

45. Ibid., 34, 39.

46. Ibid., 83.

47. J. C. [John Cleveland], *A Character of a Diurnal-Maker* (London: n.p., 1654), 1–3; idem, *The Character of a London-Diurnall: With Several select Poems* (London: n.p., 1647), 1–6.

48. John Cleveland, *The Character of Mercurius Politicus* (n.p., 1650), 2.

49. Siebert, *Freedom of the Press*, 196f.

50. Frank, *Nedham*, 88.

51. Siebert, *Freedom of the Press*, 227.

CHAPTER FOUR

1. *Letters of the Lady Brilliana Harley*, Camden Society Publications, 58 (1854), 19, 32, 69.

2. *Memoirs of the Verney Family During the Civil War*, ed. Frances Parthenope Verney (London: Longmans, Green, 1892), 2:82.

3. *Mercurius Politicus* 20 June 1650.

4. *Scotish Dove* 10 November 1643.

5. See the issues of *Moderate Intelligencer* for 3 April, 19 May, and 3 July 1645.

6. *Mercurius Aulicus*, 8 January 1643.

7. *Mercurius Aulicus*, 29 January 1643.

8. *Mercurius Britanicus*, 19 September 1643; 26 September 1643; 5 September 1643; *Mercurius Politicus*, 13 June 1650.

9. *Mercurius Politicus*, 13 June 1650.

10. *Moderate Intelligencer*, 31 July 1645.

11. [John Cleveland], *The Character of a Moderate Intelligencer* (n.p., [1647?]), 4.

12. *Perfect Diurnall of the Passages in Parliament*, 2 November 1642.

13. *Mercurius Aulicus*, 13 July 1644.

14. Frank, *Beginnings of the English Newspaper*, 164.

15. Thomas, *Berkenhead*, 65–67, 60.

16. *Mercurius Aulicus*, 25 February 1643.

17. *Mercurius Aulicus*, 12 February 1643.

18. Thomas, *Berkenhead*, 94f.

19. Ibid., 160–63, 170.

20. Ibid., 157.

21. Ibid., 92, 102–4, 120f.

22. Ibid., 128f, 145f, 183f, 199, 201f, 263.

23. Ibid., 34.

24. Ibid., 157, 161–63, 170f.

25. Cust, "News and Politics," 73–90.

26. *Hamilton Papers, Relating to the Years 1638–1650*, Camden Society, n.s., 27 (1880), 187f.

27. Adam Eyre, *A Dyurnall, or Catalogue of All My Accions and Expenses from the 1st of January 1646* (–7), Surtees Society 65 (1875): 93, 41.

28. *The Memoirs of Edmund Ludlow* (Oxford: Clarendon, 1894), 1:72.

29. *The Correspondence of Bishop Brian Duppa and Sir Justinian Isham, 1650–1660*, Northamptonshire Record Society, 17 (1955), 8, 77, 93.

30. *Sydney Papers*, ed. R. W. Blencowe (London: John Murray, 1825), 79 (6 August 1649). See also 95.

31. *The Marlborough-Godolphin Correspondence*, ed. Henry L. Snyder (Oxford: Clarendon, 1975), 330, 456, 679, 702, 1594, 1613f.

32. Dahl, *Bibliography of English Corantos*, 125, 135; cf. Blanche B. Elliott, *A History of English Advertising* (London: B. T. Batsford, 1962), 22, 26.

33. Walter Graham, *The Beginnings of English Literary Periodicals* (Oxford: Oxford University Press, 1926), 1; Robert P. McCutcheon, "The Beginnings of Book-Reviewing in English Periodicals," *PMLA*, 37 (1922), 691–706.

34. Frank, *Beginnings of the English Newspaper*, 146, 172, 219, 226.

35. Frank Presbrey, *The History and Development of Advertising* (Garden City: Doubleday, 1929), 42.

36. R. B. Walker, "Advertising in London Newspapers, 1650–1750," *Business History*, 15 (1973), 125.

37. Muddiman, *English Journalism*, 159–69, 184; Frank, *Nedham*, 105.

38. Muddiman, *English Journalism*, 145; quotation from Cranfield, *Press and Society*, 16f.

39. Quotation in Ibid., 17.

40. *Mercurius Bellicus*, 29 November 1647.

41. Frank, *Nedham*, 104.

CHAPTER FIVE

1. E.g., Harold Love, *Scribal Publication in Seventeenth-Century England* (Oxford: Clarendon, 1993), 192.

2. Siebert, *Freedom of the Press*, 228.

3. Frank, *Nedham*, 105–7.

4. Ibid., 123; Thomas, *Berkenhead*, 210.

5. It only lasted a month, February–March, 1660, until the dissolution of that Parliament. The earliest daily on record appeared in Leipzig in 1650, see Stephens, *History of News*, 180.

6. Muddiman, *English Journalism*, 174; idem, *The King's Journalist, 1659–1689* (London: Bodley Head, 1923), 125; Siebert, *Freedom of the Press*, 202–6, 279f.

7. Thomas, *Berkenhead*, 215.

8. Ibid., 218–28.

9. Ibid., 223; Siebert, *Freedom of the Press*, 291–302.

10. Fraser, *Intelligence of the Secretaries of State*, 1–5, 9, 28, 54.

11. *Intelligencer*, 31 August 1663. In his *Considerations and Proposals In Order to the Regulation of the Press* (London: A. C., 1663), L'Estrange did not treat periodical news as representing a different sort of problem within his notion of a national conspiracy against the monarchy, or as requiring special treatment. He cites *Mercurius Britanicus* and *Mercurius Politicus* along with other pamphlets in his examples of actionable publications (12, 15).

12. *The Lauderdale Papers*, Camden Society, n.s. 34 (1884), 1:185f.

13. *The Diary of Samuel Pepys*, ed. Robert Latham and William Matthews (Berkeley: University of California, 1970–83), 4:297.

14. George Kitchin, *Sir Roger L'Estrange* (London: Kegan Paul, Trench, Trubner, 1913), 146.

15. Muddiman, *King's Journalist*, 164f, 173.

16. *Newes*, 14 January 1663.

17. *Newes* 29 December 1664, 18 February 1663.

18. *Newes*, 2 June 1664.

19. *Newes*, 13 October 1664.

20. Kitchin, *L'Estrange*, 147f.

21. *Pepys*, 6:305.

22. P. M. Handover, *A History of the London Gazette, 1665–1965* (London: HMSO, 1965), 11.

23. Muddiman, *King's Journalist*, 178.

24. *Pepys*, 4:297 n.2, 3:35f. Pepys also had the *London Gazette* bound (6:305 n.3).

25. Nelson and Seccombe, *Periodical Publications*, 50–52.

26. Handover, *London Gazette*, 17.

27. C. H. Josten, ed., *Elias Ashmole (1617–1692)*, 4:1359; 3:1049.

28. Barbara Shapiro, "The Concept 'Fact': Legal Origins and Cultural Diffusion," *Albion* 26 (1994): 227–52.

29. Julian Martin, *Francis Bacon, the State, and the Reform of Natural Philosophy* (Cambridge: University Press, 1992), 72, 77f; Francis Bacon, *The Great Instauration*, in *The Works of Francis Bacon*, eds. James Spedding, Robert Leslie Ellis, Douglas Denon Heath (London: Longman, 1857–74), 4:28.

30. Bertrand Russell, *Human Knowledge: Its Scope and Limits* (New York: Simon and Schuster, 1948), 143.

31. Bacon, *Parasceve*, in *Works*, 4:260.

32. Bacon, *De Augmentis*, in *Works*, 4:292.

33. Morison, *English Newspaper*, 31.

34. *Spie, Communicating Intelligence from Oxford*, 30 January 1644.

35. Thomas, *Berkenhead*, 41–47.

36. On the basis of Nelson and Seccombe, *British Newspapers and Periodicals*. This count was suggested by Barbara Shapiro.

37. E.g., Michael MacDonald and Terence R. Murphy, *Sleepless Souls; Suicide in Modern England* (Oxford: Clarendon, 1990), 306, 316; Shapiro, "The Concept 'Fact,'" 238f.

38. John Graunt, *Natural and Political Observations Mentioned in a Following Index, and Made Upon the Bills of Mortality* (London: for John Martin, James Allestry and Thomas Dicas, 1662), 17; Reginald H. Adams, *The Parish Clerks of London* (London: Phillimore, 1971), 51–58.

39. *The Diary of Ralph Josselin, 1616–1683*, ed. Alan Macfarlane (London: British Academy, 1976), 425, 518–32; *The Diary of Samuel Newton*, ed. J. E. Foster, Cambridge Antiquarian Society 23 (1890): 14; E. M. Symonds, ed., "The Diary of John Greene (1635–57)," *English Historical Review* 43 (1928): 599–604.

40. "The Journal of Mr. John Hobson," *Yorkshire Diaries and Autobiographies*, Surtees Society 65 (1875): 319; R. M. Wiles, *Freshest Advices: Early Provincial Newspapers in England* (Columbus: Ohio State University Press, 1965), 344.

41. Graunt, *Natural and Political Observations*, 26; Nelson and Seccombe, *Periodical Publications*, 52.

42. [John Graunt], *London's Dreadful Visitation* (London: E. Cotes, 1666).

43. Adams, *Parish Clerks of London*, 56.

44. See Nelson and Seccombe, *Periodical Publications*, 16, 33.

45. John J. McCusker and Cora Gravensteijn, *The Beginnings of Commercial and Financial Journalism* (Amsterdam: Neha, 1991), 291–352.

46. E. M. Forster, "Anonymity: An Inquiry," *Atlantic* 136 (1925): 594.

47. *London Gazette*, 5 February 1666.

48. *London Gazette*, 14 December 1665.

49. *London Gazette*, 3 May 1666.

50. Thomas St. Serfe, *Tarugo's Wiles: Or, The Coffee House* (London: Henry Herringman, 1668), 26.

51. Ibid., 24f.

52. Walker, "Advertising," 117.

53. The Shrewsbury Papers show the Privy Council deciding what addresses should be put into the *Gazette* at a somewhat later date: *Historical Manuscripts Commission: Report on the Manuscripts of the Duke of Buccleuch and Queensbury*, 2:322f. Mark Knights, *Poli-*

tics and Opinion in Crisis, 1678–81 (Cambridge: Cambridge University Press, 1994), 291–98, and Phillip Harth, *Pen for a Party: Dryden's Tory Propaganda in Its Contexts* (Princeton: Princeton University Press, 1993), consider the importance of loyal addresses and petitions within the context of Exclusion politics.

54. Henry Sidney, *Diary of the Times of Charles the Second*, ed. R. W. Blencowe (London: Henry Colburn, 1843), 1:253.

55. Mark W. Hopkins, *Mass Media in the Soviet Union* (New York: Pegasus, 1970), 303–5; Ellen Propper Mickiewicz, *Media and the Russian Public* (New York: Praeger, 1981), 58–62, 67–70.

56. Hopkins, *Soviet Union*, 318–23; Mickiewicz, *Russia*, 44, 51f.

CHAPTER SIX

1. Park, "News as a Form of Knowledge," 677, my emphasis.

2. Ibid., 683.

3. Gouldner, *Dialectic of Ideology*, 98.

4. See Hugh Baxter, "System and Life-World in Habermas's *Theory of Communicative Action*," *Theory and Society* 16 (1987): 39f.

5. Habermas, *Structural Transformation of the Public Sphere*, 32–42, 159f.

6. Steven Pincus, "'Coffee Politicians Does Create': Coffeehouses and Restoration Political Culture," *Journal of Modern History*, 67(1995), 822–27. See also Aytoun Ellis, *The Penny Universities; A History of the Coffee-Houses* (London: Secker and Warburg, 1956), 49, 57, 86.

7. *Pepys*, 10:70f.

8. Pincus, "Coffee Politicians Does Create," 813f; Ellis, *Penny Universities*, 192.

9. *Coffee-Houses Vindicated* (London: J. Clarke, 1673), 3.

10. *Character of A Coffee-House*, 2; *A Cup of Coffee: Or, Coffee in its Colours* (London: broadside, 1663).

11. *The Diary of Abraham de la Pryme*, Surtees Society 54 (1869): 176.

12. Edward Robinson, *The Early English Coffee House* ([1893]Christchurch: Dolphin, 1972), 202; *The Coffee Scuffle* (London, broadside, 1662); Anon., *News from the Coffee-House* (London: Thomas Vere, 1667); Anon., *A Brief Description of the Excellent Vertues of that Sober and wholesome Drink, called Coffee* (London: Paul Greenwood, 1674).

13. *Coffee-Houses Vindicated*, 3.

14. Pincus, "Coffee Politicians Does Create," 815; Robinson, *English Coffee House*, 110; Ellis, *Penny Universities*, 45f.

15. Bryant Lillywhite, *London Coffee Houses* (London: George Allen and Unwin, 1963).

16. [John Tatham], *Knavery in All Trades: Or, The Coffee-House* (London: W. Gilbertson, 1664).

17. *The Maiden's Complaint Against Coffee* (London: J. Jones, 1663). This was advertised as by "Mercurius Democritus, . . . in the World in the Moon," which, with the obscenity, points to John Crouch.

18. Robinson, *English Coffee House*, 80; Anthony a Wood, *The Life and Times of Anthony Wood*, ed. Andrew Clark (Oxford: Historical Society, 1891–1907), xix, xxiii, lxxix. Only on 3 August 1693 did Wood mention seeing a newspaper, when the *Gazette* reported the public burning of the second volume of his own *Athenae Oxonienses*.

19. Roger North, *The Life of the Honourable Sir Dudley North . . . and Dr. John North* (London: John Whiston, 1744), 249.

20. [John Phillips] *A Pleasant Conference Upon the Observator, and Heraclitus* (London: H. Jones, 1682), 4f.

21. *Character of A Coffee-House*, 2

22. *A Cup of Coffee.*

23. M. P., *A Character of Coffee and Coffee-Houses* (London: John Starkey, 1661), 2–4; *The Women's Petition Against Coffee* (London, 1674), 4.

24. *Character of A Coffee-House*, 1–5.

25. M. P., *Character of Coffee*, 9.

26. Quoted in Robinson, *English Coffee House*, 163.

27. Ibid., 205.

28. Roger North, *Examin: Or, An Enquiry into the Credit and Veracity of a Pretended Complete History* (London: Giles Fletcher, 1740), 141.

29. Quoted by Fraser, *Intelligence of the Secretaries of State*, 119.

30. M. P. *Character of Coffee*, 7.

31. Ibid., 6, 8.

32. Steven Shapin, *A Social History of Truth: Civility and Science in Seventeenth-Century England* (Chicago: University of Chicago Press, 1994), 352f. Shapin does not discuss the fact that periodical discourse constitutes another approach to the matter of truth warrants in factual knowledge.

33. *The Record of the Royal Society of London*, 4th ed. (London: Royal Society, 1940), 4–7.

34. Lillywhite, *London Coffee Houses*, 181, 244. *The Diary of Robert Hooke, 1672–1680*, ed. Henry W. Robinson and Walter Adams (London: Taylor and Francis, 1935), lists 154 coffeehouses and taverns frequented by Hooke and his friends (464–70).

35. *Record of the Royal Society*, 36, 46.

36. Quoted in Margery Purver, *The Royal Society: Concept and Creation* (Cambridge, Mass.: MIT Press, 1967), 73f.

37. David A. Kronick, *A History of Scientific and Technical Periodicals*, 2d ed. (Methuen, N.J.: Scarecrow, 1976), 59–61.

38. Ibid., 261, 268.

39. *Philosophical Transactions*, 5 June 1665, 63.

40. *Philosophical Transactions*, 3 April 1665, 32; 2 July 1666, 91–94; 8 October 1666, 140–43; 12 March 1666, 178.

41. Dorothy Stimson, *Scientists and Amateurs; A History of the Royal Society* (New York: Henry Schuman, 1948), 146.

42. Kronick, *Scientific and Technical Periodicals*, 137, 160.

43. Hooke recorded a price of sixpence for about half the issues and a shilling for the others, which he picked up from the Society's printer (*Hooke*, 7, 12, 26, 34, 45, 49, 67, 79, etc.).

44. Henry Lyons, *The Royal Society, 1660–1940* (Cambridge: Cambridge University Press, 1944), 57; Thomas Birch, *The History of the Royal Society* ([1756–57] New York: Johnson, 1968), 4:171.

45. *Pepys*, 7:405f.

46. Samuel Butler, *Characters*, in *The Genuine Remains in Verse and Prose of Mr. Samuel Butler* (London: J. and R. Tonson, 1759), 2:296.

47. Howard Robinson, *The British Post Office* (Princeton: Princeton University Press, 1948), 45, 54f.

48. Ibid., 37; J. C. Hemmeon, *The History of the British Post Office* (Cambridge, Mass.: Harvard, 1912), 21.

49. Howard Robinson, *British Post Office*, 69–75, 83–86; Lillywhite, *London Coffee Houses*, 19–21.

50. Ibid., 85, 108, 172, 259, 262, 457, 556.

51. Ibid., 19.

52. Howard Robinson, *British Post Office*, 77f. The government continued to open the mail of certain persons—Jacobites and organized crime—but it now required a warrant from the secretaries of state (120).

53. Edward Robinson, *English Coffee House*, 213; Lillywhite, *London Coffee Houses*, 26.

CHAPTER SEVEN

1. *Poor Robin's Intelligence*, 16 October 1677.

2. *City Mercury*, 20 March 1694.

3. *Mercurius Civicus: Or, The City Mercury*, 4 June 1680.

4. Henry Snyder, "Newsletters in England, 1689–1715, with special reference to John Dyer—a byway in the History of England," in Donovan H. Bond and W. Reynolds McLeod, eds., *Newsletters to Newspapers* (Morgantown, W.V.: West Virginia University Press, 1977), 4–12.

5. Kitchin, *L'Estrange*, 155.

6. E. S. deBeer., "The English Newspapers from 1695 to 1702," in Ragnhild Hatton and J. S. Bromley, eds., *William III and Louis XIV* (Liverpool: Liverpool University Press, 1968), 120.

7. Fraser, *Intelligence of the Secretaries of State*, 127f.

8. *Saville Correspondence*, Camden Society 71 (1858): 55, 61.

9. Sidney, *Diary*, 1:249, 2:146.

10. Butler, *Characters*, 199.

11. *Conway Letters*, ed. Marjorie Hope Nicolson (New Haven: Yale University Press, 1930), 190, 261; Sidney, *Diary*, 1:207.

12. This was not the first time that a Proclamation had complained of the coffeehouses. One of 14 June 1672 had named them, among "other Places and Meetings," as places where the government was defamed, and warned them not to allow "any false News or Reports, or to intermeddle with the affairs of State and Government." Those who were no more than "present at any *Coffee-house,* or other publick or private Meeting where such Speeches are used" would be proceeded against.

13. North, *Examin*, 141. North oddly dates a *prior* consultation with judges to January 1676 (139).

14. Proclamation, 7 January 1676; see Robinson, *English Coffee House*, 160–62 for discussion of earlier attempts.

15. Quoted in Pincus, "Coffee Politicians Does Create," 822. My emphasis.

16. Ibid., 821.

17. Robinson, *English Coffee House*, 171–74; Muddiman, *King's Journalist*, 211. Keith Feiling and F. R. D. Needham, "The Journals of Edmund Warcup, 1676–84," *English His-*

torical Review 40 (1925): 235–60, show how important coffeehouses were in the political negotiations, as well as the intrigues, of the Crisis. Wilmer G. Mason, "The Annual Output of Wing-Listed Titles, 1649–1684," *The Library* 39 (1974): 219f, indicates that 5,000 titles appeared from late 1678 through 1681, at a rate of five per working day.

18. E.g., Fraser, *Intelligence of the Secretaries of State*, 114.

19. Love, *Scribal Publication*, 12.

20. Muddiman, *King's Journalist*, 219.

21. Siebert, *Freedom of the Press*, 299; Muddiman, *King's Journalist*, 222.

22. Fraser, *Intelligence of the Secretaries of State*, 116f, 122.

23. Siebert, *Freedom of the Press*, 298.

24. Ibid.

25. Ibid., 269f.

26. Frank, *Nedham*, 153–63.

27. John Kenyon, *The Popish Plot* (London: Heinemann, 1972), 237f.

28. Ronald Hutton, *Charles the Second* (Oxford: Clarendon, 1989), 392.

29. John Childs, "The Sale of Government Gazettes during the Exclusion Crisis," *English Historical Review* 102 (1987): 104.

30. *Domestick Intelligence*, 16 January 1680.

31. *Domestick Intelligence*, 23 December 1679.

32. Kitchin, *L'Estrange*, 278f.

33. Ibid., 249, 357.

34. Marjorie Plant, *The English Book Trade*, 2d ed. (London: George Allen and Unwin, 1965), 251–53.

35. Fraser, *Intelligence of the Secretaries of State*, 127.

36. Kitchin, *L'Estrange*, 335. Thomas Benskin was another, publishing Whig pamphlets until February 1681, and a Tory newspaper from 13 May of that year: Harth, *Pen for a Party*, 78.

37. Childs, "Sale of Government Gazettes," 104.

38. Kitchin, *L'Estrange*, 327, 339.

39. Iser, *Prospecting*, 10f.

40. *Observator*, 13 April 1681.

41. Siebert, *Freedom of the Press*, 298f.

42. *Heraclitus Ridens*, 1 March 1681.

43. Lillywhite, *London Coffee Houses*, 264; Brown, *Knowledge is Power*, 28–41.

44. Siebert, *Freedom of the Press*, 299.

45. Love, *Scribal Publication*, 11f.

46. Muddiman, *L'Estrange*, 204, 245.

47. Cranfield, *Press and Society*, 25; *Dictionary of National Biography*, 3:954f, "Care, Henry."

48. *Publick Occurences Truely Stated*, 21 February 1688.

49. Lillywhite, *London Coffee Houses*, 20.

50. Fraser, *Intelligence of the Secretaries of State*, 132.

51. Lois G. Schwoerer, "Propaganda in the Revolution of 1688–89," *American Historical Review* 82 (1977): 859, 874; idem, "Press and Parliament in the Revolution of 1689," *Historical Journal* 20 (1979): 567.

52. *Diary of Abraham de la Pryme*, 15f.

53. *Diary of Samuel Newton*, 96.

54. Sir John Oglander, *A Royalist's Notebook*, ed. Francis Bamford (New York: Benjamin Blom, 1971), 16–18.

55. *The Diary of John Evelyn*, ed. E. S. deBeer (Oxford: Clarendon, 1955), 4:487; 4:609.

CHAPTER EIGHT

1. R. B. Walker, "The Newspaper Press in the Reign of William III," *Historical Journal* 17 (1974): 695.

2. Siebert, *Freedom of the Press*, 299f.

3. *Monthly Account of February*, February 1645.

4. *Modern History, or, The Monthly Account*, November 1688, 79–81.

5. *Politicks of Europe, Or, a Rational Journal*, 2 July 1690.

6. Nelson and Seccombe, *British Newspapers and Periodicals*, lists five publications with Poor Robin in their titles, running intermittently between 1676 and 1691.

7. Joseph Moxon, *Mechanick Exercises*, 2d ed. (London: J. Moxon, 1693–94), Preface.

8. Birch, *History of the Royal Society*, 4:7, 4:19; *Diary of Robert Hooke*, 439f.

9. *Weekly Memorials for the Ingenious*, 30 January 1682.

10. Kronick, *Scientific and Technical Periodicals*, 135.

11. Stimson, *Scientists*, 90–94.

12. Kronick, *Scientific and Technical Periodicals*, 251.

13. Ibid., 279. Hooke's *Diary* indicates that he paid sixpence for half the issues and a shilling for the rest.

14. McEwen, *Oracle of the Coffee House*, 3–25; John Dunton, *The Life and Errors of John Dunton* (London: S. Malthus, 1705), 256–62; Jonathan Swift, *The Poems of Jonathan Swift*, ed. William Ernst Browning (London: G. Ball, 1910), 1:16–24. A letter from Swift published in *The Supplement to the Fifth Volume of the Athenian Gazette* (London: John Dunton, 1692) shows that his ode was not ironic, but sincerely panegyric. See also, Stephen Parks, *John Dunton and the English Book Trade* (New York: Garland, 1976), 90–93.

15. Dunton, *Life and Errors*, 261.

16. Ibid., 278.

17. Kathryn Shevelow, *Women and Print Culture: The Construction of Femininity in the Early Periodical* (London: Routledge, 1989), 74.

18. McEwen, *Oracle of the Coffee House*, 143.

19. [Elkanah Settle], *The New Athenian Comedy* (London: Camanella Restio, 1693). For examples of versified answers, see *Athenian Mercury* for 27 February and 8 March 1692.

20. *Athenian Mercury*, 23 February 1692.

21. *Athenian Mercury*, vol. 2: Preface.

22. Bertha-Monica Stearns, "The First English Periodical for Women," *Modern Philology* 28 (1930–31): 45–59, offers evidence that Dunton edited the *Ladies Mercury* also.

23. McEwen, *Oracle of the Coffee House*, 105–9.

24. Shevelow, *Women and Print Culture*, 4, 34, 50–53.

25. McEwen, *Oracle of the Coffee House*, 114.

26. MacDonald and Murphy, *Sleepless Souls*, 309–19.

27. Kronick, *Scientific and Technical Periodicals*, 245.

28. Chandos Michael Brown, *Benjamin Silliman; A Life in the Young Republic* (Princeton: Princeton University Press, 1989), 186.

29. *Gentleman's Journal*, April 1692, 19.

30. McEwen, *Oracle of the Coffee House*, 198f.

31. Shevelow, *Women and Print Culture*, 75.

32. Settle, *New Athenian Comedy*, 5–7.

33. [Charles Gildon], *The History of the Athenian Society* (London: James Dowley, 1691), 3–17.

34. Parks, *John Dunton*, 104f.

35. Richmond P. Bond, *The Tatler: The Making of a Literary Journal* (Cambridge, Mass.: Harvard, 1971), 123–25.

CHAPTER NINE

1. *The History of Learning*, July 1691, Preface. This was the title for the first issue only, before de la Crose changed publisher.

2. Ibid.; *The Works of the Learned*, August 1691, Preface.

3. Walker, "Advertising," 126.

4. I. G. Philip, "Advice on Advertising Publications, 1701," *Bodleian Library Record* 11 (1984): 263f.

5. *Works of the Learned*, August 1691, Preface.

6. *History of Learning*, July 1691, Preface.

7. Robert Newton Cunningham, *Peter Anthony Motteux, 1663–1718* (Oxford: Basil Blackwell, 1933), 14.

8. *Gentleman's Journal*, April 1692, 19; June 1692, 19.

9. Donald Kay, *Short Fiction in the Spectator* (University, Al.: University of Alabama Press, 1975), 16; Cunningham, *Motteux*, 28.

10. *Gentleman's Journal*, August 1693, 251; toward the end he hints that most of his submissions are from women (November 1693, 359).

11. *The Compleat Library: Or, News for the Ingenious*, May 1692, sig. A2. On the rivalry between Dunton and de la Crose, see Parks, *John Dunton*, 111–28.

12. *British Mercury*, 2 August 1712.

13. MacDonald and Murphy, *Sleepless Souls*, 316–19.

14. Robert D. Mayo, *The English Novel in the Magazines, 1740–1815* (Evanston: Northwestern University Press, 1962), 2–23. See also, Davis, *Factual Fictions*; McKeon, *Origins of the English Novel*; J. Paul Hunter, *Before Novels: The Cultural Context of Eighteenth-Century English Fiction* (New York: Norton, 1990).

15. Cranfield, *Press and Society*, 32.

16. Joseph M. Levine, *The Battle of the Books; History and Literature in the Augustan Age* (Ithaca: Cornell University Press, 1991), 29f, 144, 228.

17. Alexander Pope, *The Dunciad*, ed. James Sutherland (London: Methuen, 1943), 184.

18. Aubrey Williams, *Pope's Dunciad* (Baton Rouge: Louisiana State University Press, 1955), 13, 31, 97, 102–10.

19. Bond, *Tatler*, 97, 106–14.

20. [Archibald Campbell], *Lexiphanes* (London: J. Knox, 1767), 159–66. I owe this reference to Howard Weinbrot.

21. Richmond P. Bond, ed., *Studies in the Early English Periodical* (Chapel Hill: University of North Carolina Press, 1957), 36.

22. McEwen, *Oracle of the Coffee House*, 15.

23. R. M. Wiles, *Serial Publication in England Before 1750* (Cambridge: Cambridge University Press, 1957), 4f, 25, 32, 37, 239; idem, "The Relish for Reading," in Paul J. Korshin, ed., *The Widening Circle: Essays on the Circulation of Literature in Eighteenth-Century Europe* (Philadelphia: University of Pennsylvania Press, 1976), 114 n.28.

24. Mayo, *English Novel in the Magazines*, 2.

25. John Feather, *The Provincial Book Trade in Eighteenth-Century England* (Cambridge: Cambridge University Press, 1985), 16, 19, 65.

26. Quoted in Shevelow, *Women and Print Culture*, 32.

27. Quoted in Stephens, *History of News*, 270.

CHAPTER TEN

1. Jack R. Censer, "Recent Approaches to the Eighteenth-Century Press," *Comparative Studies in Society and History* 31 (1989): 775–83.

2. Jeremy Black, *The English Press in the Eighteenth Century* (London: Croom Helm, 1987), 286.

3. Snyder, "Newsletters in England," 9.

4. Black, *English Press*, 234f.

5. Hanson, *Government and the Press*, 7.

6. Raymond Astbury, "The Renewal of the Licensing Act in 1693 and its Lapse in 1695," *The Library*, 5th series, 33 (1978): 298–305.

7. Hanson, *Government and the Press*, 57–61.

8. Ibid., 2–11.

9. Astbury, "The Renewal of the Licensing Act," 307.

10. [Matthew Tindal], *A Discourse for the Liberty of the Press*, in *Four Discourses* (London, 1709), 293–329. Three pages from the end (326), Tindal remembered to mention that there were "News-papers besides the *Gazette*, which would hardly be permitted if the Press were regulated."

11. Astbury, "Renewal of the Licensing Act," 317–20.

12. *Observator*, 23 May 1702.

13. *Observator*, 10 June 1702.

14. *Observator*, 27 June 1702.

15. *Rehearsal*, preface to the first collected volume, published in 1708.

16. Parks, *John Dunton*, 83.

17. This and other twists in Defoe's career can be followed in *Dictionary of National Biography*, 5:730–43.

18. Morphew's *Tatler* was recognized as Whig in its sympathies, while his *Examiner* and *Post Boy*, were the main Tory organs.

19. Hanson, *Government and the Press*, 94.

20. Handover, *London Gazette*, 34–40.

21. The reasons that Steele dropped news from the *Tatler* are explored in Robert Waller Achurch, "Richard Steele, Gazetteer and Bickerstaff," in Bond, *Early English Periodical*, 50–72.

22. J. A. Downie, *Robert Harley and the Press: Propaganda and Public Opinion in the Age of Swift and Defoe* (Cambridge: Cambridge University Press, 1979), 153–60, credits Harley with the idea, though Siebert (*Freedom of the Press*, 308) took Bolingbroke himself to be the originator of the notion.

23. Black, *English Press*, 144.

24. *Medley*, 20 November 1710.

25. John Gay, *The Present State of Wit* (1711), in *John Gay, Poetry and Prose*, ed. Vinton A. Dearing (Oxford: Clarendon, 1974), 2:450f.

26. Siebert, *Freedom of the Press*, 309–18; Cranfield, *Press and Society*, 39f.

27. *Tatler*, 6 April, 18 April, 30 May, and 3 October 1710.

28. *Tatler*, 21 May 1709.

29. *London Journal*, 31 December 1720.

30. *London Journal*, 3 January 1721.

31. *London Journal*, 7 January 1721.

32. *London Journal*, 21 January 1721.

33. Jeremy D. Popkin, *Revolutionary News: The Press in France, 1789–1799* (Durham, N.C.: Duke University Press, 1990), 4.

34. Downie, *Robert Harley and the Press*, 53.

35. Hanson, *Government and the Press*, 106f.

36. Robert Harris, *A Patriot Press: National Politics and the London Press in the 1740s* (New York: Clarendon, 1993), 26–28.

37. William Thomas Laprade, *Public Opinion and Politics in Eighteenth Century England* (New York: Macmillan, 1936), passim; Cranfield, *Provincial Newspaper*, 125, 136.

38. Cranfield, *Press and Society*, 44.

39. Quoted in Harris, *Patriot Press*, 32.

40. Siebert, *Freedom of the Press*, 361f.

41. Laprade, *Public Opinion*, 292; Hanson, *Government and the Press*, 84.

42. Quoted in Laprade, *Public Opinion*, 228.

CHAPTER ELEVEN

1. See my *Popular Religion in Restoration England* (Gainesville: University Presses of Florida, 1978), and *The Secularization of Early Modern England*, on this subject.

2. Michael Hunter, "Science and Heterodoxy: An Early Modern Problem Reconsidered," in David C. Lindberg and Robert S. Westman, eds., *Reappraisals of the Scientific Revolution* (Cambridge: Cambridge University Press, 1990), 442.

3. Black, *English Press*, 248.

4. Josef Altholz, *The Religious Press in Britain, 1760–1900* (New York: Greenwood, 1989), 7.

5. Quoted in Frank, *Beginnings of the English Newspaper*, 200.

6. Quoted from Ned Ward, in Bond, *Tatler*, 148.

7. Cranfield, *Provincial*, 86f.

8. Frank, *Beginnings of the English Newspaper*, 77, 89, 93, 107, 120, 125, 196, 248.

9. Black, *English Press*, 249–53; R. K. Webb, "Flying Missionaries: Unitarian Journalists in Victorian England," in J. M. W. Bean, ed., *The Political Culture of Modern Britain: Studies in Memory of Stephen Koss* (London: Hamish Hamilton, 1987), 16–19.

10. Barthes, "Structure of the *Fait-Divers*," 185–95.

11. Ibid., 188f, 194.

12. *Mercurius Catholicus* (11 September 1648) was simply a treatise in refutation of Protestant claims to be a universal or apostolic church. There was nothing but the title to suggest that it was meant to continue, but on 11 December another issue appeared, with a different appearance, which was called "Numb. 2." *A Monthly Intelligence Relating to the Affairs of the People Called Quakers* (September 1662) was one of many types of publications that were meant to hold that hard-pressed sect together. No second issue can be found.

13. The titles were *Impartial Protestant Mercury, Loyal Protestant and True Domestick Intelligence, Observer Observ'd; or Protestant Observations upon Anti-Protestant Pamphlets, Protestant Courant, Protestant (Domestick) Intelligence, Protestant Observator, Protestant Oxford Intelligence, Smith's Protestant Intelligence, True Protestant (Domestick) Intelligence, True Protestant Mercury.*

14. *Protestant Mercury. Occurances, Foreign and Domestick, Protestant Post-Boy, Protestant Mercury; or, the Exeter Post-Boy, Churchman's Last Shift, or Loyalist's Weekly Journal.*

15. Dudley W. R. Bahlman, *The Moral Revolution of 1688* (New Haven: Yale University Press, 1957). Dunton specifically meant his *Post-Angel* for the encouragement of the societies (*Post-Angel*, January 1701, 2).

16. McEwen, *Oracle of the Coffee House*, 142; Graham, *Literary Periodicals*, 48–51. Dunton's *Night-Walker: or, evening rambles in search after lewd women, with the conferences held with them, etc.* (September 1696) combined reform and prurience, and ran for eight monthly issues.

17. Swift, *Poems*, 1: 16–24.

18. McEwen, *Oracle of the Coffee House*, 169, 174.

19. Daniel Defoe, *A Letter to a Member of Parliament, Shewing the Necessity of Regulating the Press* (Oxford: George West and Henry Clements, 1699).

20. Graham, *Literary Periodicals*, 48–51; Bond, *Tatler*, 128f.

21. *Occasional Paper*, no. 1 (1697), 2–7.

22. *Weekly Entertainment*, 24 October 1700.

23. Dunton met Mather in 1686 and again in 1689: Parks, *John Dunton*, 28, 45.

24. David Paul Nord, "Teleology and News: The Religious Roots of American Journalism, 1630–1730," *Journal of American History* 77 (1990): 9–38.

25. *Post-Angel*, January 1701, sigs. B3–B4. There was a contemporaneous, but unsuccessful attempt to do something similar, in *Memoirs for the Curious; or, an Account of What Occurs That's Rare, Secret, Extraordinary, Prodigious and Miraculous through the World, Whether in Nature, Art, Learning, Policy, or Religion* (February 1701).

26. The "second edition" of *Christian's Gazette* (1713) was entirely different, but was likewise unsuccessful.

27. C. N. Greenough, "The Development of the *Tatler*, Particularly in Regard to News," *Publications of the MLA* 31 (1916): 655.

28. Bond, *Tatler*, 119f.

29. Gay, "Present State of Wit," 451f.

30. These were *Serious Thoughts; or, a Golden Chain of Contemplations* (1710), *Balm of Gilead* (1714), *Scourge* (1717), *Church-Man* (1718), *Jesuite* (1719), *Christian Priest* (1720), and *Protestant Advocate* (1724). Samuel J. Rogal's "Religious Periodicals in England during the Restoration and Eighteenth Century," *Journal of the Rutgers University Library* 35

(1971): 27–33; Josef Altholz's "The First Religious Magazines," *Notes and Queries* n.s. 32 (1985): 223f.

31. Antagonism toward Dissent was also the theme of *Scourge* (1717), one of the party papers mentioned above, which survived for almost a year.

32. Susan Durden, "A Study of the First Evangelical Magazines, 1740–8," *Journal of Ecclesiastical History* 27 (1976): 257, 267, 272.

33. *George Whitefield's Journal*, ed. Iain Murray (London: Banner of Truth, 1960), 87, 213, 217.

34. *Weekly History*, no. 4 (1741); Durden, "First Evangelical Magazines," 261.

35. Harry S. Stout, *The Divine Dramatist: George Whitefield and the Rise of Modern Evangelicalism* (Grand Rapids, Mich.: William B. Eerdmans, 1991), 134.

36. Altholz, *Religious Press*, 141f.

37. Albert M. Lyles, *Methodism Mocked; The Satiric Reaction to Methodism in the Eighteenth Century* (London: Epworth, 1960).

38. Cranfield, *Provincial Newspaper*, 105; Black, *English Press*, 249.

39. Christopher Hill, *The English Bible and the Seventeenth-Century Revolution* (London: Allen Lane, 1993), 20, 32–34, 199.

40. Norman Sykes, *From Sheldon to Secker: Aspects of English Church History, 1660–1768* (Cambridge: Cambridge University Press, 1959), 140–187.

41. Anderson, *Imagined Communities*, 39.

42. *Spectator*, 12 March 1711.

43. Carey, "Cultural Approach," 8.

44. Park, *Social Control*, 678.

CHAPTER TWELVE

1. Howard William Troyer, *Ned Ward of Grubstreet* (Cambridge, Mass.: Harvard University Press, 1946), 59.

2. *Tatler*, 6 April, 18 April, 30 May, and 3 October 1710.

3. Snyder, "Newsletters in England," 9.

4. Clark, *Public Prints*, 61, 216.

5. Wiles, *Freshest Advices*, 142, 153.

6. Bond, *Tatler*, 31–34.

7. Walker, "Advertising in London Newspapers," 126.

8. Lawrence Lewis, *The Advertisements of the Spectator* (London: Archibald Constable, 1909), 80–100, 111; Henry Sampson, *A History of Advertising from the Earliest Times* (London: Chatto and Windus, 1875), 159.

9. Quoted in Henry Fielding, *Jonathan Wild*, ed. David Nokes (Harmondsworth: Penguin, 1982), 10f.

10. Bond, *Tatler*, 144; Kay, *Short Fiction*, 20; Benjamin Boyce, *Tom Brown of Facetious Memory: Grub Street in the Age of Dryden* (Cambridge, Mass.: Harvard University Press, 1939), 143f.

11. Black, *English Press*, 302.

12. McEwen, *Oracle of the Coffee House*, 24.

13. Troyer, *Ned Ward*, 108–116, 151–58.

14. James T. Hillhouse, *The Grub-Street Journal* (Durham, N.C.: Duke University Press, 1928), 5.

15. Shevelow, *Women and Print Culture*, 151, 168.

16. Ibid., 101, 108; Bond, *Tatler*, 139.

17. Shevelow, *Women and Print Culture*, 46–48.

18. Ibid., 36, 69, 93–98.

19. Peter Borsay, *The English Urban Renaissance; Culture and Society in The Provincial Town, 1660–1770* (Oxford: Clarendon, 1989), 269, 287f.

20. Gouldner, *Dialectic of Ideology*, 96.

21. M. Dorothy George, *English Political Caricature to 1792: A Study of Opinion and Propaganda* (Oxford: Clarendon, 1959), 141.

22. Herbert M. Atherton, *Political Prints in the Age of Hogarth* (Oxford: Clarendon, 1974), 27–33; Ronald Paulson, *Hogarth: His Life, Art, and Times* (New Haven: Yale University Press, 1974), 46, 52, 126, 163–67, 171.

23. M. Dorothy George, *Hogarth to Cruickshank: Social Change in Graphic Satire* (New York: Walker, 1967), 13.

24. David Kunzle, *History of the Comic Strip* (Berkeley: University of California Press, 1973), 1:357–59.

25. George, *English Political Caricature*, 85.

26. Atherton, *Political Prints*, 34, 260f.

27. John Mottley, *The Craftsman: or, Weekly Journalist, a farce* (London: J. Roberts, 1728), 13.

28. George, *Hogarth to Cruickshank*, 13.

29. Atherton, *Political Prints*, 62.

30. Ibid., 66, 261f.

31. Ibid., 261; George, *Hogarth to Cruickshank*, 33f, 41, 85, 103, 133.

32. *Tatler*, 26 August 1710, 12 January 1710, 12 October 1712. See also 26 April 1709.

33. *Tatler*, 13 April 1710, 3 May 1709. See also 29 April 1710.

34. *Tatler*, 7 March 1710.

35. Fielding, *Jonathan Wild*, 9.

36. Frank McLynn, *Crime and Punishment in Eighteenth-Century England* (London: Routledge, 1989), 68. Also see Lincoln B. Faller, *Turned to Account: The Forms and Functions of Criminal Biography in Late Seventeenth- and Early Eighteenth-Century England* (Cambridge: Cambridge University Press, 1987), 194–200, on the "reporting" of crime.

37. Shevelow, *Women and Print Culture*, 1f, 11, 21.

38. C. Lennart Carlson, *The First Magazine: A History of the Gentleman's Magazine* (Providence, R.I.: Brown University Press, 1938), 5–9, 60; John Feather, *A History of British Publishing* (London: Croom Helm, 1988), 110–12.

39. Carlson doubts this figure, since Cave only claimed a monthly sale of three thousand in 1746. But that was some time after the excitement of the printing of the parliamentary debates (begun in 1738) and probably ignored reprints, which sometimes reached a fourth or fifth edition (62f, 92, 102).

40. A. S. Collins, "The Growth of the Reading Public during the Eighteenth Century," *Review of English Studies* 2 (1926): 289f.

41. Quotations from Black, *English Press*, 30–47.

42. *London Magazine*, April 1732, Preface.

43. Mayo, *English Novel in the Magazines*, 162.

44. Carlson, *First Magazine*, 150.

45. Ibid., 198. Even some of these shameless aspirants had to be refused. After 1747,

when the printing of Parliamentary debates was stopped, the *Gentleman's Magazine* began to devote more attention to literary criticism (136–50).

46. Ibid., 167f.

47. Black, *English Press*, 246.

48. *Diary of John Evelyn*, 1:89; 5:366.

49. P. J. Corfield, *The Impact of English Towns, 1700–1800* (New York: Oxford, 1982), 8, 143.

50. Cranfield, *Provincial Newspaper*, 21f. The figures given in Wiles, *Freshest Advices*, 25, differ slightly.

51. Feather, *Provincial Book Trade*, 19.

52. Harris, "Structure, Ownership and Control of the Press," 90.

53. Cranfield, *Provincial Newspaper*, 103–106.

CHAPTER THIRTEEN

1. Sykes, *From Sheldon to Secker*, 173

2. Frye, *The Double Vision*, 14–18.

3. Quoted in Stanley Green, *Shaftesbury's Philosophy of Religion and Ethics: A Study in Enthusiasm* (Athens, Ohio: Ohio University Press, 1967), 14.

4. Ibid., 38f, 204–8.

5. Samuel Johnson, in the *Adventurer*, 28 August 1753.

6. Hunter, *Before Novels*, 99, 297, 167–70.

7. William King produced a parody literary journal, *Useful Transactions in Philosophy and other sorts of Learning*, in 1709.

8. Dahlgren, "TV News and the Suppression of Reflexivity," 102f.

9. Gouldner, *Dialectic of Ideology*, 107.

10. The *Critical Review* (London: for R. Baldwin, 1756), vol. 1, Preface.

11. Quoted in Tuchman, *Making News*, 169.

12. Carey, *Media, Myths, and Narratives*, 11, 17.

13. Black, *English Press*, 246, 259–72.

14. The new dailies were the *Daily Post* (1719) and the *Daily Journal* (1720). Anon., the *Case of the Coffee-Men of London and Westminster*, 5; Stephens, *History of News*, 223–38.

15. Black, *English Press*, 139; John Brewer, *Party Ideology and Popular Politics at the Accession of George III* (Cambridge: Cambridge University Press, 1976), 139.

16. Golding, "The Missing Dimensions," 76–80.

17. Gitlin, *The Whole World is Watching*, 263, 290f.

18. Stephens, *History of News*, 294.

19. Tom Koch, *Journalism for the 21st Century* (New York: Greenwood, 1991), 307.

20. Francis Bacon, "Of Studies," in *Selected Writings of Francis Bacon*, ed. Hugh G. Dick (New York: Modern Library, 1955), 129.

21. Quoted in Robert Gambee, *Princeton* (New York: Norton, 1993), 17.

Index